Language of the Heart

Language of the Heart

How to Read the Bible: A User's Guide for Catholics

NOEL COOPER

NOVALIS

Cover design and layout: Caroline Gagnon
Cover images: Getty Images (top left), Corbis (centre)

Published by Novalis

Publishing Office
10 Lower Spadina Avenue, Suite 400
Toronto, Ontario, Canada
M5V 2Z2

Head Office
4475 Frontenac Street
Montréal, Québec, Canada
H2H 2S2
www.novalis.ca

National Library of Canada Cataloguing in Publication Data

Cooper, Noel
Language of the heart : how to read the Bible : a user's guide for Catholics / Noel Cooper.

ISBN 10: 2-89507-401-1
ISBN 13: 978-2-89507-401-4

1. Bible–Introductions. 2. Catholic Church–Doctrines. I. Title.

BS587.C66 2003 220.6'1'08822 C2003-904383-5

Printed in Canada.

We acknowledge the financial support of the Government of Canada through the Book Publishing Industry Development Program (BPIDP) for our publishing activities.

6 5 4 3 14 13 12 11

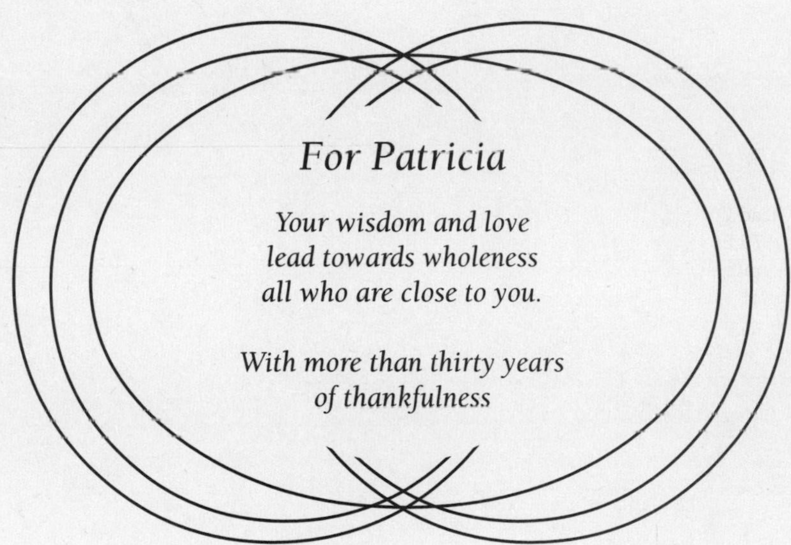

For Patricia

Your wisdom and love
lead towards wholeness
all who are close to you.

With more than thirty years
of thankfulness

In loving memory
October 6, 2002

CONTENTS

INTRODUCTION

This is a book of personal memories. Thoughts and opinions, gleaned and reflected upon over three decades of reading and teaching, have been woven into my impressions about the Scriptures.

This book expresses what the Bible means to me. I hope that the overriding positive spirit of the Scriptures can be conveyed through these pages. Through the Bible, we learn that God responds to the deepest yearnings of humanity, reaches into our lives to lead us to wholeness, and gives meaning and purpose to our journey. The study of the Bible is not just an interesting literary adventure: through the Bible, God can change our lives.

During and after a rather extensive formal education in theology and Sacred Scripture, I learned most of the understandings presented in this book from the great Scripture teachers and scholars of our time. *Language of the Heart* is also the product of many years' experience offering courses for teachers and developing curriculum for students in Catholic schools in Ontario. Canadian catechetical programs for elementary and high school students have been based on Scripture for almost 30 years at this writing. I have continually learned from students' questions and from the alternative interpretations they have proposed, with the result that this book is significantly different from what it would have been 20, ten or even two years ago.

Colleagues who have contributed to my education by co-teaching our courses have included Paul Devlin, Michael Nasello and Patrick Collins. Ann Murphy, my colleague in Religious Education for more than 20 years, and Mary Ann Takacs and Cathy Gross, co-workers in the York Region Catholic School Board, have taught me the meaning of the Bible and its value for children through years of thoughtful sharing and living. This book would never have been published except for the intervention of Maura Hanrahan of Newfoundland, and I am very grateful for her support.

My wife, Patricia, and sons, Andrew, Paul and John, are living examples of faithful love and enduring hope. With great sadness I must report that Patricia died of cancer in October 2002, and her support now can be felt only in spirit.

The thoughts in this book are offered in the hope that readers will want to study the Scriptures more deeply with a contemporary understanding, and will perceive the relevance of the Word of God for their lives. The book is built on the conviction that believers of long ago were people very much like us, living in societies surprisingly similar to ours. Technology has changed immensely, but human nature has changed very little. The ancient people had to find God in their experiences, just as we do. They asked unanswerable questions, as we do. And they shared their insight and their faith by writing prayers and poetry, telling stories, proposing theories, commenting on their times – using many of the forms of expression that human beings have used since mental activity was first recorded in writing.

Their reflections came to be recognized as the Word of God for us – in a language that can indeed speak to our hearts and give us lasting strength for the journey.

A Note About How to Identify Texts and Abbreviations of Scripture Books

First, we call them "books of the Bible" because at one time they were separate scrolls, written by many different authors. The Bible is a collection of short "books" rather than one book written by a single author.

When we cite a particular text, we give the name of the book, then the chapter number, followed by a colon, then the verse(s). So "John 1:1-12" means the Gospel of John, chapter 1, verses 1 to 12.

Complications arise when there is a number before the name of the book: "1 John 1:1-3" doesn't refer to the gospel of John, but to the First Letter of John, chapter 1, verses 1 to 3. That little book is found very close to the end of the Bible.

"1 Kings 12" (with no colon) means the first book of Kings, chapter 12 (the whole chapter).

Perhaps the most complicated kind of citation is one that "jumps across" two chapters in a book. For example, the famous story of the seven days of creation at the beginning of the book of Genesis includes all of chapter 1, and the first 4 verses of chapter 2 (the story ends halfway through verse 4, and the next story [the story of Adam and Eve] begins in the second half of verse 4).

Thus the story of the seven days of creation is cited as Genesis 1:1–2:4a, meaning that it begins at chapter 1, verse 1, and continues to chapter 2, verse 4a (the first half of verse 4).

Another very famous passage, which is read in church every Good Friday, is cited as Isaiah 52:13–53:12: it begins at verse 13 of chapter 52 in the book of the prophet Isaiah, and continues to verse 12 of chapter 53. "He was led like a lamb to the slaughter" is one of the memorable phrases in this reading.

Most Bibles and books about the Bible use abbreviations for the names of the books, like *Gen* for Genesis and *Exod* for Exodus. Most of them can be figured out with the help of the Table of Contents at the beginning of a Bible – or the page near the beginning of the Bible that lists the abbreviations for all the books of the Bible.

1

WHY READ THE BIBLE?

The Bible is a collection of the greatest religious writing of one particular ancient culture of western Asia, as it developed over the course of a millennium.

The people of that society were mostly farmers and herders rather than city-dwellers. Few of them were literate, let alone educated. Most people were economically poor and politically oppressed. Their lives were short and usually miserable. Women led lives of continual servitude, and often died at a young age, in childbirth or from infections that could easily be cured today. Their culture was patriarchal, racist and violent. Their religion suffered from superstition among ordinary people, and power-seeking among religious leaders.

In some ways, their world seems hopelessly far away and long ago.

And yet the Bible continues to be the bestselling book in prosperous 21st-century societies that are highly technological, devoted to personal freedom, suspicious of religious institutions, superstitious in their own way, struggling towards equity, and still frighteningly violent.

What could the Bible possibly offer to the sophisticated people of our time?

The Same Profound Human Concerns

It is true that the culture of biblical times was significantly different from ours. Those people were not able to travel on pathways 10 kilometres above the earth at speeds of hundreds of kilometres an hour. They didn't heat their meals by using carefully targeted electronic waves. They couldn't watch faraway events by trapping invisible rays out of the air and turning them into pictures. They couldn't communicate instantly by voice or in writing with people beyond the sea.

But those differences are about technology, not about humanity.

Fundamentally, the people of the Bible were people like us.

At times, like us, they marvelled at the beauty of the world around them. Sooner or later, most of them wondered what life was all about. Many of them had a sense of nobility, a desire to do what is right. At the same time, they recognized harmful behaviour in themselves and in others; they had to struggle to be true to themselves; they felt the need to be forgiven.

Their dreams were often crushed by reality. Poverty and sickness surrounded them, casting a pall of misery over their lives. Like us, they loved some people and feared others, admired some and hated others. They worried, and often they lost hope. They wished for good things for their children, but rather than wondering what their children would do when they grew up, parents in biblical times had to wonder whether their children would even live long enough to become adults. Death came for them and their loved ones at very early ages. Like us, most of them were afraid to die, and they wondered if death meant the end of their being.

And they frequently asked the greatest of religious questions: Why? If God is good, why is there so much pain? Why is life so unfair? Why are some people luckier than others? What makes my life meaningful?

In spite of human progress in many areas of culture and comfort, people's deepest needs have changed very little. At heart, we are as frail as the people of 2,000 years ago, whose humanity we share. Our yearnings are the same.

What Does Faith Offer to a Person's Life?

Religion is fundamentally a search for meaning and wholeness.

Humans wonder about the meaning of their lives, and seek to engage in activities that bring peace of heart, that provide a sense of personal and communal well-being, that lead towards wholeness. Religion offers a sense of direction in life; it proposes that people need a focus or centre to bring their experiences together into a meaningful pattern.

At its best, religion knows that loving and being loved are far more meaningful for human beings than the pursuit of power and wealth. Wholeness is found in being free to set the course of one's life, but only when that freedom is expressed in a community built on mutual respect and love, and, when necessary, forgiveness.

And religion believes that human beings are not expected to pursue wholeness and meaning solely by their own efforts. There is spiritual power in the world that is greater than any human power, and we call that spiritual reality "God."

A Distinctive, Challenging Sense of God

The people of biblical times dealt with their deepest hopes and fears in the light of their sense of God. Thoughtful and faithful authors wrote what they believed in a collection of works of art that has been preserved and continues to be read many centuries later. Their faith was so comforting and challenging that it has stood the test of centuries, and endures as comfort and challenge to people of our time.

Those early believers came to know a God who loves people, who gave us our lives and our world as an act of kindness to us. They believed in a God who is entirely on our side and in no way against us. They came to know God who offers us meaning and direction, speaks to us in a language that touches our hearts and reaches into our lives to lead us to wholeness.

We have been taught that God helps us to be wise, gives us understanding so that we can make sense of our lives, helps us to make good judgments, and gives us the courage to do what we know is right. Remarkably, almost incredibly, we believe that God loves us as we are, no matter what happens to us, even no matter what we do.

These biblical understandings are so fundamental to our faith that we often take them for granted, and yet they are so unprecedented that we consider them to be revealed to us by God.

The God of the Bible makes demands on people as well. God teaches us how to live as faithful people, and challenges us to do what is truly best. God's challenges and demands are not signs that God is against us, but gifts to help us be faithful to God and true to ourselves. Most important, God doesn't leave us to struggle and strive alone in the face of the challenges of life, but gives us strength for the journey from birth to death and beyond.

This book offers to guide contemporary readers through the memorable documents of faith found in the Bible. The first few chapters provide some necessary background – a discussion about what it means to call the Scriptures "the Word of God," an outline of the techniques used by scholars to distill meaning from the wide range of biblical documents, a discussion of great importance in our time about the use of gender-inclusive language in talking about both humans and God, and a brief narrative of the history of the people who shared their faith in the Scriptures.

After these introductory chapters, we will explore the most important parts of the Bible, always considering its relevance to the ultimate yearnings of every human heart – our search for meaning and hope and peace.

2

THE WORD OF GOD IN HUMAN WORDS

For centuries, Jewish believers expressed their faith in writing – poetry and prayer, sagas and legends, narratives and stories, preaching and laments. Those works of art came into existence as separate books (really, scrolls) written over a period of more than a thousand years by many different authors, most of whose names we don't know. When we read them now, bound together into a single volume, we must remember that they were once more than 70 different books – a small library.

Through these works of literary art, there emerges a picture of people who believed that they were loved and led by a God who reached into their lives and changed them for the better. It is a centuries-long process – from early, primitive practices and beliefs towards more sophisticated religious thought and behaviour.

Problems in Accepting the Scriptures as the Word of God

In the course of that journey of communal faith, some early beliefs and traditions were rejected. Early biblical faith was frankly superstitious, a magical view of life that blamed divine or demonic power for every bad thing that happened. Further, some believers thought of God at times as a vicious warrior who helped the people to annihilate their enemies, and who commanded them to kill
Deut 20:13-18 every living thing in defeated villages, to kill all the male children
Num 31:17-18 and all females who are not virgins in a defeated town, and to set
Josh 8:18 the city on fire. Their sense of God evolved over time, as did their
sense of humanity.

The Christian community has come to accept that further evolution in wisdom and faith – beyond the fundamental proclamation found in the Scriptures – will always be necessary.

For example, it took the Christian community more than 1,500 years to realize the wrongfulness of Paul's admonitions (and Jesus' silence) on the subject of people who have been enslaved by wealthy owners.

Slaves, obey your earthly masters with fear and trembling… Eph 6:5
as you obey Christ… Col 3:22

That text is found in a setting that also orders wives to submit Eph 5:22-23
to their husbands – a moral dictate from which it has taken the Col 3:18
Christian community even longer to emerge.

What endured throughout the long biblical history, and the journey of the community beyond it, has been the people's conviction that God was with them, leading them forward, responding with love to their quest for meaning and wholeness.

We read their works of art so that we may consider the validity of their insight about the deepest questions of human life, and share the beautiful and enduring aspects of their relationship with God.

Inspiration and Revelation

Revelation

Since ancient times, the believing community has perceived that somehow God is speaking to us through these works of literature. It is not that God dictated thoughts or words into an author's mind, but that human beings searching for God came to believe that God was with them, leading them somewhere, revealing truth to them.

'Revelation' means that some of our deepest beliefs about God and about human life have been given to us by God. They are not simply the products of human invention. To believe in revelation is an act of faith; what we believe cannot be 'proven.' Beliefs that can most appropriately be called 'revealed' are beliefs that are unprecedented – not inherited from previous cultures and not obviously predictable. Some of our most familiar and basic religious teachings are distinctive, not shared with other ancient religions, and thus credibly understood as revealed by God. Examples could include the fundamental Jewish beliefs that God loves people (remarkable!) and invites people to love God in return, that God's love extends to generous forgiveness of our sinfulness, and that God defends the most vulnerable members of the community and rejects the insincere worship of the respectable and prosperous.

Christians believe that God is One, and at the same time triune (three in one) – an unprecedented teaching. And we marvel in our faith that God's greatest self-revelation was embodied in the life of a small-town craftsman whose death taught us more about God than any of his miraculous deeds. Revelation makes us say, "Who would ever have imagined that God is like that?"

Inspiration

When we say that Scripture is inspired by God, we mean that God was involved in the human journey of searching and learning and living.

God inspired the authors, and in that spirit they wrote what they believed, using art forms that were familiar to their culture.

God's inspiration did not preserve the authors from scientific or historical error. They weren't scientists, so they had no idea that our earth is a minuscule sphere of rock, molten at its core, whirling around a dying star at the edge of a galaxy that is at once indescribably immense (to us) and yet ridiculously tiny among the myriad galaxies in a literally immeasurable universe. Most of the biblical authors were not historians (as we now use the term); they would not have understood the hunger of contemporary humans for precision about exactly what happened. Those authors cared about the meaning of events, not the bare facts.

Inspiration doesn't even mean that the authors' understanding of God was always accurate, because we now perceive that God has led us beyond early misunderstandings to a deeper vision of who God is, through centuries of living and praying together in a community of faith.

The biblical authors made use of a great variety of forms of literature, some of which are listed in the opening paragraph of this chapter. To understand the profound meaning that those authors were trying to express, a modern reader must become acquainted with the literary art forms of that long-ago culture. We must seek to get inside the mind of the writers, to read history as history, saga as saga, poetry as poetry.

One important art form used by the ancient peoples was the story. When great thinkers wanted to express insight about the most profound human questions, they didn't write conceptual treatises. They told stories. The parables of Jesus are one famous type of fictional story told to express an important and sometimes unexpected truth about God and about life. There never was a specific 'good Samaritan' or 'prodigal son' – those are fictional characters invented by Jesus to teach us about God and about life.

The greatest ancient art form for expressing spiritual insight is a genre we now call 'myth.' Don't understand that word to mean fairytale, or something basically untrue. Myths are used in every culture to teach truth – not necessarily facts, but deep religious or spiritual insight. Storytellers who lived before Jesus developed unforgettable myths to express religious truth about the relationship of God and the world, the reality and the consequences of sin, the meaning of life and the mystery of death.

When we say that Scripture is the inspired Word of God, we mean that God has led humanity forward in the search for meaning and wholeness in life, and for an ever-deeper relationship with God. We view all of the Scriptures – errors, misunderstandings, questions and profound revelations – as the inspired Word of God for us. And we search in our sacred books for the seeds of understanding, of faith, of love, of hope; we search for the voice of God who speaks to us in a language that reaches the depths of our hearts; we search for the face of God who responds to our deepest yearnings.

Contemporary Biblical Interpretation

For centuries, most Christians were under the impression that the Bible should be taken literally. In reality, our great scholars and saints always understood that the Bible should be read not primarily for facts, but for meaning. Preachers and teachers have probed the symbolic depths of Scripture, going far beyond the facts to offer insight and support to believers.

Roman Catholic leaders realized many centuries ago that poorly educated people would experience problems dealing with superstition presented as valid belief, with variations in reports about the same event, or with harsh understandings of God. As a result, 'untrained' Catholics were not permitted to read the Scriptures in their own languages. That practice was one of the factors that gave rise to the Protestant Reformation, as Martin Luther and others insisted on providing the Scriptures to the people in a language they could understand, and declared individual interpretation of the Bible to be a fundamental principle of the life of faith.

At the same time, the Reformed Churches maintained strong community interpretation of the Scriptures to guide believers in their search for meaning. In the past 200 years, Protestant scholars have led the way to our modern historical-critical method of understanding the Bible.

In 1943, Pope Pius XII called the Bible "the Word of God in human words," to authorize Catholic acceptance of the underlying principles of modern scriptural study while maintaining a faithful Catholic community interpretation of the texts. If we are going to understand the Bible properly as modern believers, said the pope, we must respect "the modes of writing the authors of that period would use" (*Divino Afflante Spiritu* [By the inspiration of the Divine Spirit], par. 35).

Fundamentalism

Originally, 'literalism' was a term used to define the viewpoint of believers who take every word of the Bible as factually true, and justify their point of view by devising explanations for every difficult phrase. They tend to treat the text of the Bible as if it were dictated verbatim by God, and they use it to justify rigid doctrinal and moral points of view. Thus, some believers are sure that God created the world in six days only a few thousand years ago; that during human history a flood once covered the earth to the tops of the mountains; and even that God has a human body, since the Bible talks about God's face and hands. Such interpreters can use the Scriptures to support racism, slavery, and discrimination against women or any number of groups. Every reader could develop a list of scriptural sayings that cause problems for people who would take the Bible literally, but fundamentalist believers have an answer for every objection, and are unshakeable in their opinions.

The Catholic Church and the mainstream Protestant Churches are now firmly opposed to such a literal or fundamentalist approach, and advise believers to learn about and respect the literary art forms used by the scriptural authors to express the faith that is Word of God for us. The Churches also provide adherents with careful interpretations that are accepted within the community of believers.

A great many believers and faith communities still accept a strictly literal interpretation of the Scriptures. Such fundamentalism exists in Christian, Jewish and Muslim communities, and presumably in all religions. Fundamentalism inevitably involves political as well as spiritual understandings, with the result that some states and nations are governed by fundamentalist leaders. Most mainstream religious communities decry fundamentalist groups as dangerous, and insist that they do not represent the great religions at their best.

Thus, Muslim fundamentalists justify the use of violent means to drive 'infidels' (as well as other Muslims with whom they fiercely disagree) out of Islamic territories, while a majority of Muslim leaders insist that such violence is not worthy of the teachings of Mohammed enshrined in the Qur'an. Jewish fundamentalists may believe that God truly gave the land of Palestine to Jewish people as their Promised Land, even though it was already home to people of other cultures. Most Christians fear and loathe Christian fundamentalists who believe, for example, that God has called them to murder doctors who provide legal abortions, or that the devil has possessed their child and must be driven out by means that do irreparable harm. And, tragically, Muslim, Jewish and Christian fundamentalists may believe that their political enemies are God's enemies, that God favours only them, and that God urges them to annihilate their opposition.

No doubt the most significant problem for a thoughtful believer is how to decide which parts of our written and oral tradition should be taken literally, and which parts are to be understood symbolically. That question is best dealt with in a community of faith that does not leave the believer to search alone, but offers the benefit of centuries of tradition combined with the best insight of contemporary scholarship and thought. We don't have to make sense of the Bible all by ourselves; we do it with the help of scholars and faith leaders who help us to explore the Scriptures, and to face the most difficult questions, in a context of mutual support.

Methodology

So how can we find out what the Scriptures really mean? Modern scholarship has built up an array of methods to help discern the true intent of the authors. These tools are indispensable for intelligent Scripture study; but as footings in a building are the invisible supports for the useable structure, scriptural methodology provides only an invisible foundation for the search for truth. The essential purpose of Scripture study is to enable believers to seek strength and meaning in the Scriptures. Some may say that academic tools have been given too large a role in books and courses about the Bible, trapping students in the study of detail to the detriment of the real purpose of Scripture study. If you are familiar with the subject of this Methodology section, please go on to the material that follows.

Textual Criticism

The initial step in academic Scripture study must be to establish exactly what words the author wrote in each biblical document. We don't have a single original copy. The best we have are ancient handwritten copies of copies. Yet one would be mistaken to think that we can't know what the authors wrote. Scholars compare texts (in the original languages, mostly Hebrew and Greek) written centuries ago in Russia and Spain and Africa and Syria and Rome, and find substantial agreement, despite many discrepancies. With regard to the Old Testament, the Dead Sea scrolls provide an amazing time capsule, containing almost the entire Hebrew Scriptures, apparently as they were being read when Jesus was alive – and they agree in remarkable detail with the Scriptures that are read in synagogues and Christian churches today.

When textual variations exist among copies, scholars of what is called "Textual Criticism" study the variations carefully, and try to decide which of the variant readings is most likely to have been written by the original author. And though many people instinctively say, "How could they know?" the scholars' methods of discernment are very carefully constructed. For example, scholars think that the more difficult a reading is to explain, the more likely it is to be the original reading. Most versions of Mark 1:41 say that Jesus was "moved with pity" when the leper approached him, and only a few read that he was "moved with anger." Scholars note that 'anger' is the more difficult reading, and many think it is more likely that a copyist changed 'anger' (which he saw in the text he was copying) to 'pity,' than the other way around.

There are a few parts of the Bible (especially in the Hebrew Scriptures) whose original text cannot be figured out with certainty. Still, scholars generally agree that we can be reasonably sure of what the original authors wrote in more than 95 per cent of the texts, especially in the New Testament.

Linguistics

Perhaps the most important element in academic exploration of Scripture is the study of language. In seeking the meaning of important terms, scholars compare every use of a given word throughout the Bible, learn what they can from the use of the word in the literature of the time and even in the marketplace, and consider how the word was translated into other languages, ancient and modern. Careful study of language has been a great help in understanding the Scriptures, especially considering that they were created in a culture very different from ours. To people of Hebrew heritage (such as Jesus and Paul), words like 'body' and 'soul', 'flesh' and 'spirit' meant something quite different from what the same words mean to people of European heritage. (See Chapter 14, on Resurrection, for an explanation.) Careful Scripture study is an exacting exploration of the meaning of words.

Study of the Oral Tradition

For hundreds of years, in the case of Jewish tradition, and for decades after the death and resurrection of Jesus, teachings and events and their interpretations were conveyed only by word of mouth. Elders retold stories to succeeding generations around dinner tables and campfires, and in the course of community worship. Preachers carried the word to new communities, and stayed to tell what they knew until the new community could carry the tradition forward.

Scholars, including anthropologists, have examined the characteristics of oral tradition in many cultures. Contrary to popular misunderstanding, oral tradition is very conservative as well as creative – repeated retellings tend to ensure that at least essential components of narratives are preserved, even as later generations add interpretations and insights as part of ongoing community life.

Source Criticism

It has long been perceived that some stories in the Bible are duplicated. Noah and his kin and the animals enter the ark, and

Gen 7:6-17 the floods cover the earth. Shortly thereafter, Noah and his kin
and the animals enter the ark, and it begins to rain. It appears
that the same episode is being narrated twice in a row. Many of
Exod 20:1-17 the Laws of Moses, including the Ten Commandments, are
Deut 5:1-22 reported more than once, with variations. Several accounts of
Jesus' miracles are repeated, almost word for word, in three
gospels. There are many other examples in both the Old and New
Testaments of narratives that are duplicated, or that seem to be
copied almost verbatim from another part of the Bible.

It is now widely accepted that, much like essay-writing students today, the authors of many parts of the Bible wove together pre-existing written sources in creating their narratives. Often they had such respect for their written sources that they included more than one version of the same event, as found in different sources. The first five books of the Hebrew Bible were written not by Moses, but by authors who lived centuries after Moses, and made use of written versions of the saga of the Jewish people that had developed in different places during earlier centuries. Scholars are convinced that the authors of the gospels according to Matthew and Luke had the Gospel of Mark on their desks, and literally copied almost all of Mark in composing their own versions of the good news of Jesus.

Using a method known as "Source Criticism," scholars carefully 'unweave' the strands of tradition that underlie the Scriptures as we have them, study any changes that were made by the later authors, and draw conclusions about the characteristics and preoccupations of the faith communities in which the documents were created.

Form Criticism

In addition to exploring the oral stage of tradition and the written sources that the authors used, scholars also study the characteristics of the literary genres represented in the Scriptures, and the use that was made of them in the communities of faith. Since the texts are made up of a series of small components, scholars describe the format of a miracle story, or a parable, a coronation psalm, or a blessing used at a wedding.

Narratives of Jesus' Last Supper were likely shaped by being repeated in communal worship, just as we hear them now during our eucharistic services.

The Lord Jesus on the night when he was betrayed took a loaf of bread,
and when he had given thanks, he broke it and said,
"This is my body that is for you.
Do this in remembrance of me."

1 Cor 11:23 see also Mt 26:26 Mk 14:22 Lk 22:19

Other reported sayings of Jesus are affected by Christian practices decades after his death. For example, "…baptizing them in the name of the Father and of the Son and of the Holy Spirit" (Mt 28:19) really reports not the words of Jesus in the days after his resurrection, but the baptism formula used in the author's community more than 50 years after the resurrection.

Some reflective expressions about the greatness of Jesus are likely examples of early Christian creeds.

He is the image of the invisible God, the firstborn of all creation; for in him all things in heaven and on earth were created…

Col 1:15-20 see also Phil 2:6-11

Redaction Criticism

Finally, it is important to realize that the biblical authors, while they made use of oral and written forms of their traditions, also drew upon their own genius, their faith, their insight, their point of view. Thus, one preoccupation of scholars is to decipher the contribution of the *rédacteurs*, the 'editors' who gave us the final version of each document that we accept as the Word of God. The main point made in redaction criticism is that each author was more than a redactor – they were faithful and inspired believers who shaped the message as they expressed it.

In addition to all the above methods, Scripture scholars recognize that interpretation depends on the living relationship between the text and the reader. When a text leaves an author's pen, it takes on a life of its own, and is read in the context of all the other sacred writings of which it forms a part, and in a social context generation after generation. Scholars use modern social sciences, including sociology and anthropology, to understand the development of interpretations through the years, in the confident understanding that no single generation or interpretation can exhaust the meaning of the Scriptures. The discussion of the Scriptures that follows in this book is invisibly dependent on all those branches of scriptural scholarship. The focus of the discussion, however, will be on the influence the Scriptures can have upon our search for meaning and direction in our lives, and our awareness of the presence and action of God within us and among us.

Translations

Almost everyone reads the Bible in a language other than the language in which it was written. Most of the Old Testament was written in Hebrew; some was written in Aramaic or in Greek. All of the New Testament was written in Greek. Since Jesus likely spoke and taught in Aramaic (a language related to Hebrew), we know that when we read the gospels, his teachings come to us twice translated – first to Greek, and then to English.

The study of the original languages of the Bible by scholars has improved immensely in the past 200 years. While there are still uncertainties and disagreements about the proper translation of certain words or concepts, we can be reasonably confident that what we read in English is very close to what the authors intended to express.

Still, there are major differences among available translations. The best English translation, the one that is used in Catholic churches in Canada, is the New Revised Standard Version (NRSV). The NRSV is the accomplishment of a committee of Roman Catholic, Anglican and Protestant scholars, and offers the most accurate literal translation of the words of the authors into English. As much as possible, for example, the NRSV uses the same English word to translate the original word every time, rather than using synonyms that might seem to make the meaning clearer. The NRSV is the best choice for adults, but the quality of its English makes it too difficult for children to understand easily.

The Good News translation (Today's English Version) is much more readable and understandable, but it attempts to include interpretation in its translation, so it is not as literally accurate as the NRSV.

A classic example of translation for meaning and readability rather than literal translation is found in one of Isaiah's famous prophecies about the future Messiah. (Isaiah 11:1 – see Chapter 10 for a more complete introduction to this text.) The NRSV translates the verse accurately as "A shoot shall come out from the stump of Jesse, and a branch shall grow out of his roots." The

Good News translators apparently thought that their readers would not be aware that Jesse, whose name appears in the "Jesse tree" activity practised in Advent by many Christian families, was the father of King David. As a result, Isaiah 11:1 in the Good News Bible reads, "The royal line of David is like a tree that has been cut down, but just as branches sprout from a stump, so a new king will arise from David's descendants." That really is what the words of Isaiah mean, but the Good News translation conveys neither the terse intensity of the original words, nor the significant reference to Jesse.

The New Jerusalem Bible, a fairly recent translation by Catholic scholars, and the New American Bible are also good translations for use by contemporary students of the Scriptures.

The King James Version (KJV) is a paragon of the English language, but unfortunately it is the English of 400 years ago. The Bible was written in the language of ordinary people, and most ordinary people today would find the KJV archaic and distant from their experience. As well, our knowledge about the original meaning of the scriptural texts has developed immensely since 1603, so the KJV should be read and appreciated for its elegance, but a more contemporary translation should be used by adults who want to explore the meaning of the Scriptures.

Older Catholics may have the Douai-Rheims translation, which was developed in France by English Catholics in exile in the 1600s. This translation was based on a Latin translation of the original texts, and it is simply not good enough for contemporary use.

Finally, there are a few versions of the Scriptures that are more accurately called 'interpretive paraphrases' than translations (e.g., "The Way"). Though they may be attractive to some people, they suffer because they represent the opinions of their authors more than the thoughts of the original scriptural writers.

Revelation Continues

In the years that have passed since the last book of the Bible was written, new images and concepts have been developed about God. Humanity's scientific understanding of the world has improved. We are generally less credulous, more skeptical, perhaps less open to superstition. Our awareness of the complexities of the human personality has grown in directions that were unimagined 2,000 years ago. Our communal sense about right and wrong with regard to some areas of behaviour has become clearer. Especially in economically developed societies, our prosperity has expanded far beyond the imaginings of the biblical peoples. Yet our capacity for evil and cruelty and selfishness seems, if anything, to have increased. We need to be challenged to share, and we need to be forgiven for our sins. Our deepest questions remain, to be engaged anew in each generation.

In many ways, God continues to speak to us and to lead us onwards – in the words of the poets and preachers, storytellers and prophets of our generation, and in the shared wisdom of the faith community.

Revelation, in a sense, continues, as God continues to speak to our hearts in our own time.

But Christians and Jews agree that the Bible remains the foundation for our ongoing journey. Both communities are convinced that, though God continues to speak to us, there will be no additions to the Bible; no further writings will be described as the inspired Word of God. The foundation is set; everything else is commentary. Communities of faith strive to be faithful to their origins, while developing new understandings and expressions of faith that respond to the needs of contemporary believers. That's why we need a Church – so that our continuing quest for understanding and for a deeper communion with our God takes place in a setting of mutual support, in continuity with the past, in touch with present society, under the guidance of our leaders in faith.

Despite the immense changes that have taken place in society and in religion, many of us continue to turn to the Scriptures, and find a sense of God and life that responds to our needs, a kind of foundational faith upon which we can build our lives in our complex societies.

That's why the Bible is still a bestseller. That's why people still want to learn about the faith that is expressed in the Scriptures. In the coming chapters, we will consider many aspects of biblical faith in an effort to explore again the meaning of human existence and the God who through the ages has spoken words of life to the human heart.

3

THE STORY OF A PEOPLE

The Age of the Patriarchs

Abraham and Sarah

The first historical characters in the biblical epic were Abraham and Sarah.

The term 'historical' is used to refer simply to the remembered
past. What we know of Abraham and Sarah (from the narratives Gen 12–23
that begin in Chapter 12 of the book of Genesis) is based on memories that were preserved within their clan, and passed from generation to generation by word of mouth for centuries before they were written down.

The biblical narratives in the first 11 chapters of the book of Genesis, on the other hand, describe 'pre-historic times' – a time we can't remember, literally "once upon a time." The well-known
narratives of the creation of the world, the first sin, the people Gen 1–3
who lived to be 800 and 900 years old, the flood that covered the Gen 5
entire earth to the tops of the mountains, and the Tower of Babel Gen 6–9
are all the creations of thoughtful and imaginative believers who Gen 11:1-9
were exploring some of the great religious questions of humanity, using an art form known as myth to express their insights.

We will explore those myths in greater detail in later chapters.

The narratives about Abraham and Sarah and their offspring Gen 12–50
aren't myths, but might better be called sagas – tales about our ancestors that are based on memories, but are not simply factual accounts, because they evolved in oral form for centuries before being written.

Abraham and Sarah lived more than 1,800 years before the
Gen 11:29-31 time of Jesus. They grew up as city-dwellers in Ur, in what is now
southern Iraq, not far from Kuwait and the Persian Gulf. After
they married, they migrated a thousand kilometres northwards
with Abraham's clan, and settled in Haran, a city in today's Turkey.

The dateline on the next page depicts the twists and turns of the Jewish community of faith during the centuries when the Bible was being written. On the right side of the dateline are listed some famous people and events in sequence. Left of the line are many of the books of the Hebrew Scriptures, listed approximately at the time they were written. This chapter offers a brief narrative of the history of the Jewish people in biblical times, as a foundation for a more thorough exploration of their religious writing in future chapters.

Unfortunately for them, however, economic times had become
desperate. Cities were no longer able to support their population.
In a scenario that has been repeated all over the world in our
time, people began to leave their homes in search of survival.
Abraham and Sarah and their extended family became nomads.
Abraham became the head of a clan of herders who lived in tents
Gen 12:8-10 and wandered the lands of the eastern Mediterranean. The story
of their family is told as a story of faith, a story in which God
plays an active role in daily life and in the events that make up
the history of a family.

We will discuss the religious importance of the stories of the
patriarchs and their families in Chapter 5. For the purposes of
this chapter, let us only report that the rest of the book of Genesis
Gen 16–50 provides numerous sagas about Sodom and Gomorrah, Sarah and
Hagar, Isaac and Ishmael, Isaac and Rebekah, Jacob and Esau,
Jacob and Rachel and Leah and their 12 sons and who knows
how many daughters with amazing stories of their own? The most
famous of their sons was Joseph (of the amazing technicolor
dreamcoat). The sagas about Joseph fill 14 chapters in the book
Gen 37–50 of Genesis; these tales of folk history are so colourful and
memorable that they formed the basis of a 20th-century rock
musical.

At the death of Joseph, at the end of the book of Genesis, the curtain goes down on Act One of the drama of the Jewish people – and it won't be raised again for 400 or 500 years. We have no

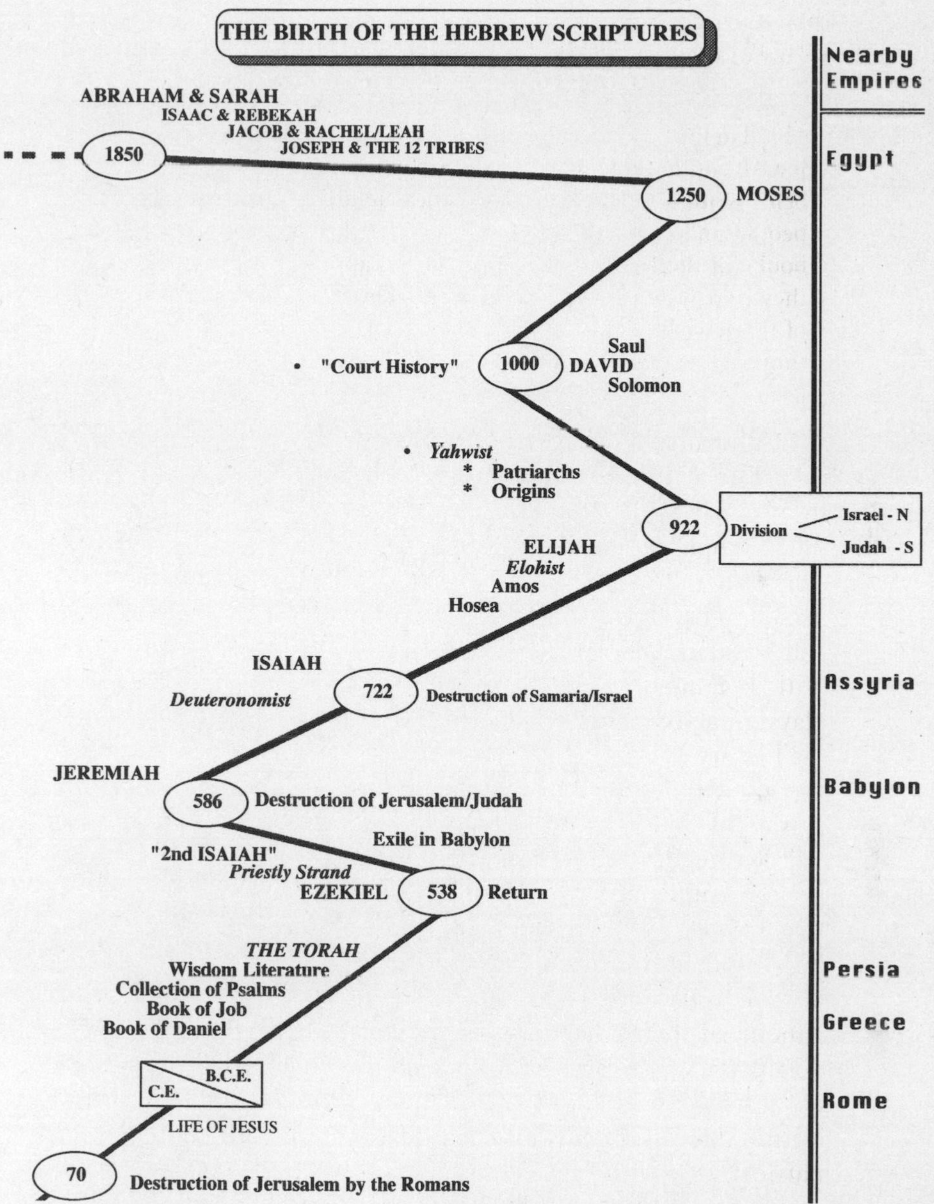
THE BIRTH OF THE HEBREW SCRIPTURES
Nearby Empires
ABRAHAM & SARAH
ISAAC & REBEKAH
JACOB & RACHEL/LEAH
JOSEPH & THE 12 TRIBES
1850
Egypt
1250
MOSES
Saul
"Court History"
1000
DAVID
Solomon
Yahwist
* Patriarchs
* Origins
922
Division
Israel - N
Judah - S
ELIJAH
Elohist
Amos
Hosea
ISAIAH
Deuteronomist
722
Destruction of Samaria/Israel
Assyria
JEREMIAH
586
Destruction of Jerusalem/Judah
Babylon
Exile in Babylon
"2nd ISAIAH"
Priestly Strand
EZEKIEL
538
Return
THE TORAH
Wisdom Literature
Collection of Psalms
Book of Job
Book of Daniel
Persia
Greece
B.C.E.
C.E.
LIFE OF JESUS
Rome
70
Destruction of Jerusalem by the Romans

memories of what happened to the descendants of Abraham and Sarah until the curtain rises for Act Two, the most important period in Jewish history – the time of Moses.

> Out of respect for people of many faiths all around the world who now use the familiar year-numbering system that originated in Christian Europe, some Bible scholars prefer not to use the designations B.C. (before Christ) and A.D. (*Anno Domini*, Latin for "In the year of our Lord"). Since people who are Hindu, Sikh, Muslim, Jewish or atheist do not think of Jesus as their "Lord," we use the designations CE (the Common Era) and BCE (Before the Common Era).

Moses

According to the book of Exodus, by the year 1250 BCE the descendants of Abraham and Sarah had been reduced to slavery, labouring in camps in the fertile delta of the Nile, surviving as an oppressed underclass in a prosperous and sophisticated Egyptian civilization. Moses was born a Hebrew but grew up in Egyptian
Exod 1:15–2:10 society – indeed, according to the saga, he was adopted by a princess in the court of the Pharaoh.

As an adult, so the story goes, Moses was wanted for murder after he killed an Egyptian overlord for beating a Hebrew labourer.
Exod 2:11-22 Now a fugitive, he fled eastwards, joined a clan of desert nomads, married, and fathered a child.

In that setting, Moses had a profound religious experience,
Exod 3 after which he was convinced that God was leading him to return to his kinsfolk and to set them free from servitude. By taking advantage of a combination of circumstances, Moses did indeed lead his people into freedom, and taught them to resume their ancestral ways as desert nomads.

It was in that setting that the religious awareness of the Jewish tradition first took shape. Here began the people's faith in God as their Saviour, who set them free, established a covenant with them and gave them the Law to guide their lives as faithful children of God. The religious experiences at the time of Moses were so significant that they shaped the telling of the stories about Abraham and Sarah and their descendants, and they have shaped the self-understanding of the Jewish people to this day. Chapters

7 and 8 will discuss the meaning of the foundational events at the time of Moses in more detail.

Settlement in Palestine

Perhaps a generation later, the Jewish people invaded or infiltrated
Palestine, and settled as 12 informally linked clans living in loosely Josh
defined territories in the hill country.

The people's sense of God at this time is particularly difficult
for modern believers to accept: "The LORD" was clearly thought
of as a ruthless (male) warrior-God. At times (especially in the
book of Joshua), it seems that the Jewish invaders practised Josh 8:24-25
genocide and claimed that their God ordered them to kill everyone Josh 10:34-42
in village after village. Some narratives claim that God did the Josh 10:11
smiting and killing. Josh 11:6

Faith in a God who orders genocide is part of the history of our tradition. In time, the tradition itself disavowed this teaching, and we no longer believe that God is male, brutal or a warrior. This primitive aspect of the tradition is seen as a product of human misunderstanding rather than of divine revelation.

In some accounts of the period during which the Jewish people
first became settlers in Palestine, it seems that the newcomers
moved in as relatively peaceful neighbours beside the previous Judg 3:5-6
inhabitants of the land, known as Canaanites. Another group of
settlers, who lived mainly along the Mediterranean seacoast, were
known as Philistines.

The narratives that have been preserved from the period of the settlement portray vicious tribal warfare and petty heroics. Though there are some religious themes in the books, they are far from the most edifying sections of the Scriptures.

The Period of the Monarchy

After 200 years of turmoil, Jewish society grew more politically sophisticated when the scattered clans arranged to unite under a single ruler.

The Story of Ruth

Prior to the rise of the monarchy is the story of a woman who was
born in the land of Moab, east of the Jordan River. Ruth married Ruth
a Jewish man who had migrated into Moab because of famine;
before long Ruth's husband died, and she was left childless in the

company of her Jewish mother-in-law, Naomi. In a remarkable act of personal loyalty, Ruth left her homeland and travelled with Naomi back to the birthplace of her husband. There, the two women contrived to enable Ruth to seduce and marry Boaz, a wealthy landowner, and bear a son. The term 'seduce' is justified when you read the following text knowing that 'feet' was used as a euphemism for 'genitals' in Hebrew. Naomi advises Ruth to wait until Boaz falls asleep from over-indulgence: "[When] he has
Ruth 3:3-4 finished eating and drinking…observe the place where he lies; then go and uncover his feet and lie down."

Three generations later, the outcome was that a Moabite woman became the great-grandmother of David, the greatest king the Israelites ever had. The writer could only marvel at God's ability to bring greatness out of tragedy, human deception and interracial marriage between an Israelite man and a foreign woman.

King Saul

The first king of the Jewish people was a warrior named Saul. The book of Samuel portrays the misgivings of many people, including the prophet Samuel, who opposed the idea of a
1 Sam 8 monarchy, believing that only God should be called king of the
1 Sam 9:16-17 Jewish people. But the view prevailed that God had chosen Saul to act in God's place as leader and defender of the people.

It was a regrettable choice. Saul fought real and imagined enemies at home and abroad, could tolerate no rivals for the affection of the people, is reported to have suffered spells of raving, dabbled in the occult in search of favourable omens, and died by suicide in the course of losing a battle that he should not have undertaken in the first place. "How the mighty have fallen," wrote
2 Sam 1:27 a poet, "and the weapons of war perished!"

King David

Saul was succeeded by the legendary King David, whose career was the more remarkable because he was born not as a prince in a royal family, but as a member of a family of herders, people at the lowest levels of society who lived in tents and barely survived.

David became famous when he caught by surprise the champion of the Philistines, felling him with a rock between the eyes when Goliath was expecting to demolish David in a sword
1 Sam 17 fight. At first, David was welcomed as a hero into Saul's court,

becoming a close friend of Saul's son Jonathan, and being given 1 Sam 18:1-5
Saul's daughter Michal as his wife. But when it became obvious 1 Sam 18:20-22
that David was more popular than the king, Saul began to hate 1 Sam 18:19-20
David and to plot against him, eventually driving him into exile.

When Saul died, David returned to become king, at first of
the southern tribes from which he came, and eventually of all
Israel. He established his capital at Jerusalem, "the city of David," 2 Sam 1
and enjoyed a 33-year reign of unprecedented peace and
prosperity.

Numerous stories about David portray a man who was predictably as brutal as any person with such power, but who also had a depth of humanity that has been respected for centuries. Two examples follow.

David and Bathsheba

Like any despot of his time, David had a selection of wives, and a
palace full of concubines to satisfy every sexual whim. Strolling
on his palace roof one day, he saw a woman bathing and sent
minions to bring her, willing or not, into the palace. Though 2 Sam 11
Bathsheba was married to Uriah, one of David's soldiers, the king
had his way with her, and soon she realized that she was pregnant.
The penalty for adultery under the Law of Moses was death for
both partners. David's efforts to cover his tracks resulted in the
death of Bathsheba's husband, Uriah, leaving David guilty of both
adultery and murder. But he was off the hook: Bathsheba moved
into his palace and became his favourite wife and the mother of
the next king, Solomon.

Nathan, an observer in David's court, had the wisdom and
courage to protest. Risking his life, he told the king a story about
a poor shepherd whose only lamb had been snatched and killed
by a rich owner of many herds. When the king demanded
punishment for the rich herder, Nathan pointed the finger of
challenge and declared, "You are the man!" To his credit, David 2 Sam 12:1-14
recognized and lamented the evil he had done.

The Revolt of Absalom

Later in his life, David's son Absalom attempted to succeed him
in power by having himself declared king by his followers while
the old king was still alive. David suffered the humiliation of 2 Sam 15
having to flee his own capital city disguised, barefoot and weeping

before the looming invasion by the forces of his rebel son. Yet when David regrouped his troops to regain his throne, he commanded his generals not to harm his son, and when Absalom
2 Sam 18:33 was killed despite his father's orders, David wept bitterly and wished he had died instead.

Such is the portrait of David the king in the Scriptures – likely a fairly accurate impression of a man of heroic exploits and exploitative power, a man of human strength and human weakness, a man like many others whose faith seemed to affect his life only occasionally.

The Beginnings of Hebrew Literature

The reign of David was a time of relative peace and growing prosperity. No enemy empire threatened his welfare, and the borders of the tiny nation expanded to dimensions that were never reached again until 1967 CE.

In David's kingdom, for the first time in Jewish history, the benefits of leisure began to be enjoyed, and thus it was that a literature could finally begin to develop.

Thoughtful, creative artists poured out a remarkable variety of literary works. One type of writing could be described as a kind of court history of the king – possibly written by someone who was there.

2 Sam The stories about David include no voices from heaven, no angel messengers, no miraculous events. They are very realistic, portraying the good and the bad in the career of a significant political and cultural leader. Of course, like modern reporting and history-writing, the narratives are based on a point of view: they were written by someone who recognized the source of his daily bread, and who therefore was very sympathetic to the king, and supported the claim that God chose David and his family to rule over Israel forever.

Some time later, during the reign of Solomon, a writer was recording the traditions about Abraham and Sarah and their offspring, stories that had been remembered in oral form for some 800 years before being committed to writing. Those accounts had evolved significantly over the centuries, and while they are based on some kind of communal memory, they are more aptly described as sagas than as history in our sense of the word. Primitive and magical tales, voices from heaven, cataclysms portrayed as acts

of God: all give us an impression of the generations of early Gen 12–50
believers who kept and shaped the sagas of their ancestors.

Also being recorded for the first time were the accounts of the foundational period in Jewish history – the people's departure from Egypt under Moses and the subsequent origins of the covenant and the Law. Those stories had been preserved for almost 300 years in oral form; they, too, evolved in oral form before taking Exod
the shape in which we know them as written narratives.

One highlight of this early literature was the product of a genius whose name we will never know, a profound believer and poet and thinker and storyteller who created tales about a time that no one can remember. Using myth, the art form by which the ancient peoples expressed their deepest insights about life, this author struggled with profound religious questions about the origins of our being, the relationship of God with the world and the people in it, the sources and consequences of evil. And so the stories of Adam and Eve, Noah and the Flood, the Tower of Babel, and several other episodes and genealogies were written Gen 1–11
by a nameless writer in the time of maturing civilization that marked the reigns of King David and King Solomon.

One significant characteristic of these stories must be mentioned. Although it seems clear that the sacred name YHWH was first used at the time of Moses, the author(s) of these first written accounts of Hebrew tradition, who lived about 300 years *after* the time of Moses, used the name YHWH for God from the *beginning* of their narrative. (Hebrew writing of the Name used only consonants; although the Name was not to be spoken aloud, scholars think that the word would have been pronounced "Yahweh." See also Chapter 8, on the third commandment.) They made it appear that the sacred name YHWH was known in the days of Adam and Eve, Noah, Abraham and Sarah and their descendants. The use of YHWH throughout the narrative has led us to give a name to this earliest strand of tradition – and to its anonymous author: both are known as "the Yahwist."

King Solomon

David was succeeded by Bathsheba's son, Solomon, and the political decline of Israel began almost at once. Although Solomon has an enduring reputation for being a fair judge and a speaker of wisdom, he became a very unpopular ruler, largely because of his policy of conscription.

As soon as a young man went through puberty, at the age of 13 or 14, he was considered an adult, and his first duty as an adult was to serve in the king's army. Unwisely, the king used his army as a source of forced labour, and made these young men
1 Kings 5:13-18 build for him palaces, stables, ships, mines and other public works. Before their military duty was complete, many of the young soldiers died as a result of being forced to work in the brutal heat. Those who survived were returned to their families, often broken in body and spirit. Thus the king's despotism affected every family in the nation, and the people's hatred for Solomon grew and festered.

Most notable among the edifices constructed for the honour and glory of Solomon was the magnificent Temple in Jerusalem. Built of "great costly stones" and equally costly cedar from the hills of Lebanon, the Temple featured courtyards surrounding the altar of sacrifice and the inner sanctum, which housed the ark of
1 Kings 6 the covenant containing the stone tablets of the Ten Commandments.

There was only one Temple in the entire country, and the worship that took place there was distinctive. Managed by a hereditary High Priesthood, almost a royal family in itself, the Temple was the site of daily animal and grain sacrifices, and of the official institutional celebrations of the high holy days.

Only members of the clan of Levi can serve as Jewish priests, but of course far more people belonged to that clan than could be employed as priests at the Temple. A family of high priests established themselves in power at the Temple, and passed on the role from generation to generation. Other members of the clan of Levi were given occasional assignments at the Temple, but otherwise lived as ordinary citizens. Contemporary members of the clan of Levi continue to preserve their awareness of their priestly heritage in their family names: the Hebrew word for priest is 'cohen,' a name that is also preserved in contemporary Jewish family names.

In later centuries, rabbis in the towns and villages taught the people and led them in prayer in the synagogues, but from the time of Solomon, Jerusalem claimed pre-eminent status as the centre of Jewish faith and culture. The priests required that true believers should journey to the Temple to take part in the high holy days and the sacrifices, the most significant and authentic forms of Temple worship.

The Division of the Kingdom

So unpopular was Solomon that immediately upon his death, ten of the 12 provinces (or clans) declared themselves unwilling to be ruled by any son of Solomon. They seceded from the federation and established their own kingdom in the northern part of the territory. They called their new country 'Israel,' established a capital city at Samaria, and began their own royal family. 1 Kings 12

Only Judah, David's clan, and Benjamin, the clan of King Saul, remained subject to the royal family of David. They called their little southern kingdom 'Judah,' and retained Jerusalem, David's city, as their capital.

Despite the reduction in size of their kingdom, the leaders of Judah retained their sense of self-importance. They continued to claim that authentic worship was to be found only in Jerusalem; they denounced the northern kingdom as corrupt and idolatrous, and they repeated the mantra that God had chosen the family of David to rule over the people forever. In reality, the northern kingdom of Israel did preserve the religious traditions of Moses, and their society was probably no more corrupt or idolatrous than the southern kingdom.

Indeed, during the first century after the division of the kingdom, a writer in the north gave us a second written version of the Jewish religious tradition as it was remembered by the people of the northern kingdom (Israel). Throughout his narrative, this writer used the word '*elohim*' (translated into English as 'God,' unlike the Hebrew name of God, YHWH, which is not translated: it's a name, not a noun). This second strand of tradition, and its anonymous author, is known as 'the Elohist.'

The Destruction of Israel (The Northern Kingdom)

Of course, two small kingdoms are not nearly as strong as one larger, united kingdom. To make matters worse, the two tiny Jewish domains began to consider each other as enemies, and formed alliances with neighbouring countries to battle each other. Soon they both came under attack as larger empires arose to the east.

The first conquering army came from Assyria, whose capital city, Nineveh, is now in eastern Iraq, not far from Baghdad. In 721 BCE, the Assyrians destroyed the 200-year-old kingdom of Israel and smashed Samaria, the capital city of the northern

kingdom. They besieged the southern capital, Jerusalem, at the
same time, and David's city seemed to be doomed until the day
the citizens awoke to find that the Assyrians had departed
2 Kings 17:1-5 overnight. The siege of Jerusalem was probably lifted for military
reasons, but the people of Judah celebrated, confirmed in their
opinion that God was on their side, and not on the side of the
conquered northerners. The prophet Isaiah, however, did not share
the enthusiasm of his compatriots, believing that, because of the
corruption of society, the destruction of Jerusalem was also
imminent. Instead of cheering, Isaiah lamented:

What do you mean that you have gone up,
all of you, to the housetops,
you that are full of shoutings…?
Your rulers have all fled together…
All of you who were found were captured…
do not try to comfort me
Is 22:1-4 *for the destruction of my beloved people.*

One result of the destruction of Israel and its capital city, Samaria, was that people from throughout the Assyrian empire settled among the hills of Palestine and married Israelite women. Thus began a people of mixed race who were known as Samaritans. They became victims of racial prejudice by the people of the south. Guerrilla warfare, ambushes and incidents of destruction were characteristic of the relationships between Jews and Samaritans.

That antagonism is background for two memorable incidents
Lk 10:25 in the life of Jesus: making a 'good Samaritan' the hero of a parable
that he told to a Jewish audience, and entering the old town of
Jn 4 Samaria and revealing the gospel to a Samaritan woman whom
he met at the well.

The Samaritans have survived as a people to this day. They have preserved their religious traditions and identity for more than two millennia, but they have suffered the genetic effects of their strong racial solidarity, and are likely to disappear as a distinct people in the near future.

The Destruction of Judah (The Southern Kingdom) and the Babylonian Exile

One hundred and forty years after the destruction of Israel, a new imperial power, the Babylonians, surged into Palestine and destroyed the tiny kingdom of Judah. Solomon's Temple was smashed into rubble; the ark of the covenant and the stone tablets of the Ten Commandments were destroyed; and many of the leading citizens were transported to Babylon (now in southern Iraq). The 50-year Babylonian exile marks the political low point 2 Kings 24:10 ff. in the classical period of Jewish history. Many good believers, who had accepted the traditional teaching that God was their all-powerful protector, found their faith shattered by the decline and destruction of their society. How could they continue to believe in a God whose faithful people were decimated, whose promised land was overrun by unbelievers, whose chosen royal family was dethroned and imprisoned, and whose earthly home – the Temple – was in ruins?

The great believers who saved the faith of the people during this long period of decline and eventual destruction are the preachers whom we know as the prophets.

The Prophets

In popular language, the term 'prophet' means 'someone who can foretell the future'. Christianity's primary awareness about the prophets has been centred around their expectation of the coming of the Messiah.

In fact, however, the term 'prophet' means 'someone who speaks on behalf of' someone else. In this case, the prophets spoke on behalf of God. These passionate preachers interpreted the events of their time in the name of God. In a community that was becoming progressively more critical of God and religion, the prophets forcefully declared that God was not to blame for the decline and destruction of Jewish society. Instead, they urged the people to realize that they had brought destruction upon themselves by their decadent and selfish lifestyles.

More than 90 per cent of the prophets' preaching was forceful criticism of their society at every level. They criticized kings and priests for being corrupt rather than fulfilling their responsibility to the people. They attacked the richer strata of society for greed and oppression of the poor. They demanded integrity, declaring that God remained faithful and loving towards the people, and that the people were to blame for their own demise because they had been unfaithful to the covenant.

Indeed, the hope for the Messiah was really a corollary of the prophets' criticism of their kings. "Your kings now are corrupt," they would proclaim, "but someday God will send us a great king who will be a faithful shepherd of God's people, and will call the people back to their senses, so that God will once again rule in our land and in our hearts."

The dateline on page 31 records the names of the prophets at approximately the time when they lived. More detail about their teaching is found in Chapter 10.

Torah

Next in the succession of conquering foreign rulers, the Persian emperor Cyrus overran the Babylonians and earned the Israelites' gratitude by permitting them to return to their ravaged homeland.
Is 45:1 (One of the prophets was so grateful that he called Cyrus God's 'anointed' – the phrase that was used to describe the Messiah.)

Thus the prisoners returned and tried to re-establish their society and culture amid the ruins. They never recaptured their former freedom, however, and remained an impoverished tribute-paying people, subjects first of the Persians, then of the Greeks under Alexander the Great, and eventually of the Romans.

The religious leaders among the prisoners who returned to Palestine in 538 BCE under the rule of Cyrus the Persian soon began to resume their traditions in the rubble of the Temple Hill in Jerusalem. They could not afford to rebuild in the style of Solomon, though they did erect a modest structure to house their worship services. Five hundred years later, a pretentious restoration project was undertaken under the patronage of Herod the Great, the king who was alive when Jesus was born. That was the structure that had been under construction for 46 years when
Jn 2:22 Jesus seemed to proclaim that he could raise it up in three days. The renovation project was completed in 63 CE, only to be destroyed forever by the Romans seven years later. A beautiful Muslim shrine topped by a golden dome sits today on the former site of Solomon's Temple.

The religious leaders returning from exile in the late 500s BCE also undertook a major literary project, as they began to compile and synthesize the written material that had been created in Jewish culture over the previous 500 years.

Weaving together the two major narrative strands of tradition (the Yahwist version dating from the time of David, and the Elohist version from the northern kingdom in the 900s), a committee of priests working in Jerusalem created the first four books of the Hebrew Scriptures as we know them today.

As compilers sometimes do, the editorial committee could not resist composing some material of their own to enhance the written material they were using. Their most famous original composition is Chapter 1 of the book of Genesis – the story of the seven days of creation. Thus we have two very different stories about creation – the story of Adam and Eve, part of the Yahwist strand, written around the year 950 BCE; and the story of the seven days of creation, written some 400 years later as part of a 'priestly strand,' which was included in the book of Genesis as we know it. We will discuss both creation narratives in Chapter 9.

As well, the compilers added other pre-existing material, including another version of the law of Moses, now found in the book of Deuteronomy (a Greek word meaning 'the second law').

Thus, five scrolls were created: the books of Genesis, Exodus, Leviticus, Numbers and Deuteronomy. Known in Hebrew as *Torah*, they form the core of the Hebrew Scriptures to this day. The Greek term *Pentateuch* (meaning 'five books') is also used in scholarly books to refer to Torah.

Soon, Torah was recognized to be more than just great religious literature, and came to be honoured as Scripture. People believed that God inspired these writings and was using the vehicle of sacred literature to speak to their minds and hearts. From that time, Torah was revered as "the word of God in human words."

The prophets had habitually begun their proclamations with the remarkable phrase "Thus says the LORD." With the creation of Torah, it was immediately recognized that the recorded preaching of the prophets was also "the word of God," and the core of the Scriptures soon included both "the Law and the Prophets."

The Writings

Jewish religious literature continued to develop despite the travails of Persian, Greek and Roman occupation. Although several different types of literature were produced during the ensuing 500 years, the most significant was Wisdom literature.

Prov

Sir (aka Ecclesiasticus)

Wis

Song

Eccl (aka Qoheleth)

Job

Characteristic of Wisdom writing is the insight that God is involved in every aspect of human life. Everything is sacred; nothing is merely secular.

Other books in Wisdom literature exult in the sensual love of a betrothed couple, struggle with the seeming futility of life's efforts, and confront the most difficult question every believer must face – the problem of God's role in the suffering of good people. As well, in the time after the Exile, the prayerful poetry of centuries was collected in the book of Psalms. Eventually, "the Writings" would be included in Sacred Scripture alongside the Law and the Prophets.

The wisdom of the sages will be discussed in more detail in Chapter 11.

Establishing the Canon

For 500 years, the Hebrew Scriptures were a collection in progress. Centred around Torah and the Prophets, any number of religious books were written, respected and considered as possible candidates for inclusion in the Scriptures.

The process came to a stop after another cataclysm befell Judaism. The Roman Empire had occupied Palestine for a hundred years, including the lifetime of Jesus. In the year 70 CE, the Roman general Titus, aggravated by several years of rebellion by Jewish militants, ordered the destruction of Jerusalem along with its newly rebuilt Temple. Jewish civilization in Palestine was almost eliminated. The Jewish people lost political control of the Holy Land, a control they did not regain until a declaration of the United Nations in 1948 created a Jewish state in Palestine.

After the disaster inflicted by the Romans, Jewish leaders met to consider the future of their culture. They recognized that if Jewish religion was to survive, it could no longer be based on the Temple and priesthood; it would have to be based on the Scriptures, which could be carried anywhere as the basis of faith and culture.

If their identity was to be based on The Book, they knew that everyone would have to be perfectly clear about what was in the book. So it was that Jewish academic and religious leaders selected a list of books and declared them to be the Word of God for the Jewish people. They realized that God continues to be revealed in new ways throughout history, and that other valuable religious writing would be created. But they believed that no later literature would have the authority and importance of these divinely inspired works of art, now known as the canon of the Hebrew Scriptures.

Further Complications

More than a millennium later, the bishops of the Catholic Church performed the same duty for the New Testament, deciding that early Christian documents would have the authority of Scripture. Their list has been accepted in all the Christian churches ever since.

Having accomplished that task, the bishops also reconsidered the Hebrew Scriptures. They were aware that many other Jewish books might have been included in the Hebrew Scriptures, had the process not been so abruptly terminated after the destruction of Jerusalem. Some of those books included writings that agreed with the thought of Jesus and could therefore be seen as preparing for the New Testament.

For that reason, the bishops in an ecumenical council confirmed that seven additional books by Jewish authors should be considered as inspired Scripture in the Christian Church. Thus the collection that Catholics call 'the Old Testament' has more Jewish books in it than the Hebrew Bible has.

When the Reformed Churches established their identity distinct from Roman Catholicism, they expressed their trust in the long-ago decision of the Jewish leaders, and declared that for the Churches of the Reformation, the Old Testament would be identical to the canon of the Hebrew Scriptures.

That decision resulted in the difference between Protestant and Catholic bibles that was familiar to Christians growing up in the twentieth century. Today, Protestant and Catholic scholars co-operate to produce many of the best modern translations of the Scriptures, and most editions of the Bible include the additional Jewish books. The Reformed Churches call those books 'the apocrypha' (which is derived from 'hidden' but can also mean 'not genuine'). The Roman Catholic and some other Churches call them 'the deuterocanonical books' (meaning 'the second canon' or 'the second list').

With that perhaps confusing historical note, we conclude this brief outline of the history of the Jewish people and of the development of their Scriptures.

After one further important introductory consideration, we will begin to explore specific portions of the Hebrew Scriptures, in an effort to perceive the profound, evolving and believable experience of God that bursts from every page.

4

GENDER EQUITY AND THE SCRIPTURES

Women and men should be equal, but until quite recently, women have not been treated as men's equal in political society or in the Christian community. Regrettably, the Bible and religious organizations are among the most significant offenders in this regard. From the beginning, our community of faith has enshrined a patriarchal understanding of society and of human life. For many of us, gender-exclusive language and images became part of our fibre as we grew up, and traditional attitudes are not easily overcome.

This chapter is an attempt to recognize and remedy exclusive and discriminatory language about people, God and faith.

Language and Imagery About People

The meaning and the connotations of words change constantly in a living language. You could probably think of several words that have acquired new meaning in our lifetime. Gay, pot and coke are a few that come to mind.

The word 'man' may have meant 'everyone' to previous generations, but it doesn't mean that anymore. Many people now perceive the word 'man' as referring only to males. Our society has become increasingly sensitive to this fact, with the result that more and more people avoid using 'man' or 'mankind' to refer to all humanity.

The best modern English translation of the Bible, the New Revised Standard Version (NRSV), consistently uses 'everyone,' 'person,' or 'humanity' (and, often, 'mortals') instead of 'man'; 'brothers and sisters' instead of just 'brothers'; 'one' or 'you' instead of 'he.' 'Brotherly love' has become 'mutual love,' and 'children of

God' replaces 'sons of God' in talking about all of us in the Christian community. Interestingly, the term 'fellowship' has been retained, though most people would probably think of males when they refer to 'fellows' (and 'community' might have expressed the concept just as well). The Canadian Catholic bishops authorized the gender-inclusive version of the NRSV for use in Catholic parishes beginning in 1992; the U.S. Catholic Church uses the New American Bible, a version that is being revised to be more gender-inclusive.

Such considerations about vocabulary may seem insignificant, but they are not. Exclusive language is everywhere, and it can be insidious. Readers who use a gender-exclusive translation of the Scriptures can train themselves to notice such language and revise it mentally as they read.

Imagery is more difficult to define than language, but it is certainly just as powerful.

Nearly every page of the Bible portrays a patriarchal society that was oppressive towards women, and one may wonder whether it does more harm than good to study these texts. Yet, biblical narratives can present effectively the power of God's love to children and adults. The oppressive aspect of our tradition must be recognized and named where it appears but, with careful teaching, people can read the Bible perceptively with an open mind, and hear God speaking to their hearts.

Rather than listing examples of gender bias in the Bible, let us consider the positive side of the scriptural tradition.

In particular, Jesus' attitude to women is a positive component of the imagery of our tradition. When the twentieth-century equity movement forced us to think about the place of women in Christianity, we found to our amazement that Jesus was 20 centuries ahead of his time in treating women as equals to men.

One summer, an adult student in a Religious Education course I was teaching asked why Jesus hadn't told parables about women, or healed women as well as men. His question was remarkable evidence of how completely male imagery has dominated our
Mk 1:29-31 tradition. Of course Jesus did heal a number of women – Peter's
Mk 5:22-43 mother-in-law, the daughter of Jairus, the woman who had been
Mk 7:24-30 hemorrhaging for years. The only person in the gospels who ever changed Jesus' mind by challenging something he said was a Syro-Phoenician woman (today she would be identified as Lebanese), who persistence resulted in Jesus' healing her daughter.

Parables often came in pairs. Jesus told two parables to express
the idea that the reign of God begins on a small scale, but will
inevitably achieve great results. One parable tells of a mustard
seed that grew into a large shrub; the second parable tells of the
yeast that a woman mixed with flour so that the dough grew to Mt 13:31-33
fill the bowl. When the opposition asked why Jesus welcomed
outcasts, he responded that God is like the shepherd who goes
looking for the one lost sheep that is most in need; God is also
like the woman who keeps searching in her home until she has Lk 15:1-10
found the money that she lost.

Why do we think of God primarily as the planter of the mustard seed and as the shepherd, and almost never think of God as the baker-woman or the woman searching for her lost coin?

Jesus had several women friends, among whom Mary Magdalene is the most familiar to us. Mary is listed among several
women who travelled with Jesus, and who supported him out of
their own resources. Thus, the only known financial supporters
of Jesus were women. Mary Magdalene was among the few friends Lk 8:1-3
of Jesus who were loyal and courageous enough to stay nearby as Mk 15:40
he was dying, and to witness his entombment. In all four gospels, Mk 15:47
Mary Magdalene is reported to have been among the first (all of Mt 28:1
them women) to know that the tomb of Jesus was empty, and to Mk 16:1
have been commissioned to proclaim the news of his resurrection Lk 24:10-11
to the other disciples. They, of course, didn't accept the women's Jn 20:1
testimony. In the Gospel according to John, Mary Magdalene is
the first person to whom the risen Jesus reveals himself after the
resurrection. Jn 20:11-18

Jesus' friendship with women is a surprising aspect of his ministry – unexpected and challenging in such a rigid and patriarchal society.

Jesus spoke to women to whom he shouldn't have spoken,
such as the Samaritan woman who had been divorced by five Jn 4:17-18
different husbands. (Since a woman could not divorce her husband
no matter what he did, Jesus' recognition that she had had five
husbands identifies her not as a promiscuous woman, but as a
repeated victim of the one-sided divorce practices in Jewish
society.) In John's gospel, that woman is the first person to whom
Jesus clearly announces that he is the Messiah. She becomes the Jn 4:25-26
first missionary, proclaiming her discovery to her townspeople.

Jn 8:1-11 In another episode reported only in John, Jesus saves a woman's life when she is about to be executed for adultery.

All of these anecdotes form part of our imaginative portrait of Jesus – our imagery about how he dealt with people. He seemed to accept some measure of gender equity almost 2,000 years before the term was invented in a society that is proud of its progressive and humanistic attitudes.

Our Language and Imagery About God

The Spiritual Reality of God

In the image of [God] created them;
Gen 1:27 *male and female [God] created them.*

What is 'the image of God' in humanity?

Because of traditions based on the creation narrative, many people in our culture have grown up in the belief that people 'look like' God. A great many of us have imagined God as a man, often as an old, bearded man sitting on a throne. People of European heritage have perceived no anomaly in their confident imagining of God as a white-skinned man, as in Michelangelo's famous portrayal of the creation of Adam. Children hold those images quite literally; when pressed, most adults agree that God is a Spirit-being who doesn't have a human body.

People of the Jewish tradition were so aware of the spiritual nature of God that they never attempted to draw a pictorial representation of God. The second of the Ten Commandments forbade the people to make an image of God. (Such was the original meaning of Exodus 20:4.) As a result, Jewish art has been predominantly literary; Muslim visual art, for the same reason, is not representational, and has been confined to the elaborate and intricate designs that grace their places of worship. Until the tradition-shattering work of Marc Chagall in the 20th century, Jewish artists did not draw religious pictures, but instead wrote books, in part because they knew that God is too great, and too different from us, to be portrayed in a picture.

Regrettably, Christian art has not respected the original meaning of the second commandment, and we have grown up with pictures that are poor depictions of the greatness of the Creator God.

How, then, are we to understand Genesis 1:27? Human beings are 'images of God' not because of how we look, but because of what we can do. People are like God in that we can think, we can make decisions, we can be creative, we can give ourselves generously in love.

To imagine God as a Spirit being rather than a body-being, use words that describe love. Is love real? Certainly. Is it powerful? Indeed, it can change a person's life. Where is love? Love is everywhere – in our hearts, all around us, all over the world. Love has been forever, and love will be forever. But can you see love? Can you trap it in a bottle? Can you prove scientifically that it is real? Can you measure it? No. Love cannot be seen in itself, but only in its expressions.

The New Testament states quite simply that "God is love" – 1 Jn 4:16
not a body-being, but spiritual, real, powerful, personal, forever, everywhere in the world, within us and visible only in God's expressions of love.

Adults feel, accurately enough, that young people need concrete images to help them get in touch with spiritual reality. But the image of God as an old man in the sky surely does more harm than good, and may result in adults living their whole lives with an inadequate sense of the greatness of the spiritual God. If children – or adults – were invited to draw pictures of love, they would realize that their drawing is symbolic. When they are reminded that God is love, they may understand that their drawings have explored something of the spiritual reality of God as it is expressed concretely in our world.

Father/Mother

Psalm 18:2 proclaims that God is "my rock, my fortress, and my deliverer." That image of God's protective strength was immortalized 500 years ago in a magnificent hymn by Martin Luther.

Although our tradition considers it appropriate to think of God as a rock, many people are opposed to our thinking of God as a mother. A rock is only a symbol, they might say; we're not saying that God is a rock, but that God is reliable like a shelter made of rock. Agreed – but 'mother' is 'only a symbol' too – and so is 'father,' and they are all valuable symbols of the reality of God.

In fact, the Scriptures do occasionally portray God as being like a mother, giving birth to the people, nursing her children at the breast:

Is 66:13 *As a mother comforts her child, so I will comfort you.*

Is 42:14 Elsewhere, God cries out as does a woman in labour.
Or, as a mother eagle, teaches her eaglets to fly:

Exod 19:4 *You have seen…how I bore you on eagles' wings*
and brought you to myself.

Hos 13:8 God is also portrayed as being like a mother bear, protecting
Lk 13:34 her young. Even Jesus, who was assuredly a man, described
himself as a mother hen, wishing to gather the people under her
wings.

Why shouldn't we appreciate the beauty of those feminine images of our God as we do the other symbols?

The image of God as father, like all the other images, is both valuable and ambivalent. In the closing decades of the 20th century, we have become aware of how badly the image of fatherhood has been corrupted by the human sinfulness of some male parents and clergy. We must be able to express the reality of God's love through a variety of images.

Ps 68:5 Still, since fathers at their best are benevolent, we must not
Ps 89:26 lose the image of God as the best of fathers. God was compared
Ps 103:13 to a merciful father occasionally in the Jewish Scriptures, but not
Is 63:16 as often as one might expect: fewer than ten times in the Hebrew
Is 64:8 Bible, and only in Psalms, Isaiah and Jeremiah.
Jer 3:19
Jer 31:9

'Father' was surely the most important image of God in Jesus'
mind. He taught his followers to pray to God as 'Our Father'; he
Mt 6:9-13 referred repeatedly to his mission from his Father; he spoke of
God as "your heavenly Father."

In a remarkable moment of intimacy, as Jesus prayed fearfully
Mk 14:36 in the garden the evening before his death, it is reported that he
even used the language a young child would use for a father. The
Hebrew word for father is '*ab*'; '*abba*' is the term used for a father
by a little child. Jesus' prayer to his Abba as he confronted the
prospect of death is profoundly moving in its tenderness,
vulnerability and childlike quality.

The image of God as Father has endured through centuries of human experience as a deep expression of God's faithfulness and loving-kindness. But we should supplement the father image with other images as well. A version of the Lord's Prayer developed by the Maori people in New Zealand begins this way: "Eternal Spirit, Earth-maker, Pain-bearer, Life-giver, Source of all that is and shall be, Father and Mother of us all, Loving God...." Perhaps it would be beneficial to use a thought-provoking variation for our image of God from time to time. God loves us as our creator and our saviour. God loves us like the best of fathers; God loves us like the best of mothers.

King

Some people may find it troublesome to change our traditional language about God. Their concern must be respected, but they must also consider the possibility that better balance in our religious language can improve our awareness about God, and therefore enrich our lives.

There isn't much balance there yet. The constant repetition of images of God as male causes profound sadness in the hearts of many sensitive women and men. For example, God is often portrayed as a king, the "king of kings." You may say, "I don't pray to God as a king very often." But we do, every time we say "thy kingdom come"; the imagery is so deep in our hearts that we don't even notice it.

Many thoughtful Christian writers now use 'reign of God' instead of 'kingdom of God' to translate the phrase that was so important in Jesus' teaching. Although 'reign' seems to be a more abstract concept than 'kingdom,' it is closer to what the scriptural term really means – it's about the benevolent influence of God ruling our lives and giving us the power to live in love, to be true to ourselves, to become whole.

It may be too large a step to change the word 'kingdom' in the Lord's Prayer, but perhaps the occasional use of a paraphrase of the whole prayer in modern language would help all of us to be more reflective and thoughtful when we pray that beautiful prayer.

The Lord

Another patriarchal image of God is expressed in the ever-present term 'The Lord.' By definition, a lord is a dominant male. Some women and men are not comfortable repeatedly addressing God (or Jesus) in the language of a servant before a master. Others don't feel that the image is oppressive, usually stating that they really never consider the meaning of the term. Perhaps we could agree that other words than 'LORD' could be used more often. 'LORD' does not have to be the most common designation of the God of love.

The main reason for the ubiquity of that term is the Jewish practice of never pronouncing the sacred Name of God (YHWH). Out of reverence, readers never pronounced the Name itself even when reading the Scriptures in religious services. Instead, they used the Hebrew word *adonai*, meaning 'my Lord.'

Every time 'the LORD' appears in capital letters in the Bible, you need to realize that the word in the text is not 'Lord' but the sacred Name. To begin to move beyond this dominant male image implied in the title 'Lord,' try to replace it with YHWH or 'the Name' sometimes as you are reading.

At the same time, all of us, female and male, should reflect on the meaning of addressing God as our Lord. If we accept God's authority over us, we are willing to act as our God commands. In other words, when we pray to 'our Lord,' we should realize that we are expressing our obedient acceptance of our place as creatures in God's world. The expression is meaningless unless we are conscious of it, and live it.

Many other great and equally traditional terms can also express the reality of God faithfully. So instead of habitually saying, "Lord, hear our prayer," consider using such phrases as 'Gracious God,' 'God of Love,' 'God of all kindness,' 'God our Saviour.'

Pronouns About God

Finally, we must also consider our use of pronouns that refer to God. Pronouns must express our awareness that God is personal. It is not appropriate to call God 'it.' Unfortunately, in English, personal pronouns also designate gender. The New Revised Standard Version of the Bible uses masculine pronouns in referring to God. But God is neither male nor female; God is Spirit. Surely there are ways of avoiding the use of exclusively masculine pronouns for God.

One simple, though sometimes awkward, expedient is to use the word 'God' as often as possible in order to avoid using any gender-exclusive pronouns. That will be the practice in this book.

The problem jumps off the page in many of the hymns we sing. Recently published hymn books are systematically reducing the use of third-person pronouns by addressing God as 'you,' rather than referring to God as 'he.' Choir leaders might also decide to change 'Lord' to 'God' (and 'the Lord' to 'our God') as often as possible. 'Man' can be changed to 'people.' 'He' and 'his' can become 'they' and 'their.' When hymns use images of war in referring to God, the verses may have to be rewritten, or the songs may have to be dropped from our repertoire. Some of the newest hymns have been written with this awareness in mind, but many traditional hymns cry out for rewording.

Conclusion

Some readers may feel that those who object to gender-exclusive imagery take offence too easily. But people of all ages and both genders are being hurt by our male-dominated tradition; we must face the problems and do what we can to redress the harm.

Some may be disheartened by the extent of the changes that must be made: it feels as if we should be changing every sentence we read or sing. That may almost be the case, but that's what we have to do – one line at a time, consistently and courageously.

Some readers may feel that the issues raised here are of little importance. Rather, this chapter is talking about a major revolution and maturation in our religious thinking. We are challenged to realize, at the level of imagination and not just intellect, that God is a Spirit-being. The great number of small details can't hide the fact that the instinctive foundations of our consciousness are being changed.

When we reflect on our language and imagery about God, we are dealing with our awareness of the very roots of our being.

And now, with the historical outline and the considerations about language in our minds, let us explore in detail some of the more significant sections of the Hebrew Scriptures.

5

ABRAHAM AND SARAH

People of Faith in a World Like Ours

Now the Lord said to Abram,
"Go from your country and your kindred
and your father's house
to the land that I will show you.
I will make of you a great nation,
and I will bless you, and make your name great,
so that you will be a blessing.
I will bless those who bless you,
and the one who curses you I will curse;
and in you all the families of the earth shall be blessed."
Gen 12:1-4 *So Abram went, as the Lord had told him.*

With those few brief sentences begins the odyssey of the Jewish people, a journey of faith that continues almost 4,000 years later.

Abraham and Sarah are presented as a young married couple who have grown up in a city in the area now known as the Persian Gulf. They have moved from one city to another with Abraham's father and clan.

From what archaeologists have learned about that period in history, we now think that Abraham and Sarah were living in a time of economic crisis. The cities were falling apart; they couldn't support their populations any longer. People were facing severe hardship, even starvation. What naturally happened in such times was a wave of nomadism, as families left the cities behind and became herders and wanderers, living in tents and following their flocks in search of pasture.

The Bible story portrays the transition as their response to the voice of God, uprooting them from their homes and sending them out into the unknown in search of a promised blessing.

A Format for Exploring Scriptural Narratives

Let us use this apparently simple text to establish a three-stage process for dealing with any biblical passage.

Step 1. Consider the narrative at face value, including its connotations.

Most readers naturally take biblical narratives at face value, but don't explore them fully enough at that level. Our natural flaw is to speed along, especially when we are familiar with a passage, and to take the passage for granted as it stands. As a result, we sometimes fail to appreciate fully the implications of the story, or we miss details of vocabulary or symbolism that could add depth to our understanding of the text.

The call of Abraham offers some examples of vocabulary that deserve attention and perhaps a little reflection. God's promise that Abraham will become a great nation refers, of course, to all the people of the Jewish nation – all the people who look back to Abraham and Sarah as their ancestors. (The same language is used to speak of the First Nations people of Canada.) God is not only changing the course of this young couple's lives; God is initiating a community.

"You will be a blessing" sounds strange in modern English, but still today at weddings, we pray that the couple may have long and happy lives, and see their children and grandchildren as Abraham and Sarah did: that ancient couple has indeed become a blessing for us.

Just as important in the study of every text is the exploration of the connotations – the emotional implications of the situation. For example, consider: How did that couple feel, being told by God to leave their homes and families and to set out into the unknown? (God was extremely vague, promising to lead them to "a land that I will show you.") There would be no social system out in the desert to protect them; they had no idea where they were going; they would have to live in tents instead of in their urban homes. Consider Sarah's part in the decision: How would she feel? Did she have any choice? Maybe she co-operated in deciding to leave home, or maybe she had to do whatever her husband ordered her to do. In either case, the couple had to do something, but every choice caused great distress.

Awareness of the couple's feelings brings the story into the present, because many people today have experienced the same uprootedness.

Step 2. Focus on the human side: Does anything like this ever happen today?

Especially if you have imagined God's directive to Abraham as being spoken in a powerful voice, you may feel that there is little similarity between the biblical story and the life of people today. God no longer tells us what to do in a big booming voice.

But in this narrative, as in all biblical stories, it is important to draw your attention away from the miraculous or the unusual, and focus on the human element in the episode. Thus, for this story, realize that Abraham and Sarah were a young married couple who lived in the same town as their parents, but who had lost their income and had no hope of surviving in that town in the future. They believed in their hearts that they had to leave home and seek their livelihood elsewhere. Does anything like that ever happen today?

Abraham and Sarah faced the same heartbreak as do many people of our time. Their dilemma was the same as that of a couple in New Brunswick when the fish plant closed down, who had to go and try to find work in the oil patch in Alberta. Or the family that left Viet Nam by crossing the South China Sea with a hundred people in a boat meant for 20. Or the *nonno* and *nonna* who came from Calabria and landed in Halifax with no money, only the address of a cousin in Toronto.

To consider the same issue on a more spiritual level, Abraham and Sarah are like people today who experience a change of heart about ideas that they have held dear their whole lives. Perhaps they have been brought up in total dedication to the pursuit of wealth, but decide that they will turn down an opportunity for career advancement and spend more time with people they love. Perhaps they have been members of a faith community and feel themselves drawn to a different way of believing, either rejecting the past or proceeding into the future in the name of new understanding. Perhaps they finally admit to themselves that they must separate from a spouse to whom they had once committed their entire future.

Yes, the human dimension of the biblical stories continues to be part of contemporary experience. But what of the divine dimension? Is God part of our world in the same way as God was part of the world long ago?

When a mother leaves Jamaica with four children and no husband and moves to Canada in the middle of winter, would we perceive that God told her to "leave your country and your kindred and your father's house"? Most adults would answer in the negative: God doesn't talk to people like that anymore.

Yet, God might have had something to do with her decision. She might have prayed that God would be with her when she moved to a new country; she might have asked God to help her make the right decision; she might have asked God for strength and courage.

Did God speak to her at all? Perhaps God spoke to her in her heart. What about Abraham? Did God speak out loud to Abraham in the words reported in the book of Genesis? Many believers today would understand that God probably spoke to Abraham in much the same way that God spoke to the woman of Jamaica – it was a word to the heart. The biblical narrative (which first took written form 800 years after Abraham and Sarah lived) uses a literary way of telling what happened inside a person's heart.

Some readers may resist such an interpretation, preferring to believe that the Bible's account is literally accurate, and that the world was different long ago, when God's intentions and actions were far more obvious and frequent than they are now. That position is reasonable, but many scholars and people of faith agree that it is also reasonable and faithful to understand that the biblical narrative has evolved, and is not intended to be read as simply a report of facts.

The great advantage of this way of interpreting the narratives is the realization that the people of the Scriptures were people like us; they faced the same kinds of human problems that we face, and they had to find God the same way we do.

Does anything like this ever happen today? People who lived in biblical times met God in the experiences of their lives and in the depths of their hearts. People today may still hear the voice of

God calling them to head out into the unknown, in search of economic security or deeper relationships or peace of heart or new wisdom.

The ancient people expressed their faith in various kinds of stories. When we read their stories to share their insight and their faith, we realize that God is part of our lives, too.

Step 3. Application: What does the story teach us about God and about life?

This generic question can be applied to any biblical passage by rephrasing it to deal directly with any specific text. Thus, for the episode we are discussing, one might ask, "Why do we remember Abraham and Sarah now, almost 4,000 years after they lived? What's so great about Abraham and Sarah? In what ways should we try to be like them?"

What we can perceive in this brief narrative is that Abraham recognized what God was asking of him, and did it. That's what faith is, stripped down to its essentials: a person's way of life being in tune with God.

Abraham and Sarah are presented to us as pure believers. They had no creed to express their faith, no Ten Commandments to tell them what to do, no sacraments, no Church to support them or confuse them. They were simply people who built their lives on their relationship with God. If we could do the same, we would be great believers also.

Another aspect of this story is that it deals with part of normal human life. If, as we think, economic circumstances forced Abraham and Sarah to leave home and set out into the unknown, and they perceived in this decision the presence and support of God, then their decision was much like choices that believers make today.

We looked at contemporary situations of migration and uprooting as being parallel to the situation of Abraham and Sarah. So are many other kinds of decisions people make in our world, often without thinking that the decisions are religious. But God can provide wisdom and courage and peace and strength to us who have to make choices in our world.

Who ever thinks that taking on a mortgage is a religious decision? And yet, if faith is about one's identity as a person, about being true to oneself and to God, even such mundane decisions contribute to one's self-identity. The suburban areas around North American cities are full of people who have gone deeply into debt to buy a family home, and have discovered that both parents must work endless hours just to service their debt. They have less time for each other and for their children; they worry constantly about money, sometimes they quarrel about it. In the 1990s, many couples were trapped under the burden of enormous debt because the value of their home had decreased to less than the size of their mortgage. Older children in the family may have had to take on the role of parent, because one or both parents had to be away from home for all three meals, most days of the week. The decision to enter that mortgage shaped the lives of all the people in that home. It's not that the decision should be seen as sinful, but that it should be seen as meaningful, as identity-shaping – as a religious decision.

Such is a possible application of the story of Abraham and Sarah's call by God to leave their home city and head out into the desert to search for a new way of life.

What does the story teach us about God? God can be part of all the significant decisions of our lives. God provides wisdom and meaning and courage and strength to all who are open to God's powerful action in our lives. We can live as people of faith in everything we do. But not all people are conscious of the strength and peace that God offers. Many of us prefer to go it alone, and we're poorer because of this choice.

When Disaster Strikes

From time immemorial, humans have been confronted with disastrous events, and have asked a profoundly religious question: Why? Why me? Why here? Why did some live and some die?

We ask these questions ourselves: when an earthquake kills several thousand people, when a tidal wave drowns tens of thousands, when a lightning bolt kills one baseball player who is standing with a group of teammates at a tournament.

Often the question is phrased "Why did this happen?" The 'why?' usually does not mean "What does this death mean for my life and the life of the person who has died?" Rather, the question means, "How can I understand the role of God in this death?" Often the question implies that God has caused the tragedy, or could have prevented it. In a way, the questioner is asking God to explain or justify a particular suffering.

One of the narratives about Abraham provides a fascinating
Gen 18:20-33 glimpse of the efforts of early believers to reconcile their faith in a loving God with their fear after a natural disaster. The narrative is based on a very human portrayal of God as a powerful prosecutor pursuing justice without forgetting mercy, seeking evidence, discussing alternatives, being persuaded.

As the narrative begins, God decides to go into the towns of Sodom and Gomorrah and investigate whether the rumours about the people are true. If they are, God is going to unleash punishment. Abraham boldly reminds God, "Shall not the Judge of all the earth do what is just?" and proposes that if there are 50 good people there, God should spare the cities rather than destroy the good people with the bad. When God agrees, Abraham becomes a dealmaker in a style familiar to many Mediterranean (and other) cultures. He calls himself "mere dust and ashes" daring to bargain with God, but argues that if he falls five short of the magic number of 50, surely God wouldn't destroy the cities for the lack of five good people? Having remade the agreement at 45, Abraham says, "Now, don't get mad, but would you take 40?" After several more steps in the negotiations, the final deal is set at ten. And Abraham and God walk away from the bargaining table with an agreement.

The story is amazing. It may make you shake your head and laugh, marvelling at those people's sense of God. But it is dealing with an important question, for Abraham couldn't find his ten good people in those towns. Shocking stories of violence
Gen 19:24 (especially violence against women) are told in Chapter 19 of the book of Genesis, and the episode ends with God raining sulphur and fire from the sky. This dramatic closing scene finds Abraham standing on the hilltop where he had bargained with God, looking
Gen 19:27-28 out across the plain where the cities had been, and watching the smoke rise off the land "like the smoke of a furnace."

It seems the story of the bargaining session was written after a shocking event, to try to make sense of a natural cataclysm (volcanic action or earthquake) that destroyed two towns without warning.

Does anything like that ever happen today? Perhaps not if we're thinking about a man bargaining with God for the life of a city. But we have seen videotape of people in other parts of the world fleeing from explosive volcanoes, with fire and ash raining down upon them from the sky. And, as always, we ask why. What does it mean? Where is God in this event?

The only answer that primitive believers could devise after a natural disaster was that God was punishing the evil actions of people. (The fact that the people in the doomed towns were not of Abraham's race made the episode all the more satisfying for the storyteller.) That was the only rationale they could find, since they believed that God is good, and in no way evil.

Still today, some people are convinced that God is punishing us when natural disasters strike, be they earthquakes, volcanoes or epidemics.

Many more people in our world, however, are not content with the primitive understanding reflected in this narrative. Neither was the biblical tradition. Some centuries after the story of Abraham was written, the book of Job argued forcefully with the 'punishment' theory, claiming that good people do suffer, and that suffering cannot be understood simply as God's punishment for evil-doing.

The Problem of Pain

The suffering of good people is the hardest question for believers to face. It is very difficult, for example, to reconcile the painful fatal illness of a child with faith in a loving God who has the almighty power to prevent that suffering. Many people feel scornful outrage when believers respond with platitudes: "It was God's will," "God must have a good reason for letting this happen," "God sent this suffering to teach us a lesson about life," or "God will never give us more suffering than we can handle." Who can believe in a God who would inflict pain on a baby to teach adults a lesson?

The crucial flaw in traditional exploration of this important question is its portrait of God on high, manipulating events in the world, hearing prayers of petition from millions of believers, deciding which ones to answer and which to ignore. Even as we revere God as the source of all that is, and we give thanks to a God who has given us the universe and our lives as a gift of love, there are believers who are not satisfied with the notion that God causes (or is able magically to prevent) individual events in our lives.

During the dramatic months leading up to the death of cancer crusader Terry Fox, many believers instinctively prayed to God to make Terry well. Others knew that Terry was going to die, and were afraid that some people's faith would die with him. Who can believe in a God who could easily take away the cancer, but who rejected the prayers of thousands of adults and children pleading for the life of an inspirational young man?

Doubtless, the problem is ours: we have limited ability to understand the greatness of God, but we are mistaken if we think that God causes everything that happens in our world.

Instead of thinking about God always as the cause of specific happenings, always in language of 'power and might,' we can think of God in terms of Love and Meaning (and Wisdom, and Understanding, and Truth). God isn't the magical manipulator of phenomena; God is the personal presence of Love in our hearts. It is God who gives meaning and direction to our lives, who helps us to make sense of life, to be wise and true to ourselves, courageous and free – no matter what happens.

The life and death of Jesus provide the ultimate assurance that good people do suffer and die too young; that the suffering of good people is meaningful; and that somehow God is part of our lives, loving us and strengthening us whatever happens, even when we are not able to perceive God's presence.

Is there any value to prayer of petition? Yes, but not if it is based on fanciful belief in God pulling strings from on high. When we pray, we are expressing our needs and our hopes. The bond of love that unites the people who are praying and the people who are being prayed for is the Spirit of God, for God is Love. Hoping together in love helps us all: those who pray perceive the strengthening presence of God within us, pulling us together in love. The people who are prayed for are helped by the power of love flowing among everyone who cares about them. Those many years ago, we prayed that Terry Fox would die surrounded by love, and that he and his family would have courage and wisdom as he lived through his fatal illness. And we believed that the bond of love that united all of us with Terry and his family is the Spirit of God.

That same search for understanding is what was at stake more than 30 centuries ago, when a tiny group of fledgling believers tried to understand the role of God in the fire that rained upon them from the sky.

Family Crisis

Home is the place that "When you go there, they have to take you in," wrote Robert Frost.

At their best, families are where people go to be loved. Young and old go home to many different kinds of families; the one fundamental gift they ask from their family is love. Yet a quick reflection on family life in our society reveals that families can also be a source of pain, conflict and destruction in the lives of children and adults. The horrifying violence that occurs in some families, and the current radical restructuring of family life, may seem unprecedented in human history.

And then we read another episode from the life of Abraham and Sarah.

Couples who are unable to bear children in our society often experience enduring distress. They undergo tests, try to decide which partner's reproductive system is defective, and sometimes spend thousands of dollars and months of anxiety in an effort to have a child. Children are a blessing deeply desired by most married people; most adults' identity as human beings is profoundly connected to their sense of themselves as sexual beings and as parents.

It should come as no surprise that a childless couple in the fiercely patriarchal clans of biblical times experienced similar distress. So deeply rooted was a man's need to have a male heir that nomadic society allowed him to father a child even after his death! If a husband died without an heir, it was the duty of the dead man's brother to impregnate the widow, and the child thus conceived was considered to be the child and heir of the dead husband.

In such societies, the pressure on women to be fertile was
unrelenting: "Now Sarai, Abram's wife, bore him no children." Gen 16:1
After several years of marriage Sarah must have felt ashamed and sad, for herself and for her husband. And she knew what she was supposed to do. Sarah gave her husband permission to have
intercourse with one of his slave women, with the understanding Gen 16:2-4
that the child thus conceived would be taken from his mother and raised by Abraham and Sarah as their heir. Whatever the feelings of Sarah and of Hagar, the slave woman, were, such were the demands of family structure in their society.

> The ages ascribed to Abraham and Sarah during this episode are undoubtedly legendary. Most likely the historical basis of the story is that Abraham and Sarah married at puberty, and were childless for several years. At some time during 800 years of oral tradition, to make sure that everyone understood that Isaac was the result
> Gen 16:16 of God's intervention, a tradition developed that Abraham's first
> Gen 21:5 child was born when he was 86 years old, and the second when he was 100.

Gen 21:2 Then, to complicate the situation further, Sarah herself later became pregnant. But Sarah's child would not be Abraham's first-born son and heir as long as Ishmael lived. So, as in many situations through centuries of human family life, competition and jealousy entered into the picture.

Sarah couldn't stand watching Ishmael grow up as the older brother of her son Isaac. She demanded that Abraham banish
Gen 21:9-21 Hagar and her child from the camp. When your clan is living in tents in a desert wilderness, and you turn a woman and child out of the camp with bread and a skin of water, today's name for the deed is 'attempted murder.' The fact that the pair were saved from death, presumably by another nomadic clan, does not absolve Abraham and Sarah of responsibility for their action, though they might plead 'extenuating circumstances' because of the inexorable pressure of their society.

Society's pressures today are just as strong. Many young men still feel that they must prove their virility with a succession of sexual partners. Many young married women are still expected to be subject to their husbands and to play the traditional role of housewife in addition to whatever career responsibilities they undertake. Children continue to be the objects of competition and jealousy between adults, particularly after marriage break-down, and uncertainty still afflicts children of different partners living in the same household (blended families including her, his and our children).

Family crisis has been part of life forever. The Bible reports and reflects on the people's pain; it tries to find the presence of God in what happens; it even tries to cover up some of the drama of the situation by providing a happy ending to the story. But the community had to face the destructive side of family dynamics, and in reporting these traumatic events seemed to shrug and say, "What can you do? Such is life."

Our society has no right to scorn their helplessness. Despite our vaunted sophistication and openness, we are apparently no closer to overcoming the destructive elements of family life than were the members of that clan of herders living in tents in the southern desert of Palestine almost 4,000 years ago.

They were people like us.

6

MOSES: A NARRATIVE OF FREEDOM

Something significant happened about 3,250 years ago, when a small band of ragamuffin labourers slipped out from under the thumb of the most powerful civilization of their world. Most likely, it didn't happen as it has been portrayed in the movies, with the water flowing up out of the sea to form a wall that allowed people to walk through on dry land. Both Cecil B. deMille's classic *The Ten Commandments* and the late-20th-century animated feature *Prince of Egypt* give the impression that the biblical story should be taken literally, with little concern for the depth of meaning that is enshrined in the account.

In this brief chapter, we will discuss what might have happened at the time of Moses to give rise to the memorable narratives that are preserved in the book of Exodus. Exactly what happened is of little importance. The meaning of those events is of supreme importance, because the people who escaped from the slave camps came to know God in a new way, and their faith became the foundation of three of the world's most significant religious traditions: Judaism, Christianity and Islam.

The story of Moses begins with a fanciful tale about the
Exod 1:8-12 Pharaoh fearing that this little band of enslaved nomads would
increase in population and power until they took over the
magnificent civilization of Egypt. That unlikely scenario sets the
stage for a typical example of 'childhood legends of the heroes,'
in which Moses' life is saved by the clever actions of his mother
Exod 2:1-10 and sister, and he spends his childhood being raised by a princess
in the royal court of Egypt.

One detail in the story that may be factual is that Moses' family had become culturally influenced by Egyptian society. His name is Egyptian rather than Hebrew; it is related to the familiar name 'Ra-mses.' (Ra was the name of the sun god in Egyptian tradition.)

As a grown man, Moses apparently remembered his roots, for the story goes that when visiting the slave camps one day, he killed an Egyptian guard who was beating an Israelite worker. Exod 2:11-15

Now wanted for murder, he fled eastward into the desert from which his ancestors had come. He joined a nomadic clan, married, fathered a child and presumably learned much about desert life Exod 2:16-22 that had been forgotten, since recent generations of his ancestors had lived as labourers in the fertile delta of the Nile in northern Egypt.

In that setting occurred one of the most significant religious experiences of human history. Moses came to believe that God was sending him back into the slave camps of Egypt to bring freedom and faith to his people. As the experience is narrated, God revealed to Moses the sacred name YHWH, a word that is Exod 3:13-15 linguistically linked to the verb 'to be' The story makes the connection when God responds to Moses, "I am Who I am." The sacred Name may mean 'He causes to be' or 'Being Itself.'

The God who spoke to Moses was understood to be the same God whom Abraham and Sarah had known some 600 years before. Yet, except for the existence of the narratives themselves about the times of the patriarchs, there is no evidence that a lasting religious or liturgical tradition had been preserved among the Hebrews. The people to whom Moses returned with the message that God would set them free don't seem to have been practising a worship of the God of Abraham, Isaac and Jacob in the Egyptian camps.

With the permission of his father-in-law, the desert chieftain Jethro, Moses did return to the forced-labour camps where his kinfolk were imprisoned. As the story tells us, Moses goes to the Pharaoh in the name of God to demand freedom for his people. The Pharaoh responds with scorn ("Who is the LORD, that I should Exod 5:2 heed him?") and imposes increased hardship on the Israelite workers. A memorable contest of wills ensues.

The Plagues

In a series of dramatic episodes, Moses repeatedly confronts the Pharaoh, is refused, and confidently produces one consequence Exod 7–12 after another to dismay the Pharaoh and to secure the Israelites' freedom. The river turns to blood; frogs, gnats, flies and locusts infest the land; animals are diseased; there is thunder and hail and unnatural darkness; the people are afflicted with boils. Finally, the first-born son of every Egyptian family dies, and eventually the Israelites escape after the angel of death passes over their homes without doing harm.

What might have happened to give rise to this gripping and frightening narrative? Quite likely, the narrative reports actual events, somewhat exaggerated, using a brilliant storytelling technique that spins out the tale for maximum dramatic effect.

The story of the plagues seems to be based on a reasonably accurate memory of a time of natural disaster in Egyptian society – a time of drought, famine and epidemic similar to what has been experienced in central Africa in our time. During such a period, it could be expected that the river would change colour and "stink," and that fish would die; that unexpected numbers of frogs and insects would swarm across the land as their natural enemies declined in numbers; that storms and sandstorms would darken the sky; and that animals and people would suffer illness and death. It is unlikely that only first-born male children would die in a plague. That detail could be the product of the storyteller's art, but almost certainly, the magnificent Egyptian civilization was crippled by natural disaster, economic crisis and devastating disease. The story is told, event by event, for dramatic effect. The Pharaoh is repeatedly given opportunities to change his mind, but always refuses.

Thus the Hebrews took advantage of the distress in Egyptian society, and made good their escape. They also interpreted their success as being due to the hand of God. What their experience taught them about God is the topic of the following chapter, but there are a few movie scenes to be discussed beforehand.

The Crossing of the Sea

What sea are we talking about? On a map of the southeastern Mediterranean region, notice the route that people would take if they were travelling east into the Sinai desert from the Nile Delta region, where they lived in forced-labour camps. It would make no sense at all to travel south towards the nearest major body of water – which isn't the Red Sea, but the Gulf of Suez (between Egypt and the Sinai Peninsula). The Red Sea is much farther south, between modern Eritrea and Arabia.

The Bible narratives of the crossing of the sea never mention
the Red Sea but instead speak of a "sea of reeds" – in other words,
a marsh. How it became known as the "Red Sea" in English seems Exod 13:18
to be a mystery. Most likely, the escaped slaves fled eastwards
from the Nile Delta into the desert where Moses had recently
been living as a member of a nomadic clan. Towns named in the
story are located where the Suez canal is now. In that area were a Exod 14:2
series of tidal saltwater marshes – sometimes submerged,
sometimes above water, but always muddy.

As we saw in Chapter 3 of this book, the book of Exodus as we now have it was compiled by a committee of priests in Jerusalem, some 700 years after the events it describes. The authors of Exodus wove together two pre-existing versions of the story. Modern scholars try to unravel the accounts, and compare the different versions that have been preserved in Torah.

What they have found is one account that seems to describe an explainable series of natural events, interwoven with a more miraculous version that gave great scope to the imaginations of mid-20th-century moviemakers.

As the more subdued version presents the narrative, the band Exod 14:10
of slaves, escaping on foot from the strongest army in their world,
looks back and sees the clouds of dust raised by Egyptian chariots
pursuing them. They snarl at their leader, but he urges them to
keep going, and they scurry across the mud flats of the "sea of
reeds," possibly made more firm by a "strong east wind" (off the Exod 14:21
desert).

The Egyptian chariots follow the fugitives into the marsh,
but the unconquerable mud (perhaps assisted by the rising tide)
"clogs their chariot wheels" and they abandon the chase, probably Exod 14:25
saying, "Let them go; they'll all die out there in the desert anyway."
The terrified refugees, watching the departure of the military force
they fear the most, turn to each other and say, "It's a miracle! God Exod 14:31
has set us free!"

Under the guidance of the desert-experienced Moses, these
people, who had lived in green and fertile surroundings in the
Nile Delta, learned to survive in the desert. Their leader taught Exod 17:1-6
them how to find water, and what kinds of desert vegetation are
edible. (Tourists in the Sinai desert are still shown the 'manna' Exod 16:4
that the desert people eat for nourishment.) The newly freed
refugees were confirmed in their feeling that their survival was a
miracle.

And they were right! Many people think of miracles as unexplainable or unnatural events, happenings that can be caused only by God. But the key aspect about miracle, in the Bible and in our world, is a person's perception of the *meaning* of what has happened.

When a 45-year-old parent, dying of heart disease, enters a modern hospital and walks out a few weeks later with someone else's heart, have they not, as they often declare, experienced a miracle? The surgeon's skill and the amazing technology that make a transplant possible are not unnatural or unexplainable. We don't claim that only God can perform such a deed. But we nonetheless perceive the hand of God in what has happened: we understand the event as a miracle because of what we see as the *meaning* of the event.

Many a person has reflected on a miraculous escape from death, and has come to understand life in a new way: "I believe that God has given me the coming years for a reason. I plan to pay more attention to what is really important in life. I'll spend more time loving my family, and less time trying to make more money. I'll smell the roses more than I used to. My life has taken on a whole new meaning."

That is how miracles are recognized in our world – and it is very similar to how a scruffy band of labourers more than 3,000 years ago recognized the hand of God in a series of natural events and coincidences that freed them to set their own course in the world.

What they learned about God and about life from those experiences was the foundational insight of Jewish faith. The Jewish sense of God has also shaped the faith of millions of Christian people and Muslim people across a wide spectrum of cultures.

It is the meaning of those experiences that we will now explore.

7

A GOD WHO SAVES

The Foundations of Jewish Faith

Christians are heirs of the Jewish tradition. We share the Hebrew Scriptures; many of our rituals have Jewish roots; we know that Jesus was a faithful Jew throughout his life.

But many of us don't really know our roots very well. If you were to ask an average Christian to define Judaism in one sentence, you would likely be told that Jews are the people who are still waiting for the Messiah to come. Such an answer is inadequate, because it defines Judaism only in reference to Christianity, and it speaks only of the future. It would be like defining Christians as the people who are waiting for Jesus to return at the end of time. Jewish believers don't define themselves in terms of their indefinite future any more than Christians do.

Fundamentally, Jewish believers are people who try to live in a way that is faithful to God, as God was revealed throughout Jewish history, and particularly through the experiences associated with Moses.

Christians are hampered by another serious misunderstanding about Judaism. Many of us have been taught that God was known to the Jewish people as harsh, angry and vengeful, whereas Jesus revealed God as loving, compassionate and forgiving. Such characterizations are evidence of our age-old prejudices. Rather, faithful Jewish people have been inspired for all these centuries by a profound and beautiful sense of God, which has held them together as a distinctive group of believers despite the persecution and devastation they have suffered through the ages. According to the Jewish tradition, God loves us and always acts to help us, to inspire us, to forgive us and to lead us to wholeness.

The Jewish Understanding of God

Jesus' teaching about God was consistent with the traditional Jewish understanding of God. As a faithful Jew, Jesus loved God, prayed to God, listened to the voice of God, obeyed God, trusted God – and taught us to do the same.

We will discuss Jewish faith about God under the following headings:

- God sets people free
- God chooses us; we belong to God; God enters a covenant with us
- God offers love to people and invites love in return
- God saves us: God leads us towards wholeness
- God teaches us how to live as worthy members of God's family, and forgives us when we fail.

These points express what the people learned about God in the course of the foundational experience of the Jewish religion: their escape from Egypt at the time of Moses.

1. *God sets people free.*

The foundational Jewish experience of God came in the people's escape from slavery at the time of Moses. They had been an insignificant group of labourers, helpless and hopeless. As they burst out of the slave camps into a new sense of self-identity as a people, they came to realize that God had taken the initiative to set them free and, more fundamentally, that freedom is a gift of God. It is a lasting insight.

We have heard with our ears, O God,
our ancestors have told us,
what deeds you performed in their days, in the days of old:
you with your own hand drove out the nations,
Ps 44:1-2 *... but them you set free.*

The New Testament also teaches that Jesus came to bring
freedom to people. "If the Son makes you free, you will be free
Jn 8:36 indeed." "You will know the truth, and the truth will make you
Jn 8:32 free." "For freedom Christ has set us free."

Gal 5:1 Freedom is a profound human need, a characteristic of humanity at its best. We humans have always desired to be free – free from constraint and from oppression, free to set our own course in life, free to shape our selves by our responsible decisions.

Do people today have more freedom than ever before? The majority of the world's people still have to devote most of their energies to survival. They don't experience much freedom, but they continue to yearn for freedom. We in the wealthier societies demand personal freedom, but we often feel oppressed by illness or tragedy, by powerful structures like governments or the Church, by hurtful relationships, by the size of our mortgage or our credit card debts, at times by our own selfishness. Rich or poor, young or old, robust or fragile, female or male, people everywhere feel a profound need for freedom.

God still stands for freedom. It is not that God is a magician who will take away the forces that distress us, or turn the world into paradise. But God will meet us at the depths of our being, and help us grow towards inner freedom, no matter what happens to us. Inwardly, Nelson Mandela was a free man through all his years in prison. In that sense, we can be free people also. With God's help we can overcome the constraints that bind us; we can shape our own lives.

For more than 3,000 years, the Jewish tradition has known that God acts to set us free.

2. *God chooses us; we belong to God: God enters a covenant with us.*

From the beginning of their religious history, the Jewish people have known what it means to belong to God. At the beginning of the narratives about Moses, the people felt that they were doomed to live and die as slaves of foreign overlords. And yet somehow, by no merit of theirs, God reached into their lives, gave them an entirely new identity, and established an enduring and faithful relationship with them.

The Bible's most important term for the bond between God and the people is 'covenant.'

Unfortunately, books about the Scriptures invariably define covenant in terms of a treaty or pact between a lord and his vassals: the master agrees to protect and defend his subjects; the subjects agree to serve the master and obey his commands. While it is true that biblical language of covenant is similar to such agreements, the Jewish people's sense of belonging to God is much more deeply felt than a treaty.

The best comparison to help us experience the meaning of covenant is not a lord/vassal treaty, but the bond of adoption.

Imagine the helplessness of a child with no parents: "I have no one to care for me; I'm all alone; no one loves me; I'll die unless someone feeds me." And imagine such a child's feelings when a couple says, "We choose you. From now on you belong to us; we will love you and take care of you forever; everything we have is yours; we will never let you go."

Rom 8:23 The New Testament uses the magnificent, generous gift of
Gal 4:5 adoption as an analogy for God's faithful covenant with people. We who live today are invited to feel chosen, adopted as God's children, just as those first liberated slaves were given a new sense of themselves as people who are cared for, who belong, who are loved.

You have seen…how I bore you on eagles' wings
and brought you to myself.
Now therefore, if you obey my voice
and keep my covenant,
Exod 19:4-5 *you shall be my treasured possession out of all the peoples.*

3. God offers love to people and invites love in return.

It has become axiomatic for believers that "God loves us." But that insight represents a revolutionary change in the history of religion: love was not a characteristic of the gods who were worshipped by the ancestors and neighbours of the Jewish people.

Ancient peoples felt that they were in the grip of unseen forces that controlled their lives. Pagan religions attempted to get those unseen forces on their side. Thus people worshipped one god to help them in battle, another to control the weather and the seasons, another to make their fields and flocks and wombs fertile. There was no concept that the gods loved people; the gods were terrifying forces, especially if they did not accomplish what was expected of them.

In that setting, the God of the Jewish people was understood as a God of love. For its time, it was such an unexpected idea about God that it must have been *revealed* to us by God and no human invention.

A classic phrase is often repeated to describe the action of God in the Hebrew Scriptures: "steadfast love and faithfulness."

A God merciful and gracious, slow to anger,
and abounding in steadfast love and faithfulness,
Exod 34:6-7 *keeping steadfast love for the thousandth generation.*

For as the heavens are high above the earth,
so great is [God's] steadfast love
toward those who fear [God]… Ps 103:11, 13
As a father has compassion for his children,
so the LORD has compassion for those who fear him. Jer 31:3

I have loved you with an everlasting love.

There are hundreds of similar passages in the Hebrew Scriptures. The phrase expresses the predominant sense of God held by the Jewish people.

Not only does God reach out to people in love, but God invites love in return.

You shall love the LORD your God with all your heart,
and with all your soul, and with all your might. Deut 6:5

Many is the Christian who thinks that Jesus was the first to give us that beautiful teaching. In fact, it is part of the Law of Moses, in the book of Deuteronomy. For 3,000 years, the daily prayer of the Jewish people has begun, "Listen, Israel: The LORD is our God, the LORD alone. You shall love the LORD your God with all your heart…."

According to the gospels, Jesus declared his belief that Deuteronomy 6:4 was the greatest commandment in the Law (meaning, the Law of Moses), more important than any of the Ten Commandments, or any of the more than 600 other laws in Mk 12:28-34 the Jewish Scriptures. Jesus' choice as the second-greatest law, to love your neighbour as yourself, is also part of the Law of Moses. Lev 19:18 Jesus didn't create those teachings; the importance of love was central to the Jewish tradition for centuries before Jesus lived.

Indeed, the gospel narratives show that Jewish scholars agreed with Jesus about the importance of these two laws: according to the Gospel of Luke, Jesus asked a Pharisee what he thought was Lk 10:25-28 the most important commandment in the Law of Moses. The Pharisee responded by citing the prayer about loving God with all our heart. "You have given the right answer," Jesus said.

This belief in a God of love is one of the most treasured aspects of the faith that we have inherited from the Jewish tradition: God loves each of us as we are, without conditions. God is faithful; God can be trusted. And God invites us to respond by loving God from the depths of our being.

4. *God saves us: God leads us towards wholeness.*

Salvation is central to our lives as children of a loving God.

"God saves us" means that God takes the initiative to make us whole.

In the Bible, salvation doesn't refer primarily to life beyond death, but to life in this world. From beginning to end, the scriptural tradition portrays God as being entirely on our side, and in no way against us.

God saves us from everything that keeps us from being true to ourselves and to God, from everything that diminishes us, from oppression outside and within, from our own selfishness, from sin. Again, there is no magical idea that God will take away all that is hurtful in our lives. Rather, salvation is about the inner life, and the initiative of God is to overcome what hurts us and to lead us towards wholeness.

The saving God comes to us and lives within us, overcoming the power of evil in the world and in ourselves, giving us the strength to be faithful to what is right. God helps us to become people of integrity, the people that we know we are meant to be – fully human, profoundly generous and loving. The more we are
1 Jn 4:8 true to ourselves, the more loving we are, the closer we are to God, because God is love.

Implicit in the idea of salvation is the recognition that we are not able to become fully the people we are meant to be without God's help. We don't achieve wholeness by our own efforts; it comes to us as a gift from God.

Thus, salvation is central to every section in this chapter. "God saves us" means:

- God sets us free;
- God chooses us and we belong to God;
- God offers us love, and invites love in return;
- God teaches us how to live in a way that is worthy of God's people, and forgives us when we fail.

Each of these statements expresses a different way in which God's saving initiative leads us towards wholeness.

5. *God teaches us how to live as worthy members of God's family, and forgives us when we fail.*

Another of the great revelations about God to the Jewish people is the recognition that God cares about our moral lives.

With some exceptions, the religions of their ancestors and neighbours were not moral religions. The God of the Jewish people was strikingly different from the pagan gods. God not only expected to be worshipped, but also asked people to live in a certain way, in order to be faithful children of God.

Many of the Ten Commandments, for example, are basic civil law. In fact, several of them are duplicates of a Babylonian civil law code that existed long before Moses lived. In the Jewish tradition (and in some other cultures) civil law is religious – God cares about daily life, and demands that believers honour their aging parents, are faithful in marriage, tell the truth in court, and respect other people's lives and property. In the next chapter, we will discuss the Ten Commandments and other laws of Moses; our purpose here is to appreciate the spirit in which the commandments were received by the Jewish people.

The Law of God, for the Jewish people, was never understood as an arbitrary burden. Instead, they knew God's Law as "a light for their path," the gift of a loving God. The Law was salvation for them: by the Law, God gave the people insight about how to live in happiness and peace, how to be truly human, how to be faithful to God, how to become whole.

Happy are those…
[whose] delight is in the law of the Lord…
They are like trees planted by streams of water…
In all that they do, they prosper. Ps 1:1-3

The law of the Lord is perfect, reviving the soul;
the decrees of the Lord are sure, making wise the simple;
the precepts of the Lord are right, rejoicing the heart. Ps 19:7-8

The Avenging God

A brief reading of the Law of Moses could easily make a reader question the accuracy of the previous paragraphs. Many Christians have been brought up with the impression that the Jewish people knew God as a harsh and punishing judge. What about the theme of the avenging God? There is no denying that this theme is present in Jewish tradition, and accompanies many of its moral teachings. For example, the law demanding that people respect the rights of widows and orphans is accompanied by God's threat to those who disobey:

If you do abuse them, when they cry out to me,
I will surely heed their cry;
my wrath will burn, and I will kill you with the sword,
and your wives shall become widows
Exod 22:23-24 *and your children orphans.*

Thus, Jewish faith about God as a moral teacher includes the realization that God is both a loving guide and a demanding judge.

The sense of God as vengeful probably grew out of people's efforts to understand the unending misery they faced in their lives. Grief was everywhere in Jewish society and family life. Average life expectancy at the time of Jesus was 22 years. Eight of every ten children died before they grew to adulthood. Everyone was poor, struggling to survive into an uncertain future.

The profound human question, then as now, was "Why?" How can the beautiful teachings about the goodness of God be reconciled with the reality of constant illness and death? The only answer those people could discover was that God is not only kind, but also just. In a tradition that had not yet come to believe in reward and punishment in life after death, the suffering of everyday life was understood as the consequence imposed by a just God in reaction to human sinfulness. Promises of God's retribution were therefore attached to moral teachings, to motivate people to do good and to avoid the consequences of evildoing.

The prophets were passionate critics of wrongdoing at every level of their society. They blasted the kings and priests for being corrupt; they censured the rich for oppressing the poor. In the name of God, they demanded that people act with integrity, and they often predicted terrible retributions for the evils that prevailed in society.

In the same spirit as the prophets, Jesus attacked corruption, demanded integrity and attached threats of punishment to his moral teaching.

'You that are accursed, depart from me into the eternal fire
Mt 25:41 *prepared for the devil and his angels.'*

[Some will be] thrown into hell, where the worm never
Mk 9:48 *dies, and the fire is never quenched.*

The heirs of the kingdom will be thrown into their outer
Mt 8:12 *darkness, where there will be weeping and gnashing of teeth.*

Jesus' images of punishment inspired centuries of medieval art, literature and preaching. Indeed, the threat of eternal punishment in life after death, which became a significant part of the Christian moral system, was a late development in the Jewish tradition. Interestingly, though Christians often think that the Jewish sense of God was harsh, it was Jesus who spoke about God sending bad people to hell forever, with no opportunity for escape. (To what extent that fearsome threat is part of authentic Christian moral teaching will be discussed in Chapter 26.)

Jesus' teaching, like Jewish teaching, clearly expressed the inexorable quality of God's demands. If we ignore the truth about how we should live, it will be worse for us. Some deeds are wrong, whether we like it or not; we harm ourselves and others when we do wrong; there is no escape from the truth.

The Forgiving God

We can recognize the binding force of God's demands and still believe that God is entirely a power for good in our lives. In fact, the loving-kindness of God is revealed most dramatically, in both Old and New Testaments, in the theme of forgiveness.

People who do wrong sometimes feel that they can do nothing to make amends for the evil they have done. They will say, "I can't forgive myself for what I did," or, "I can't really believe that God will forgive me."

But the teaching of both the Hebrew and the Christian Scriptures is that the forgiving love of God does overcome the evil we do. When we weaken our relationship with God by our decisions, God reaches out to us with love, invites us to change our hearts, heals the injury we have done to ourselves, strengthens our sense of purpose and leads us onward towards wholeness.

Absolve, O Lord, your people Israel, whom you redeemed. Deut 21:8

You are a God ready to forgive. Neh 9:17

Bless the Lord, O my soul, and do not forget all [God's]
benefits – who forgives all your iniquity. Ps 103:2-3

As far as the east is from the west, Ps 103:12
so far [God] removes our transgressions from us.

In the next chapter, we will study some of the moral teachings proclaimed in the Hebrew Scriptures. Later, in Chapter 20, we will consider Jesus' moral teaching as the fulfillment of the Law of Moses.

Conclusion

Such is the portrait of God that emerged from the Jewish people's experiences at the time of Moses. They learned of a God who reaches into people's lives to lead them to wholeness, who acts to set people inwardly free from what oppresses them, who chooses all of us to be God's own people and promises to be faithful to us forever, who teaches us how to live in a way that is worthy of God's people, and who forgives us when we fail. All of those beliefs are included when we speak of salvation – the generous initiative of God to lead us to wholeness.

The Bible invites us to open our hearts to the transforming action of God as it offers us this crucial choice: Will you accept God's offer of salvation?

8

THE LAW OF MOSES

The Ten Commandments and the Other 603

The Law of Moses provides a code of behaviour for a very wide spectrum of Jewish life. Altogether, there are 613 commandments to be observed by practising Jews. There are laws about what you can and can't eat, laws about sexual practices, laws that are recognized as idealistic and other laws that carry the death penalty, laws against revenge and laws allowing revenge, laws that are remarkably civilized and laws that clearly depict a harsh and often brutal society.

There are books full of laws in the Hebrew Scriptures. The book of Exodus presents hundreds of laws as part of the story of the people's escape from Egypt. The book of Leviticus (primarily for the priests) outlines very detailed rules of worship and many laws about the duties of priests. More laws are found in the book of Numbers. (The 'numbers' concern the number of people in each tribe that escaped from Egypt.) The book of Deuteronomy (a Greek word meaning 'the second law'), which is based on a collection of laws that was preserved separately from the book of Exodus, repeats many of the laws in Exodus and adds several details of its own.

The most famous of the laws of Moses – also called the Mosaic laws – are the Ten Commandments, but they aren't the most important. Both Jesus and many other faithful Jews considered
the laws commanding wholehearted love of God and love of Deut 6:4
neighbour to be the greatest of the laws – more important than Lev 19:18
any of the Ten Commandments.

As mentioned in Chapter 7, the people saw the law of God as a gift, because it taught them how to be true to themselves and faithful to God.

Christians have traditionally used the Ten Commandments as a convenient list of headings under which to cram all kinds of moral rules and values, and in so doing, have stretched the original meaning of the commandments almost beyond recognition. In this chapter, we will discuss only the original meaning of the Ten Commandments in the Jewish tradition – an understanding that has been almost forgotten in the Christian tradition. Later in this chapter, we will discuss a few other significant laws in the Mosaic collection.

The Ten Commandments

Exod 20:1-17
Deut 5:1-22

The Ten Commandments are reported in the book of Exodus; another version can be found in the book of Deuteronomy. The first four commandments in the Jewish numbering concern people's responsibilities towards God; the latter six commandments deal with responsibilities to other people. In this discussion, we will use the Jewish numbering of the commandments; for an explanation about why the Christian numbering is different, see the paragraph about the tenth commandment.

The list of the commandments begins with a prologue in which God proclaims the right to impose rules of behaviour on people:

Exod 20:2

> *I am the Lord your God, who brought you out of the land of Egypt, out of the house of slavery.*

This is an introduction to all the commandments. The passage follows the form of many agreements between lords and vassals, in which the lord establishes credentials: "I'm in charge in this fiefdom; in exchange for my protection, you will behave in the following manner...." But God's relationship with people is more profound than any feudal pact.

In this introductory statement, God claims the right to make moral demands, because God is responsible for the existence of the people as a free community. The commandments that follow are seen as gifts of God's love – the expression of a covenant in which God sets people free and tells them how to live as worthy people of God, for their own benefit, in pursuit of human wholeness and true faithfulness to God.

Commandments About God

1. You shall have no other gods before me.

Exod 20:2
Deut 5:7

People at the time of Moses had a choice of gods. Most of the cultures of the region were polytheistic, with different gods in charge of different aspects of life. Jewish religion was distinctive in its monotheistic belief that no other god except the LORD deserved their worship and loyalty.

Still, there were stages through which believers would pass on their journey from polytheism to monotheism. Abraham and Sarah and their descendants probably were loyal to one God ("the God of Abraham, Isaac and Jacob"), but quite comfortable with other people having their own gods, too. Melchizedek was a priest of El Elyan ("God Most High") who would be considered different from the God of Abraham. After the time of Moses, the Jewish people believed that their God was stronger than the gods of the other nations – but not necessarily that the other gods did not exist.

Gen 14:18-20

True theoretical monotheism is usually associated with the time of the prophets, who forcefully mocked the gods of their pagan neighbours. Jeremiah, preaching more than 600 years after the time of Moses, describes how artisans cut down a tree, work on it, dress it in fancy clothes, and then kneel down and worship it. The idols are like a scarecrow in a cucumber field, says Jeremiah. They cannot speak; they have to be carried because they cannot walk.

> *Do not be afraid of them, for they cannot do evil, nor is it in them to do good…*

Jer 10:3-5

Psalm 115 adds, "They have…eyes, but do not see. They have ears but do not hear." But our God is not like the idols, say the prophets; only the LORD is the true God.

see also Is 44:9-20

Thus, this first of the Ten Commandments demands that the Jewish people worship only the God of the Jewish people. It was not a practice that could be taken for granted. The Bible is full of stories of people abandoning their worship of God and reverting to the worship of other gods – perhaps because the worship of the Jewish God was austere and demanding, compared to the ecstatic and orgiastic rites of some of the pagan cultures.

Today, it has become commonplace to say that we have reverted to idol worship, in the form of money or power or other delights of contemporary life. Modern secular society may be idolatrous, or simply godless, but the first commandment continues to urge all believers to worship God alone.

In this setting we recall also the teaching that Jesus (and countless Jewish commentators before him) declared to be the greatest of all the laws of Moses.

Hear, O Israel: The LORD is our God; the LORD alone.
You shall love the LORD your God with all your heart,
Deut 6:4-5 *and with all your soul, and with all your might.*

Jewish believers understood that they were not only to worship God, but to love God, in return for the great gifts of freedom and love that God gave to them. A God whose relationship with people was one of mutual love was unheard of in the religions of their neighbours. Jewish tradition understood the profound importance of this awareness; for 3,000 years, the saying has been the opening words of the daily prayer of the Jewish people. Our God is a God of love.

2. You shall not make for yourself an idol,
Exod 20:4 **whether in the form of anything that is in heaven above,**
Deut 5:8 **or that is on the earth beneath,**
or that is in the water under the earth.

This commandment seems so similar to the first commandment that the traditional Christian remembering of the Ten Commandments includes this sentence as part of the first. But the original meaning of this commandment is distinct: for the Jewish tradition, the second commandment forbids any attempt to depict God in a visual representation.

Jewish tradition has always realized that any attempted picture of God is more false than true: God is a Spirit-being; God is too great to be depicted in a statue or a picture; God should not be portrayed in representational art.

Jewish disapproval of artistic depictions of God came to be expressed in terms of fear of idolatry: if someone creates a portrayal of God, there is a danger that people will pray to the statue rather than to the spiritual God. So great was the recognition that such a practice would be a fundamental act of disrespect for the real

God that visual art of any kind is almost unknown in Jewish culture. Jewish religious art is almost exclusively literary: they wrote about God rather than trying to make pictures of God.

Some may say that Christians have ignored the original meaning of this commandment to our detriment. Portrayals of God as an elderly bearded man sitting on a throne are pathetic misrepresentations of the reality of God, contributing to a loss of a sense of God as a spiritual being. This is not to protest against pictorial representations of Jesus – as a human being, he can indeed be portrayed in art, on stage, in video – but to help each other to know the Creator God, we must primarily imagine God as Spirit. Words are preferable to pictures for that difficult goal. Such is the original purpose of the second commandment.

3. You shall not make wrongful use of the name of the LORD your God. Exod 20:7 Deut 5:11

For the ancient peoples, a person's name was extremely significant. Your name sums up and expresses the reality of who you are. To speak the name of a god was to put a claim on the god's power. In contests of willpower or magic, a name was thought to have magical powers. For example, when Jesus is battling a horde of demons in the Gospel according to Mark, the demons try to gain power over him by announcing his name, "Son of the Most High God," out loud. Jesus brushes off their thrust, forces the demons to tell him their name, and, thus in control of them, casts them into a herd of pigs. Mk 5:7-9

Such was the respect for God enshrined in the third commandment that no Jew ever wanted to appear to be trying to get control over God by speaking God's sacred name. This reverence was extended so far that Jewish people today do not even pronounce the name of God when they read it in the Scriptures during a synagogue service. Instead of saying the Name given by God to Moses, faithful Jewish readers usually say the word *adonai*, meaning "my Lord." Sometimes they pronounce *HaShem*, meaning "the Name." Most modern English translations convey this practice by writing "the LORD" in capital letters. Thus we have learned the commandment as "You shall not take the name of the LORD your God in vain," when the Hebrew text says, "You shall not take the name of YHWH, your God, in vain."

Because Jewish people never pronounced the Name of God represented by those four consonants, there is some uncertainty about how the Name was originally pronounced, if indeed it ever was.

Is it not regrettable how irreverent towards God our society has become, when so many people repeatedly and thoughtlessly use the name of God and of Jesus as mindless expletives? We believers must regain our respect for God and for God's name; to do so will result in increased respect also for ourselves as human beings.

Exod 20:8 ***4. Remember the sabbath day, and keep it holy.***
Deut 5:12 ***Six days you shall labour and do all your work.***

The weekly sabbath holiday was a gift from God to the poor and oppressed of Jewish society. Without a commandment requiring a day's rest each week, people would have had to work from dawn until dark every day of their lives. Thus the Law of Moses represents a civilizing and humanizing advance in human history – this is another example of the action of God leading people towards wholeness.

The law was interpreted quite rigorously in orthodox Jewish practice through the centuries. No work was to be done on the sabbath. Meals could not be prepared; instead, meals prepared
Exod 35:3 on the previous day were eaten cold (since it was also forbidden to strike a fire on the sabbath). Interpretations of the law did allow for work on the sabbath in certain defined situations (for example, to save a life), but for most people, the sabbath was a
Exod 35:2 day for the more spiritual side of human life. It may come as a
Num 15:32-36 shock to realize that the penalty for working on the sabbath was death!

The sabbath law is still taken very seriously in orthodox Judaism. Conservative religious political groups have succeeded in grounding the Israeli airline El Al on the sabbath. Elevators in tall buildings (both in Israel and in Jewish buildings around the world) are set on "automatic pilot" (going up or down one floor at a time) so that no observant Jew has to push an elevator button.

Since in agrarian culture the end of each day comes when the sun goes down, the sabbath begins at sundown on Friday, and ends at sundown on Saturday. In Israel, businesses close by midday on Fridays, so that everyone can make it home by sundown and enjoy the sabbath meal with their families.

As we shall see, Jesus' interpretation of the sabbath practice
differed from that of the strictest Jewish tradition, but he clearly
knew that the sabbath rest was a gift of God for the well-being of
people. "The sabbath was made for humankind...." Mk 2:27

Hundreds of years after the sabbath observance began, the
author of the "seven days of creation" narrative supported the
weekly day of rest, writing that God created the universe in six
days, and that God was first to observe the sabbath by taking a
day of rest after six days of work. In the process of developing the Gen 2:2
final version of Torah, the connection between the creation
narrative and the sabbath law was also included in the listing of Exod 20:11
the Ten Commandments in the book of Exodus.

Hundreds of years after that, the followers of Jesus changed
the weekly day of rest and prayer to Sunday, because it was on
Sunday (the "first day of the week," not the seventh day) that Mt 28:1
Jesus rose from the dead.

To a great extent, contemporary society has departed from the original purpose of this commandment. Especially in the fields of retail commerce and entertainment, there is little difference between Saturday/Sunday and other days of the week. Our society is the poorer for it, since increasing numbers of people do not take time for prayer and other spiritual human activities. Somehow, each of us needs to hear again the call of the fourth commandment and regain perspective on the place of God in our lives and on important human values.

One aspect of faithfulness to the commandment that does endure in many contemporary families is a wonderful emphasis on family activities on Sunday. This practice is dwindling in some North American subcultures, but for many people, Sunday is still the day when the whole family gets together for a meal, when grandparents get to enjoy their grandchildren, and when people engage in relaxing and enjoyable activities. Especially if there is a conscious effort to be in touch with God as part of the Sunday practices, all of those activities are very much in the spirit of why God commanded the Jewish people to take a weekly day of rest.

Commandments About Relationships Among People

5. Honour your father and your mother. Exod 20:12

Deut 5:16

Both the Jewish and the Christian ways of life are primarily intended for adults. In fact, children were not bound to follow the Law of Moses until they reached adulthood, a stage that generally coincided with puberty and is now celebrated with the ceremony of *bar/bat mitzvah* ("son/daughter of the Law").

The fifth commandment, then, was not addressed to little children. It is a commandment that requires adult children to respect their aging parents.

No doubt there was as much intergenerational conflict in biblical times as there is now. Today, this commandment is addressed to young adults who are battling their parents (or parents-in-law), to middle-aged adults who are having difficulty with elderly parents, and even to people who continue to struggle with a parent years after the parent's death.

The commandment should not, of course, be interpreted as a sanction of the many evils some parents have inflicted on their children; it does express the conviction of the Jewish tradition that adults must honour their aging parents. In the unending "war between the generations," God sides with the older generation against the younger.

Exod 20:13 **6. You shall not murder.**
Deut 5:17

The remaining five commandments are basically civil law. The distinctive feature of biblical morality is the belief that civil law is religious. According to the Bible, God cares about the structures of human civilization and supports the fundamental rights of individuals in society. Thus, though these brief, forceful imperatives were borrowed from much earlier Babylonian law codes, the Jewish commandments are different because they are understood not simply as the law of the state, but as the law of God.

The first of the fundamental rights of individuals is the right to life itself. Jewish society never understood the commandment as a prohibition of all killing; modern translations convey the meaning correctly when they translate the word as "murder." What is forbidden is unjustified killing. As the commandment was interpreted, the killing of human beings was justified in many circumstances (and there was no thought of any prohibition of killing animals or other living things). It was believed that God supported killing during the ferocity of war, and also that God supported capital punishment as society's response to such
Deut 13:6-10 offences as worshipping other gods, rebelliousness towards

parents, falsely claiming to be a virgin at the time of marriage (females only), adultery (understood as intercourse with a married woman), homosexuality, and even lighting a fire on the sabbath day. Deut 21:18-21 Deut 22:20-21 Deut 22:22 Num 20:13 Exod 35:2

Thus the "right to life" was certainly not absolute for humans; the social order was considered to be of greater value than the life of any individual.

Jesus used the commandment against murder as the basis for one of his moral teachings. In the Sermon on the Mount, he radicalized the commandment, expanding "respect for life" to include a prohibition even of the kind of anger that results in a loss of respect for another person. The only incident that might be interpreted as a comment on the tradition of socially authorized killing is the scene where he frees a woman caught in adultery from her executioners. Was Jesus completely opposed to capital punishment? We have no way of knowing. Mt 5:21-22 Jn 8:1-11

Certainly the political and religious leaders of Christian Europe were responsible for the deaths of thousands, claiming that social order outweighs the individual's right to life. Today, Roman Catholic leaders proclaim the right of each individual to live from conception to natural death.

The original meaning of the fifth commandment is that God forbids unjustified killing. Ever since, both political and religious society have recognized some types of killing as justified. Today, society is struggling to decide whether the killing of human beings can be justified as it tackles the issues of capital punishment, abortion, assisted suicide, euthanasia and ethnic conflict.

Let's phrase the question in terms of the sixth commandment: When is killing murder? The struggle to discern has gone on for centuries; the discussions must continue in the contemporary context. What we know for certain is that unjustified killing is an act against the commandment of God.

7. You shall not commit adultery.

Exod 20:14 Deut 5:18

Adultery refers precisely to sexual infidelity by married people. In the patriarchal society in which the law originated, husbands were not bound to be sexually faithful to their wives, but they were bound to respect the rights of other husbands.

Thus the commandment against adultery was interpreted in practice as a commandment against 'wife-stealing': it did not forbid

a husband from having sexual intercourse with an unmarried woman, but it did forbid a wife from having sexual intercourse with any man except her husband, and it forbade men from having sexual intercourse with married women. Males or females who were apprehended in the act of adultery could face capital
Deut 22:22 punishment. "If a man is caught lying with the wife of another man, both of them shall die."

Mt 5:27-28 Jesus supports the commandment against adultery in the Sermon on the Mount, radicalizing it to include not just unfaithful actions, but even unfaithful and lustful intentions.

The religious demand for marital fidelity has fallen into disfavour both in practice and even in theory among many in modern society. Yet the command remains a viable standard of behaviour for believers. In fact, most people entering marriage consider sexual faithfulness to be an obligation for both themselves and their partner, and know that unfaithfulness will be harmful to the relationship and to their individual well-being. People recognize that this commandment of God is truly wise.

Exod 20:15
Deut 5:19

8. You shall not steal.

Because this commandment in its present form seems almost indistinguishable from the tenth commandment in asserting the rights of property owners, scholars think that its original meaning was not what now appears. They speculate that in its original form, it was a commandment against stealing a *person* – a law against kidnapping. In that rugged society, such a law likely had to be specifically expressed.

We will discuss the stealing of property under the tenth commandment, and leave this eighth commandment with the observation that it is another law whose original meaning remains viable today, and has bearing not only in obvious cases of violent hostage-taking, but also in cases of marital conflict and custodial rights of parents.

Exod 20:16
Deut 5:20

9. You shall not bear false witness against your neighbour.

Witnesses testify in court; this fundamental civil-religious law requires citizens to tell the truth when they testify in court under oath. The ninth commandment is a law against perjury. The law remains valid and necessary in contemporary society.

Interestingly, Jesus radicalized this commandment not just by expanding its terms of reference, but by forbidding his followers to take oaths for any reason. Such was his respect for the greatness of God that he considered it fundamentally irreverent to invoke God as a 'character witness' for someone testifying in court about some more or less trivial human dispute. Believers who are profoundly respectful of the greatness of God, says Jesus, will simply tell the truth because it's true: "Say 'yes' when you mean 'yes,' and 'no' when you mean 'no.'" Mt 5:33-37

Broadened thus in its application, the commandment continues to bind faithful believers today.

10. You shall not covet your neighbour's house; Exod 20:17
you shall not covet your neighbour's wife, Deut 5:21
or male or female slave,
or ox, or donkey,
or anything that belongs to your neighbour.

The tenth commandment, as phrased in the book of Exodus, provides a classic demonstration of the status of women in early Israelite society. A man's wife fits between his house and his slaves in the list of his chattels. The compilers of the book of Deuteronomy split the verse into two commandments, a division that has been continued in the traditional Christian numbering of the commandments. (The total number of commandments is kept to ten by combining the first and the second into one.)

God's covenant required right relations with both God and others. Strongly desiring what another person has violates the covenant. The very intention of doing so is forbidden by this commandment.

The economic sphere is, of course, a complex aspect of human social existence. Jesus advocated detachment: he feared the power money held for people and urged his disciples to free their hearts from the quest for wealth and to build their lives on a foundation of generosity rather than acquisition. Lk 14:33

This commandment, requiring justice in economic dealings, remains a challenging demand for all (especially in wealthier societies) who seek to live as faithful people of God. Lk 18:24

Summary

The Ten Commandments were originally fundamental, specific and forceful imperatives governing the way of life of believers. There are other moral considerations in life, but the Ten Commandments deal with ten key areas of human behaviour. They remain valid for believers today.

The original wording of the commandments is timeless and memorable, but paraphrases can help us reconsider their meaning.

- Realize who God is. Be conscious of God's action in your life.
- Never worship an image of God instead of God. Recognize that all human images of God are faulty, but the best ones do express some truth about God.
- Never permit yourself to be irreverent towards God, even thoughtlessly.
- Regularly take time to rest and to pray and to cultivate the spiritual side of your humanity.
- Respect your elders.
- When the issue is life and death, the initial preference is in favour of life, and any other value must be compelling to outweigh it. Unjustified killing is always wrong.
- Taking possession of an unwilling person is violent, harmful and wrong.
- Marriage depends on the sexual and emotional faithfulness of both parties.
- Honesty in communication is a fundamental human obligation.
- Respect the economic rights of others.

Other Examples from the Law of Moses

There are more than 600 laws in the Hebrew Scriptures; the meaning of each has been explored in rabbinical thought for centuries. Some of the laws of Moses are harsh expressions of the realities of an often brutal society, but many of them call forth kindness and generosity.

Concern for the Weaker Members of Society

Exod 22:22-23 *You shall not abuse any widow or orphan.*
If you do abuse them, when they cry out to me,
I will surely heed their cry.

If you lend money to my people, to the poor among you,
you shall not deal with them as a creditor;
you shall not exact interest from them. Exod 22:25

If you take your neighbour's cloak in pawn, you shall restore it before the sun goes down, for it may be your neighbour's only clothing to use as a cover; in what else shall that person sleep? And if your neighbour cries out to me, I will listen, for I am compassionate. Exod 22:26-27

You shall not oppress a resident alien; you know the heart of an alien, for you were aliens in the land of Egypt. Exod 23:9

The portrait of God that underlies these four laws is beautiful and lasting: God is the compassionate protector of the weakest members of society. In a society where the foundational rule had been "might is right," widows and orphans had no one to defend their rights, and could easily be victimized by any oppressor. The law of God declares that might is no longer right, and that faithful people must safeguard the rights of all. If a poor person can't afford to provide collateral for a loan, God will make sure that lenders don't take away the basic shelter that everyone needs. In a society (like so many others) with strong racial exclusivity, God is revealed to be the guardian of the outcast. God demands that the people care for the foreigners among them rather than oppressing them, and reminds them that they know what it is to be refugees.

These laws provide a civilizing direction in society; they portray God as leading people to a better understanding of human nobility and social well-being. They don't portray a violent and vicious society, though other laws do. They are early steps in God's guiding the people towards human wholeness, a process that eventually culminated in the life of Jesus.

These civilizing aspects of the Law of Moses were emphasized by the prophets, whose calls for integrity and justice in society are remarkably relevant in the neighbourhoods and corporate boardrooms of contemporary society. We will study the prophets and their preaching in Chapter 10.

Laws About Revenge

Lev 24:19-20 *Anyone who maims another*
shall suffer the same injury in return:
fracture for fracture, eye for eye, tooth for tooth;
the injury inflicted is the injury to be suffered.

Exod 21:23 *If any harm follows, then you shall give life for life,*
eye for eye, tooth for tooth, hand for hand, foot for foot,
burn for burn, wound for wound, stripe for stripe.

Lev 19:18 *You shall not take vengeance*
or bear a grudge against any of your people,
but you shall love your neighbour as yourself.

Christians tend to think of the famous Mosaic law of revenge as the slogan of a cutthroat society – in spite of the undeniable fact that "an eye for an eye" is the prevailing rule in the contemporary marketplace, in which Christians are enthusiastic participants. In fact, "an eye for an eye" was a civilizing factor in Jewish society, because it forbids vendetta. Before the Law of Moses, the prevailing practice was enunciated in the war cry of
Gen 4:23-24 Lamech: "I have killed a man for wounding me, a young man for striking me. If Cain is avenged sevenfold, truly Lamech seventy-sevenfold."

Under the Law of Moses, vendetta is forbidden. Revenge is permitted, but it is limited to one for one – an eye for an eye, a tooth for a tooth.

Jesus, of course, declared that revenge is unworthy of faithful
Mt 5:39 human beings, and urged his disciples to "turn the other cheek." His teaching is radical and idealistic – and is ignored by a great many Christians. But it wasn't entirely new. It was clearly foreshadowed in the Jewish tradition, in the law that Jesus considered to be the second most important in the law of Moses:
Lev 19:18 "You shall love your neighbour as yourself." In that text, the law of Moses proclaims a truly noble vision of human society, forbidding all vengeance, and declaring that human relationships should be built not on power, but on love.

9

CREATOR OF HEAVEN AND EARTH

God has given us our lives and this beautiful and awe-inspiring universe in which we grow towards wholeness in the human community and in the world.

This sentence is an attempt to express the fundamental religious teaching of the creation narratives in very simple terms. The narratives offer much more complex teaching than this, to be sure, and this chapter will discuss some of the issues found in the first three chapters of the book of Genesis.

But the underlying point of the opening sentence is that the creation narratives are concerned with religious teaching, rather than with science or history. Uncertainty about this point continues to cause unnecessary anxiety for many believers. Scientific study of the universe is entirely compatible with religious faith. For example, one can believe in God and still accept the theory of evolution. (More discussion of this topic will be found later in this chapter.) If you want to know what may have happened at the beginning of the universe, ask a scientist. If you want to know *why* it happened – the *meaning* of creation – read the Bible. The creation narratives deal with the relationships of God and the world, God and people, people and the world. The narratives are brilliant and profound and of lasting interest: people today are still concerned about the great religious issues dealt with by anonymous Jewish storytellers so many centuries ago.

Readers may wonder why the creation narratives appear as late as the ninth chapter of this book, when they are found at the very beginning of the Bible. The creation accounts are explored here because they began to be developed at this point in the history of the biblical tradition. As you will recall from the Old Testament dateline on page 30, the story of Adam and Eve – the earliest of the creation narratives – was written some 300 years after the experiences of the people who left Egypt with Moses. The "seven days of creation" account was written 500 years later, 750 years after Moses lived, in the process of the creation of Torah (the first five books of the Scriptures as we know them today).

The foundational insight that gave rise to the creation narratives was the recognition that God had been saving people, not just since the time of Abraham or Moses, but for as long as there had been people. Thoughtful believers asked reflective questions about what God was like before they came to know God, and concluded that God's love is timeless and eternal. In exploring questions about the origin of the world, they came to realize that God is not only Saviour (the first understanding they had of God), but also Creator, and that the entire universe is God's first gift of love to us. To express these profound insights, they wrote narratives so brilliant that today, 3,000 years later, they are remembered and studied by hundreds of millions of modern, technologically sophisticated people living in cultures that are remarkably different from the culture of those ancient authors.

In this chapter, we will begin with a discussion of the story of Adam and Eve; then we will go on to the account of the seven days of creation; and finally, returning to the earlier narrative, we will explore the myth of "the original sin," and its insightful teaching about the meaning of human sinfulness.

A. The Story of Adam and Eve

The story of Adam and Eve begins with the author's imagined picture of when the world was new – a remarkably childlike description of a dry land without plants or herbs, because God "had not caused it to rain upon the earth, and there was no one to
Gen 2:5 till the ground."

In the well-known narrative, God is portrayed as a sculptor, shaping the body of the first human out of dust (imagine it as modelling clay), breathing life into the statue so that it becomes a living being. Then God makes the plants grow and gives the new
Gen 2:7 human the responsibility of tilling and tending the garden "in Eden, in the east."

After God sensitively perceives the loneliness of the first human, every living thing is created and presented to the human, who gives a name to each. The naming process is understood as an act of power: in naming the creatures, the human tells them who they are. Humanity is given control over the rest of creation, according to this author. Gen 2:18-20

In the next scene, God takes the role of surgeon, extracting a part of the human's body, and wondrously shaping it into a woman. Gen 2:21-23

"Aha," says the man. "Finally, I am no longer alone." (Although the man has been exploring the garden with God in person, and has marvelled at the amazing complexity of created life, he feels lonely.) "This at last is bone of my bones and flesh of my flesh...." Gen 2:23

And so the earlier biblical story of creation is complete.

1. *What Is God Like in This Story?*

Children easily respond to this most significant theological question about the narrative by saying that God is like "a nice person" or "a magician." Children are naturally attracted to the portrait of God as very much part of our world, shaping clay into a human body (perhaps God's hands got muddy), and then breathing life into the body, walking around in the garden, feeling the loneliness of the first human, and taking steps to overcome that loneliness. Adults, too, often resort to conceptual explanations of the theology of the creation narratives, instead of reacting instinctively as children do.

This beautiful and believable sense of God, one that we continue to cherish, is to be understood symbolically rather than literally, for it expresses only part of the reality that is God.

2. *The Issue of Female/Male Relationships*

Some contemporary feminist observers decry the stereotypes that they perceive in this narrative, based on the creation of the man before the woman, and on the portrayal of the woman as the man's helpmate, created so that the poor fellow wouldn't be so lonely, and so that he would have someone to care for him. Other feminist commentators hold the opinion that the narrative was in fact fighting against those stereotypes, which were undeniably dominant in the culture in which the story was written.

One point presented in support of the latter view is that the Hebrew word *adam* really means 'human,' and does not necessarily refer to a male. *Adam* is related to the Hebrew word *adamah*, for earth – a human is an earth-being. The word for a male human is *ish*, and for a female, *ishshah*. The gender difference in humanity doesn't appear until the woman is distinguished from the man at the end of the chapter; it would be possible to translate the narrative accurately into English without ever referring to the first human as a male. That point may be considered arcane, but the following ones are more convincing.

Especially in ancient narratives, first isn't necessarily best, and last isn't necessarily worst. Indeed, most narratives (such as Chapter 1 of the book of Genesis, which portrays the humans as being created last among all the creatures) build to a culmination: the author of Chapter 2 may intend to say that woman in the story was created last and best.

We may have to concede that in Genesis 2, the woman is regrettably portrayed as having a role (as companion, partner) in relation to the man, but the most significant point is that the woman is human, distinct from the animals and from the rest of living things.

Exod 20:17 This narrative was written in a world where a man's wife was listed between his house and his donkey among his chattels (in the tenth commandment). The author of Genesis 2 portrays the woman as equal to the man and distinct from the rest of creation. The first human is not complete in a universe of marvels, even when the human walks in friendly communion with God. The woman and the man are part of each other; each is incomplete without the other; they are meant for each other. As the author perceives the original intention of God, woman should never be considered as one of a man's possessions – as she was according to the Law of Moses.

The ancient author's support for male-female complementarity and for the institution of marriage is sometimes challenged in our time by unmarried people and by homosexual people, who disagree with a statement like "man and woman are incomplete without each other." The sentence is not meant to refer to individual men and women, but to humanity in general: humanity is composed of males and females; both sexes are necessary for humanity to be what it is, and our lives would be different and would be deficient if there were only one gender. It is not reasonable to expect the ancient author to have considered such modern sensibilities. The author was writing a story to express his beliefs about the world as he knew it. He endorsed some aspects of his society and opposed others. He believed that men and women are equal as creatures of God, and he accepted marriage as the cornerstone of society. And he imbued his story with a profound belief that God is a loving presence in our lives.

At this point, we will leave the more primitive narrative, and will return to it later to discuss the first human sin. But first, let us explore another, very different account of the origins of the universe.

B. The Seven Days of Creation

Around the year 500 BCE, in the ruins of Jerusalem to which they had returned after 50 years of exile in Babylon, a team of authors brought together the various written traditions of their culture and compiled the first five books of the Bible as we know it today.

Among their collection of scrolls were different versions of the Law of Moses, and different versions of the story of their people, from Abraham and Sarah through Moses and the kings. Also among their resources were stories that had existed in written form for almost 500 years – Adam and Eve, Cain and Abel, Noah and the flood, and the Tower of Babel.

Perhaps they felt that the story of Adam and Eve was too primitive or childlike, that its sense of God was too simple and down to earth, or that the author had not been imaginative enough in portraying the beginnings of the world as they knew it. Doubtless they perceived that the existing creation narrative expressed great truth, but that more insight could be expressed in dealing with the same fundamental questions about the origins of the universe and of humanity. They decided to begin Torah with a majestic narrative of a supreme and powerful Creator God taming cosmic forces in creating a wonderful universe.

1. *The Setting*

In the beginning when God created the heavens and the earth, Gen 1:1-2
the earth was a formless void
and darkness covered the face of the deep,
while a wind from God swept over the face of the waters.

In spare, brief images, the authors have painted a verbal picture of chaos – unrelieved darkness, wind and raging waters. The Israelites were an inland people, at home in the desert and the mountains, and nothing struck terror into their hearts more forcefully than a dark and stormy sea. At the beginning of the narrative, there is no earth at all – the land is all jumbled up in the endless sea. (Our English translations that speak of a formless void are far too elegant to express the jumble-sound of the original Hebrew *tohu wabohu*.)

The power of God is present, though, in the wind – a word that in Hebrew (*ruach*) and Greek (*pneuma*) means both wind and spirit. The wind is a wonderful natural symbol for the power of God. As the Gospel of John puts it, "The wind blows where it
Jn 3:8 chooses, and you hear the sound of it, but you do not know where it comes from or where it goes." But if you've ever been outdoors in a howling wind, you certainly know that you're in the grip of an invisible, unconquerable and often destructive power. It will take you where it wants you to go, and you have very little choice in the matter. For the Israelites, the wind was a sign of the presence of God – unseen, spiritual, certainly real, of unknown origin and direction, powerful, uncontrollable by humans. Indeed, in both Genesis and John, it would be appropriate to translate the phrases using the word 'Spirit' instead of 'wind.' But you need to hear the word 'wind' to appreciate the author's visual portrait of chaos – a raging storm over a totally dark sea.

For the authors of Genesis 1, the process of creation will be a process of God's bringing order into chaos, of a divine power overcoming with a word the feared powers of nature and producing a benign and beautiful universe for the benefit of people.

2. *Let There Be Light*

Gen 1:3 The first principle of order, according to this creation narrative, is light. Light has long been used as a symbol of the reality of God in a great many cultures. Light is what our minds seek. Light is what gives us direction (like a lighthouse, or a farm window in a darkened countryside). Light makes it possible for people to communicate: in total darkness, we can't express ourselves nearly as fully.

Thus, according to the poetic vision of Genesis 1, God begins the work of creation by bringing light to the world, and demolishes one of the greatest of human fears – the fear of darkness. And God saw that the light was good.

3. *Sky, Earth and Sea*

The description of the second day of creation is based on a fascinating map of the universe as the Israelites understood it. A diagram of their world view, which was based on what could be deduced from everyday observation, appears below.

Like everyone in that era, the Israelites were sure that the world was flat. They thought of it as a disk, and as they gazed at the horizon it was obvious to them that the sky comes down to meet the earth, no matter which way you look. They therefore perceived the sky as a transparent dome, and since they had no Gen 1:6-8
scientific awareness of the principles of evaporation and condensation, they concluded that the blueness above the dome was water, which could be released through floodgates whenever God decided to send life-giving rain.

In "chambers on the waters" (above the sky) – a detail of
Ps 104:3 their universe that is not mentioned in Genesis 1 – they imagined
a heavenly court as the home of God and of myriad angelic
courtiers, including, according to the first chapter of the book of
Job 1:6 Job, the heavenly creature known as the Satan (or "the adversary").

Then as now, people marvelled at the great light that travelled
Gen 1:16 across the sky in the daytime, and the lesser light that appeared
at night. Still, despite observing that the sun is the source of the daylight in the world, they saw no contradiction in having God create the sun three days after the creation of light.

Knowing that one could also find water by digging, they concluded that there was water under the earth as well as in the sea; they called it 'the Deep' or 'the Abyss.' Rather than thinking of the world as a disk floating unsteadily in an all-encompassing world of water, they believed that God had set the world firmly
Ps 104:5 on its foundations…though they never tried to describe what the
foundations were set upon. Also somewhere under the earth, the Hebrews thought there was an underworld (*She'ol*, similar to the later Greek idea of Hades), in which lurked the life principles of dead people in a state of suspended animation, neither dead nor alive.

Thus the people of the Bible lived in a threefold universe made up of heaven, earth and the underworld. Their poetry and their mythology were built on this commonly accepted world view. Their map of the universe can easily be perceived as one reads the events of Day 2 in Chapter 1 of the book of Genesis, but it also underlies more poetic descriptions of creation, such as the following:

Bless the Lord, O my soul.
O Lord my God, you are very great.
You are clothed with honour and majesty,
wrapped in light as with a garment.
You stretch out the heavens like a tent,
you set the beams of your chambers on the waters,
you make the clouds your chariot,
you ride on the wings of the wind…

You set the earth on its foundations,
so that it shall never be shaken.
You cover it with the deep as with a garment;
the waters stood above the mountains;
At your rebuke they flee;

at the sound of your thunder they take to flight.
They rose up to the mountains, ran down to the valleys
to the place that you appointed for them.
You set a boundary that they may not pass,
so that they might not again cover the earth.

Here the creation narrative, so familiar to us from Genesis 1, is retold in poetry. As the Genesis narrative goes on, the waters of chaos are gathered into one place, and the land emerges from the Deep. God then populates the earth with plants, the sky with lights, the waters with swarms of living things, the air with winged birds, and the land with animals of every kind. Everything, as it is made, is good.

Ps 104:1-9

Gen 1:9-25

Finally, the stage is set for the appearance of humanity.

4. *In the Image of God*

In this thoughtful exploration of the meaning of human existence, and of humanity's relationship with the created world, three classic parallel lines of Hebrew poetry express a remarkable depth of insight. (The Hebrew word here translated as "humankind" is *adam*.)

So God created humankind in [God's] image,
in the image of God [God] created them;
male and female [God] created them.

Gen 1:27

What image of God did the authors perceive in humanity? Should we imagine God as some kind of exalted human, an old Jewish man? Filled with profound respect for the 'otherness' of God, the unpicturable spiritual nature of God, the authors must have realized that the image of God in humanity is not what we look like, it's what we *do*. In the ensuing verse, humanity is given the Godly right to be stewards of the world.

Other distinctively human characteristics can well be understood as the image of God in us: we can think, we can love, we can know God and communicate with God, we can choose and decide, we can even create – and be creative in many ways. All of these describe the meaning of the humanness that we share – the image of God that we embody.

Another aspect of the image of God in us is expressed in the parallelism visible in the poetic arrangement of the lines. Very often in Hebrew poetry, ideas are repeated in different words, in a parallel structure.

In the image of God [God] created them;
male and female [God] created them.

There can be no question that females and males are dealt with as perfectly equal in this poetic statement. And undoubtedly, for those authors, the male-female nature of humanity was seen to be a profound expression of the image of God in us. Certainly, they were not attempting to portray God as a sexual being, or as some combination of male and female. But they perceived that the sexual nature of humanity expresses the greatness of God. The way men and women connect with each other, and penetrate each other's lives so that they become part of each other, and create new life – all these portray for us what God is like. No doubt the writers understood their poetic lines to support the institution of marriage in their society, but the verse is also an acknowledgment of human sexuality. The Bible recognizes both the value and the ambivalence of human sexual behaviour; in this fundamental statement of the meaning of human life in the universe, the Bible says that our sexual nature is an image of God in us.

5. *Subdue the Earth*

Perceptive contemporary writers have criticized the biblical
Gen 1:28 authors and readers who perceive the earth to be the centre of the universe, the world to be made for the benefit of humans, humans to be the greatest of God's creatures, and humans to be given dominion over all creation to do with it as they wish.

In *A Planet for the Taking*, David Suzuki blames this verse of the Bible, as interpreted particularly by Christians during the Industrial Era, as the primary cause of the rape of our planet by human greed. By constructing the smokestacks that began to pollute the air in the nineteenth century and that may eventually turn our environment into an overheated swamp, by misusing chemicals and thus destroying the ozone layer, which will cause the deaths of thousands from skin cancer, and by destroying the rainforests, on which the world depends for much of its oxygen supply, believers have subdued the earth in the name of progress and profit, and have not listened when this approach has been challenged.

Carl Sagan speculated in *Cosmos* and *Pale Blue Dot* on the likelihood that other technological societies have developed somewhere among the billions of galaxies where planets may whirl around other suns. But he considered it unlikely that other such societies could develop at the same time as ours, because the billions of years of necessary evolution could occur at different rates in other worlds. Travel from here to any such planet is a matter of centuries at the fastest speeds we can imagine. Further, if other technological societies have evolved, how long have they lasted? Our history as a technological society is barely a moment compared to the 5-billion-year history of our planet, and there is every reason to wonder whether technological humanity will destroy itself in a matter of a few hundred years.

The only hope for the continuation of humankind is that believers will learn from the poets and philosophers that the Bible's gift of "dominion over the fish of the sea and the birds of the air" cannot be taken as permission for pillage, but as God's demand for careful conservation of the gifts of creation.

6. *Evolution*

Science and faith are compatible with regard to the process by which life has reached its present stage on our planet. The Bible does contain (mistaken) 'scientific' presuppositions based on the knowledge of the authors, but the Bible is a book about faith, not science.

The creation narratives were written to express the authors' faith about the relationships among God, the world and people. If you want to know what really happened, ask a scientist; if you want to consider *why* it happened – what it means – read the Bible.

Believers often protest that such a distinction implies that the Bible isn't true. We must help them to distinguish truth from facts or from scientifically demonstrable reality. The Bible is mistaken about many facts – scientific and historical. But the purpose of the Bible is to proclaim God's revelation and to explore religious truth. Facts aren't the only reality in our world; not everything can be measured by science. The best example is probably love, which is a powerful spiritual reality that can be perceived but not measured. The Bible can't be relied upon to tell us facts, but it does tells us truth about spiritual realities, such as hope and integrity and God and faith and love.

When it comes to evolution, some questioners may struggle with the idea of other primates being our ancestors. To put it simply, we can state that scientists believe that our planet began to cool down about five billion years ago (some eight or ten billion years after the Big Bang). An atmosphere including oxygen, nitrogen and hydrogen gases congregated around the planet, and water could be sustained on the surface of the sphere. Single-celled life began in the water, and became more and more complex in form, eventually including an amazing variety of bacteria, fish, birds, reptiles and mammals.

At one time, the most complex life form on the planet was the primates. Later, several types of 'proto-humans' lived; these can be identified by scientists. It's not a question of an ape giving birth to a human baby, but rather of adult creatures with increasingly complex brains becoming capable of more and more sophisticated activities.

What's the difference between human beings and other creatures of complex brain structure? Theology based on Greek philosophy would say that it is the 'infusion' of a spiritual soul, but it is possible to describe the difference without reference to a soul. Teilhard de Chardin, a Jesuit writer in the first half of the twentieth century, saw the key difference as 'reflexivity': with the arrival of humans, "evolution becomes conscious of itself." People can reflect on what they are doing, as other animals apparently cannot. In any case, reflection and spirituality are a distinctive part of human life, whether we think of them as brain activity or soul activity.

For believers, science's efforts to describe the process is an attempt to express how God went about creating us in our world, since we no longer understand that God literally shaped a human body out of clay, or spoke a series of mighty words to bring the world as we know it into existence in six days.

7. *The Seventh Day*

The epic narrative of creation comes to its climactic conclusion not in the creation of people on the sixth day, but in God's day of rest and reflection. The created world has sprung fresh from the
Gen 1:31 word, not as we experience it every day, but as it ought to be – orderly, harmonious and "very good."

God's moment of reflection is presented as the prototype of every seventh day, which Jewish tradition revered as a day of rest and prayer – a holiday, in the original sense of the English word. Gen 2:3

The observance of the sabbath day existed for centuries before this creation story was written. It was likely borrowed from Babylonian practice of taking a day of rest at each quarter of the moon. The social practice apparently became a religious practice under the Law of Moses, and the great creation myth gave it a deeper religious meaning based on the beauty of creation and the supreme power of the creator God.

8. *What Is God Like?*

The purpose of the creation narratives is to help us to know God. In Genesis 2, God walks the earth, shaping creatures with muddy hand and surgeon's skill. The sense of God in Genesis 1 is almost the opposite – God is majestic and distant from the world; God controls cosmic chaos simply by speaking a powerful word. Indeed, the intention of the authors of Torah is to say that *both* images of God are true: God is indeed close to us, and is part of our experience; God is also radically 'other,' far beyond our ability to know completely.

A further point about the sense of God in the biblical creation myths can be made by comparing the Hebrew narratives with similar documents of other cultures, before and since. The Bible shares with them the universal recognition that our world is the product of a power far greater than ourselves; the Bible clearly borrows images and sequences from pre-existing myths of the Babylonians and others.

But the Bible is also different from the other myths, and that is a significant point. Other cultures, seeking to deal with the problem posed by the existence of evil in the world, often invoke the idea of a cosmic struggle between opposed divinities. In the Bible, there is no sign of struggle in the process of creation; God is always in command; there is no other god; and everything that God makes is good. This insight of the authors is profound, distinctive and still valid.

At the same time, they too had to struggle with the question of the source of evil in the world. Their effort to face that question has come to be known as the story of the original sin.

C. The Problem of Evil

1. *The Question*

If God is entirely good, where did evil come from? Since the earliest glimmers of religious thought, that is the most difficult question that believers have had to face.

Jewish believers faced a distinctive challenge in confronting this question so long ago, since, according to Jewish faith, God is not the source of evil, but is entirely good; whatever evil power may exist in the world is in no way equal to or a rival of God.

The question of evil is fundamentally the same question as the one we looked at in Chapter 5 in connection with the cataclysm at Sodom and Gomorrah. But here in the creation narrative, the author is dealing with the more general question of the source of all the evil and grief in the world. The wisdom of the Jewish religious tradition is expressed not in a conceptual work of theology, but in a story. The author of the story of Adam and Eve, writing a thousand years before the time of Jesus, presents a magnificent mythical tale to express the viewpoint that all the evil we experience is not intended by God, nor is it a result of an evil god.

Instead, the author teaches, all the evil in our world is a result of human sinfulness.

It is a flawed answer, one that has been reconsidered and adjusted through the intervening centuries as we continue to search for a way of understanding the meaning of the evil that touches all of our lives.

2. *The Nature of Sin*

The story of Adam and Eve is the story of all humanity. Adam and Eve are everyone. Everyone sins, says the author; we need to explore the nature and the results of human sinfulness.

The author has artfully identified the key to human sinfulness as the desire to experience everything, without being limited by concerns about right or wrong. According to this story, then,
Gen 2:17 human beings want to eat from the tree of the knowledge of good and evil: to be able to do whatever they want, to set their own rules, to be God for themselves rather than to accept God's truth about what is right and wrong. That is exactly what the serpent
Gen 3:5 says: "You will be like God, knowing good and evil."

3. *The Consequences of Sin*

a) Alienation

When people attempt to be like God, what is the result? In the story of Adam and Eve, the first thing that happens is that the people are alienated from each other and from God. In covering Gen 3:7-8 their bodies, they are symbolically hiding their true selves from each other. Then they hide from God, who comes walking in the garden looking for them. Sin drives people apart.

A similar insight is expressed in another 'original sin' story, later in the book of Genesis – the story of the tower of Babel. Gen 11:1-9 There, the symbol of sin is a tower to reach the heavens: people want to be in command of their world; they aspire to the place of God. In this story as well, the result of human sinfulness is alienation: people scatter across the face of the earth, no longer able to communicate with each other.

The deliberate New Testament counterpoint to this situation is the story of Pentecost. There, people of many languages from Acts 2:5-13 all over the world understand the gospel message. The power of God's love overcomes the alienation caused by sin, and brings people together in the Spirit. Love pulls people together.

b) The Grief in Our Lives

Seeking to shed light on the question about the source of life's sadness and pain, the author continues with the theme: we must not blame God for our afflictions. God is entirely good, and God made the world good. We have wrecked God's creation by our sinfulness, and (since Adam and Eve stand for everyone) we are responsible for all the suffering that besets our lives.

This insight is expressed in the story through the conse-quences that God metes out, first to the woman, and then to the man.

Thus, to the woman in the story, God says, "In pain you shall Gen 3:16 bring forth children, yet your desire shall be for your husband, and he shall rule over you." The author is saying that the status of women as he knows it is not what God intended.

The consequence pronounced upon the man is equally telling in a society whose economy was primarily agricultural: "In toil you shall eat of [the ground] all the days of your life; thorns and thistles it shall bring forth for you; and you shall eat the plants of the field. By the sweat of your face you shall eat bread until you return to the ground…" Gen 3:17-19

Though the author may be criticized for giving Eve the leading role in the beginning of human sinfulness, the story seems reasonably equitable in its fundamental teaching that the problems faced by men and women are not intended by God, but the result of sin.

4. *Original Sin*

Strangely, the nature and origin of sin is never mentioned again in the Hebrew Scriptures. Long before there was a story of Adam and Eve, the Jewish tradition knew God as the Saviour who takes the initiative to reach into human lives and lead us to wholeness. God's generous saving action was in no way related to the sin of Adam and Eve in Jewish thought: God saved people because God loved people.

Traditional Christian teaching, on the other hand, took the story of the origin of sin rather literally, speaking of inherited guilt being passed through the generations from our first parents. We almost saw God as holding a grudge against humanity because of the sin of Adam, and thought that God demanded the death of the Son of God to make recompense for this sin. That theology was based on a sense of a punishing and vengeful God, rather than on the biblical sense of God as taking the initiative from the beginning to lead people to wholeness. Further discussion of Christian theology of salvation will be found in the closing chapter of this book.

Today, we have reinterpreted the story of the sin of Adam and Eve, and now understand it to be a symbolic description of the nature and consequences of the sin of everyone. 'Original sin' may be understood as 'the sinful heritage of humanity.' When a child comes into the world, the child's potential is limited by the oppressive forces, the evils in society, that surround the child. The author of the story of Adam and Eve recognized that it is not just the wrong that we ourselves do, but the heritage of human sinfulness that diminishes all of us.

The sacrament of baptism can still be understood traditionally in this context. Baptism was originally a celebration of death and resurrection – death to sin as the believer was submerged in water, and resurrection as the believer emerged from the water to begin a new life as a member of the community of disciples of Jesus. Using a slightly different sense of the symbolism, baptism means new birth, and the waters symbolize the waters of the womb.

'Washing away sin' is yet another sense of the symbol, but it is less significant than the use of water to symbolize death/resurrection/birth.

In seeking to express the meaning of baptism, we have traditionally said that baptism takes away original sin, though Rom 6:3
some of the effects of sin remain. Now, whether one prefers to speak of 'death to sin' or 'washing sin away,' we might say that the sacrament of baptism celebrates the powerful action of God to overcome the effects of human sin. The consequence of our sinful heritage is that we are diminished, we are kept from becoming whole, we are held back from our growth towards becoming the true person whom God calls us to be. Through the life of Jesus, the power of God bursts into our lives, transforms us, counteracts the force of sin, and leads us towards integrity and wholeness and love and full humanity.

Conclusion

We have looked at a few of the religious insights explored in these brief biblical narratives: God as part of our world and yet far beyond our experience, the universe as a gift of God's love, the interplay between humanity and the environment, the relationship of male and female, humanity – including sexuality – as image of God, the importance of rest and reflection in human life, the problem of reconciling the reality of evil with the goodness of God, the nature and consequences of sin, and the power of God's love to save us from our own sinfulness.

We cannot rely on the Bible for scientific and historical information, but if we live only on the level of facts and information, if we think that nothing is real unless we can see it and measure it, we are impoverished as human beings.

The Bible is true because it explores the spiritual realm – and finds God at the heart of human existence.

10

THE PROPHETS

Is not my word like fire,
Jer 23:29 *and like a hammer that breaks a rock in pieces?*

The word of God, as spoken by the prophets, was dynamite. Through the prophets, God demanded integrity of all believers and challenged the corruption and decadence that were synonymous with power, then as now.

The term 'prophet' means 'someone who speaks for' someone else; in this case, the prophets spoke on behalf of God. They were passionate preachers who interpreted the events of their time in the name of God. The preaching of some of the prophets was recorded by believers who were scribes; their exceptional courage and integrity have been remembered in written form, and they continue to disturb the comfortable. For other great prophets, such as Nathan and Elijah, we do not have the benefit of a scroll of 'collected sermons'; we know only a few anecdotes about them that have been remembered in the historical books of the Bible.

It is not easy to read the book of a prophet from cover to cover. The works of the prophets are like books of poetry. They have no storyline; some passages make more sense than others; they should be read slowly and reflected upon, preferably with notes that describe the context in which the prophet was preaching. In this brief summary of some important prophetic themes, we can do no more than skim the surface of this deep well of insight and faith.

A. Comments on Their Society

1. *Challenging Their Leaders*

Chapter 3 mentioned the prophet Nathan, a member of David's court who had the courage to confront the king after David arranged the death of Bathsheba's husband. How did Nathan keep his life after challenging such a ruthless and powerful despot? David had the wisdom to recognize the truth of what Nathan was saying; he may also have had enough religious fear to believe he was in danger of God's vengeance if he acted against the prophet. 2 Sam 12

The same two reasons likely account for the fact that none of the prophets whose thoughts are preserved in the Scriptures were killed immediately for what they preached, though they publicly and fiercely denounced the political and religious leaders of their time. Jesus acted in continuity with this prophetic spirit when he attacked the power structure of his society; he was killed as a result.

Your princes are rebels and companions of thieves. Is 1:22
Everyone loves a bribe and runs after gifts.

O my people, your leaders mislead you,
and confuse the course of your paths.
The Lord *enters into judgment*
with the elders and princes of [the] people:
It is you who have devoured the vineyard;
the spoil of the poor is in your houses.
What do you mean by crushing my people,
by grinding the face of the poor?
says the Lord God *of hosts.* Is 3:12-15

Woe to him who builds his house by unrighteousness,
and his upper rooms by injustice…
Are you a king because you compete in cedar?…
Your eyes and heart are only on your dishonest gain,
for shedding innocent blood,
and for practising oppression and violence.
Therefore, thus says the Lord
concerning King Jehoiakim…:
'They shall not lament for him…
With the burial of a donkey he shall be buried –
dragged off and thrown out beyond the gates of Jerusalem.' Jer 22:13-19

see Jer 22:1 The prophets who had the courage to shout messages like these to a crowd of the king's subjects gathered outside the king's palace were people of integrity and profound faith. They were also radicals who brought the word of God into the political realm with revolutionary force. And they certainly were not people who made deals with those in power, for the benefit of themselves or their institutions.

What would those prophets say about the religious and political leaders of our time?

2. *Challenging Society's 'Respectable' Citizens*

Like Jesus centuries later, the prophets knew that the truly faithful people of Israel were the poor and the outcasts, the people who were scorned by the 'respectable' members of society. According to the prophets, the rich, whose pursuit of wealth led almost inevitably to the oppression of others, could not claim to be faithful believers, no matter how often they went to synagogue and uttered all the traditional prayer formulas.

In the name of God, the prophet Amos shouted,

I hate, I despise your festivals,
and I take no delight in your solemn assemblies.
Even though you offer me your burnt offerings
and grain offerings,
I will not accept them…
Take away from me the noise of your songs;
I will not listen to the melody of your harps.
But let justice roll down like waters,
Amos 5:21-24 *and righteousness like an everflowing stream.*

Even current issues such as Sunday shopping, corrupt business practices, couch potatoes and indulgent lifestyles were on the agenda almost 3,000 years ago, when Amos proclaimed:

Hear this, you that trample on the needy,
and bring to ruin the poor of the land,
saying, 'When will the new moon be over
so that we may sell grain;
and the sabbath, so that we may offer wheat for sale?
We will make the ephah [like a bushel basket] *small,*
and the shekel [a weight measure] *great,*
and practice deceit with false balances…'

The Lord *has sworn by the pride of Jacob:*
Surely I will never forget any of their deeds.
Shall not the land on this account…? Amos 8:4-8

Alas for those who…lounge on their couches,
and eat lambs from the flock, and calves from the stall,
who sing idle songs to the sound of the harp…
and drink wine from bowls,
and anoint themselves with the finest oils,
but are not grieved over the ruin of Joseph!
Therefore they shall now be the first to go into exile,
and the revelry of the loungers shall pass away. Amos 6:4-7

Numerous similar passages can be found in the writings of the great prophets of Israel. The constant themes are the wake-up call ("Wake up and realize the implications of what you're doing!"), the demand for conversion and integrity ("You must change the way you are living!"), and the ominous threat ("You are bringing destruction upon yourselves by your actions – and this collapse is God's response to your decadence.") Is 5:1-7

One of the most amazing scenes from the prophets is found in the seventh chapter of the book of Jeremiah. We must learn to read and imagine the 'stage directions' in the text: God tells Jeremiah to stand at the front gate of the Temple in Jerusalem, and to accost the respectable God-fearing citizens who are approaching the Temple for worship. Perhaps Jeremiah is unkempt, clothed in a loincloth made of camel-skin, standing at the gate of the most sacred place in Jerusalem and shouting at the faithful. All they are doing, he says, is coming into the Temple and mouthing meaningless words ("This is the temple of the Lord, the temple of the Lord, the temple of the Lord") – and reassuring each other that they are saved – and then cheerfully going back into the city to continue robbing and murdering and committing adultery and worshipping false gods and oppressing the poor and widows and foreigners. In the name of God, Jeremiah literally screams at the people: "Has this house, which is called by my name, become a den of robbers in your sight?" Almost 700 years later, in the very same place, Jesus proclaimed the same challenge to the people of Jerusalem – and it cost him his life. Jer 7:1-15 Jer 7:11

Understandably, the prophets were not popular among the leaders of society and its more powerful citizens. But they were respected. In some way, everyone recognized the truth of what they said.

B. How Did it Feel to Be a Prophet?

Who would want to stand in front of a crowd of fellow citizens and tell them that their way of life is inherently wrong, that they must change or face the wrath of God?

Most of us prefer to hang back, to let others try to change things. Most of the prophets wouldn't have chosen to speak out. But they felt called to step out of the respectable crowd and speak the word of God with power to people who didn't want to hear it. Three examples follow.

1. Elijah's Search for a Quiet Voice

Elijah was an important prophet who preached in Israel, the northern kingdom, some 400 years after the time of Moses, 50 years after the division of the kingdoms. No one recorded the preaching of Elijah in a book of his thoughts; we have only narratives in the first book of Kings to tell us about the significant role Elijah played in his society.

The king of Israel at the time was Ahab, son of Omri. Because the narratives about the northern kings were written in the south by writers who considered the northerners to be uncivilized heathens, it is difficult to distill an accurate sense of their careers
1 Kings from the Bible. Omri, a strong ruler who reigned for 12 years and
16:23-28 founded Samaria, the capital city of Israel, is given two paragraphs in the book of Kings. The story of Ahab, who ruled in Israel for 22 years, is told in much more detail, but the narrative begins with the evaluation that Ahab "did evil in the sight of the LORD
1 Kings 16:30 more than all who were before him."

Ahab was probably a typical despot who didn't care much about religion, and likely deserved Elijah's criticism. To cement a political alliance, he married Jezebel, a princess from Sidon, a town on the Mediterranean coast in what is now Lebanon. She cared more about her heritage and religion than Ahab did about
1 Kings his, so she introduced Sidonian rituals into the court of Israel,
16:31-32 and thus incurred the rage of Elijah, who insisted that Ahab should be faithful to the worship of the God of Israel.

1 Kings 18 Elijah waged a titanic struggle against the queen and her agents in the court of Ahab, but Jezebel prevailed, and Elijah had to flee for his life into the southern desert.

It is there that we are given a glimpse into the soul of a prophet.
The defeated Elijah prays for death, being totally disillusioned by
the faithlessness of the people of Israel. He is dissatisfied with
traditional images of the powerful and dramatic presence of God
– the God who is perceived in the wind, the earthquake, the fire.
That traditionally powerful God seems to have deserted Elijah 1 Kings
when he most needed him, and Elijah wishes for death. 19:11-13

In the end, the true nature of God is revealed to Elijah's searching soul in sheer silence, in a still small voice within his heart. Elijah's purpose and mission are renewed, based on a deeper sense of who God is.

2. *The Book of Jonah*

Jonah, a book about prophecy, uses one of the less familiar literary art forms to discuss the issue of the temptation not to listen when you know in your heart that you are called by God to do something distinctive with your life. The book of Jonah is a satire.

It tells the story of a man who is called by God and given a
mission as a prophet to preach the word of God in the faraway
city of Nineveh. Jonah's response to God's call is to run in the Jon 1:1-3
opposite direction, west instead of east, away from Nineveh.
Presuming that God is most active in the land of Israel, Jonah
tries to get away from God by boarding a ship and sailing out
onto the unmarked ocean. It doesn't work.

God sends a great wind to chase Jonah. The sailors (who are
more faithful than Jonah in trying to find out which god is blowing
at their ship so hard) determine that Jonah is the cause of the Jon 1:17
tempest and throw him overboard. God sends a big fish to swallow
Jonah and spit him back out on the land; Jonah gets the point
and gives in when God repeats the call to be a prophet. Jon 2:10

Jonah does as he is told and threatens the Ninevites with
destruction if they don't change their ways in 40 days. He is
dumbfounded when they repent, saving their city from destruction
by God. At this point, Jonah gets angry at God and wants to die, Jon 4:1
because Jonah had threatened a major catastrophe, which hasn't
materialized, and now he feels foolish.

This little book is supposed to be funny, but it does offer a Jon 4:2
positive sense of God who is gracious and merciful, slow to anger
and abounding in steadfast love, and who cares even for the
animals in Nineveh as well as for the 120,000 inhabitants who Jon 4:11

"don't know their right hand from their left." It invites us readers to reflect on our own faithfulness: do we respond to God's call to integrity, or do we prefer to be like everybody else, just comfortable, respectable ordinary citizens?

3. *The Confessions of Jeremiah*

The most poignant expressions of the heart of a prophet are found in a series of lyric poems in the book of Jeremiah.

At the beginning of the book, the prophet reports his
experience of being called to be God's prophet, and admits that
he prayed to be spared the task, claiming that he was too young
and that he was not a good public speaker. But God overwhelms
Jeremiah with promises of support, and gives him a mission to
Jer 1:4-10 destroy what is bad in society and to build and to plant something
new and better.

Jeremiah accepts the task and does his duty, but he continues
to wish that life were different for him. The prophet grieves in his
heart at the oppressive selfishness of the rich; he laments that the
Jer 8:18–9:1 starving poor feel that God has abandoned them.

Jeremiah complains to God that the way of the guilty prospers
Jer 12:1-6 while he tries to be faithful, and the poor people are withering.
He reminds God that he has been suffering insults because of his
preaching, and he wants to see his tormentors punished. He
whines that he would prefer to join the merrymakers and have a
little fun, but he can't because he is ostracized for his challenging
Jer 15:15-18 proclamations.

Jeremiah is shocked when God is not sympathetic to his
Jer 12:5 prayers. "If you're getting tired racing against foot-runners, how
are you going to compete with horses?" is God's response to one
prayer, meaning, "You haven't seen anything yet; quit complaining
and keep doing what you're supposed to do."

"Stop uttering all this worthless nonsense, and change your
Jer 15:19 heart and speak what is precious – and then I'll be with you," is
another expression of Jeremiah's sense of God's relentless demands.
Being a prophet is no easy task.

In the most tragic of Jeremiah's confessions, he is overcome
Jer 20:7-18 by the trials of his life as a prophet. He feels that God seduced
him into this work, and the result has been that everyone hates
him and makes fun of him. He reports that sometimes he tries to
ignore the call of God, and not speak anymore in God's name, but

that he can't keep quiet; he feels as if he is bursting with an inner fire.

Jeremiah wishes he had never been born and, in a bitter line, curses the messenger who brought the 'good news' of Jeremiah's birth to his father. Jer 20:15, 18

Such feelings may arise in the life of any believer. If ever we feel abandoned by God or uncertain about the direction of our lives, we may remember that these feelings are not evil or wrong; they were shared by one of the most faithful believers who ever lived.

It may comfort us to know that the heart of a prophet, like that of any believer, is not always serene.

C. The God of All Consolation

The teachings of the prophets are not always predictions of doom and radical demands for conversion. The central theme in their preaching is the faithful love of God, a love that demands integrity, but remains no matter how unfaithful the beloved.

Some of the most beautiful poetry in the Bible portrays God's faithful love for an unfaithful people.

1. Hosea

The book of Hosea is based on the prophet's personal life. Hosea's wife, the mother of his three children, left him and committed adultery. Rather than demanding the death penalty, Hosea forgave her and invited her to return to their family.

In this experience, Hosea realized that he was symbolically living God's relationship with God's people, who had been unfaithful in so many ways. He recognized the meaning of God's faithful love and expressed his recognition in poetry.

Speaking in the persona of God as the loving parent of a wayward child, Hosea writes:

When Israel was a child, I loved him,
and out of Egypt I called my son.

The more I called them,
the more they went from me…
Yet it was I who taught Ephraim to walk,
I took them up in my arms;
but they did not know that I healed them.

I led them with cords of human kindness, with bands of love.
I was to them like those who lift infants to their cheeks.
I bent down to them and fed them…

My people are bent on turning away from me…
How can I give you up, Ephraim?
How can I hand you over, O Israel?…
My heart recoils within me;
my compassion grows warm and tender.
I will not execute my fierce anger…
because I am God and no mortal,
the Holy One in your midst,
Hos 11:1-9 *and I will not come in wrath.*

Images of a vengeful God are far outweighed in the Bible by passages such as this one, about the God of mercy and forgiveness. The refrain of a beautiful modern hymn captures the heart of Hosea's poetry: "Long have I waited for your coming home to me and living deeply our new life."

2. *The Poetry of "Second Isaiah"*

Some of the most inspiring poetry in the Scriptures was written during the most terrible period in the history of the Jewish people. Their capital city had been destroyed by the Babylonians, and their leading citizens had been exiled to the land of the conquerors. Reasonable people were asking, "Where is this God who was supposed to take care of us? Even the house of God, the Temple in Jerusalem, has been reduced to a pile of rubble. We must have been believing in the wrong god."

In response, there arose a wise and profound believer – a writer whose name we will never know. His poetry was collected and attached as chapters 40 to 55 of the scroll of the prophet Isaiah, who had lived some 150 years earlier. We know this great poet only as "Second Isaiah." (Chapters 56 to 66 are the work of yet another unknown writer or two.)

The work of Second Isaiah is often known as "The Book of the Consolation of Israel." Writing from Babylon, the author assures the people that God has not deserted them. The destruction they have experienced was the result of their own decadence, but God loves them still, and will restore their freedom and return them to their homeland.

Comfort, O comfort my people, says your God.
Speak tenderly to Jerusalem,
and cry to her that she has served her term,
that her penalty is paid… Is 40:1-2

Thus begins the prophecy of Second Isaiah. He continues with a triumphant image, declaring that God will smooth out the rocky badlands between Babylon and Israel and make a highway across the desert so that the people can return home singing and dancing and rejoicing:

A voice cries out:
In the wilderness prepare the way of the LORD.
Make straight in the desert a highway for our God.
Every valley shall be lifted up,
and every mountain and hill be made low;
the uneven ground shall become level,
and the rough places a plain.
Then the glory of the LORD *shall be revealed,*
and all people shall see it together….' Is 40:3-5

Christians will recognize these words, which were spoken by John the Baptist. John picked up the imagery of Second Isaiah, saying that he was that voice in the wilderness, preparing the way of the Lord.

This begins our discussion of the fulfillment element of prophecy. We have seen that most of the preaching of the prophets was not to predict the future, but to comment on the present. The original meaning of the image of a highway in the desert was related to the plight of the exiles in Babylon. But John the Baptist and the Christian community perceived a new meaning in the imagery, one that expressed their conviction that God had been preparing for the coming of Jesus in the many experiences of the chosen people. (A more complete discussion of the theme of fulfillment of prophecy will appear later in this chapter.)

The poetry of Second Isaiah offers a wealth of consolation to suffering people even today. Readers can delve in with little background information, and be inspired and renewed in hope. For adults and for youth, these texts can provide food for thought about their deepest fears or consolation in times of sadness, when people might feel that it is hardly worth believing in God anymore. Reflection will not take away the pain by itself, but it serves as a reminder that good, faithful people have felt the same way through the centuries, and that somehow their trust in a faithful God helped them to deal with their sadness.

Is 43:1-3 Modern composers have taken several images from this great
Is 54:10 prophet and shaped them into hymns: "Be Not Afraid" and "You
Is 40:9-11 Are Mine," "Though the Mountains May Fall," "Like a Shepherd,"
Is 55:1-2 "Come to the Water" and "Isaiah 49."

Is 49:14-16 To conclude this brief introduction to Second Isaiah, let's
reflect on the final verses of this poet's work. In reading these lines, try to put yourself in the frame of mind of the exiles for whom it was composed – far from home, looking out at vast, rocky, arid badlands. Flowers are little miracles when the very air you breathe is visible with swirling desert dust.

For as the rain and the snow come down from heaven,
and do not return there until they have watered the earth,
making it bring forth and sprout,
giving seed to the sower and bread to the eater:
so shall my word be that goes out from my mouth;
it shall not return to me empty,
but it shall accomplish that which I purpose,
and succeed in the thing for which I sent it.

For you shall go out in joy,
and be led back in peace;
the mountains and hills before you shall burst into song,
and all the trees of the field shall clap their hands.
Instead of the thorn shall come up the cypress;
instead of the brier, shall come up the myrtle;
and it shall be to the Lord *for a memorial,*
Is 55:10-13 *for an everlasting sign that shall not be cut off.*

D. The Hope for Messiah

As the people looked back on the glories of their past, their hope for future glory was expressed in a variety of ways.

1. *A Golden Age*

The time is surely coming, says the LORD,
when…the mountains shall drip sweet wine,
and all the hills shall flow with it.

I will restore the fortunes of my people Israel,
and they shall rebuild the ruined cities and inhabit them;
they shall plant vineyards and drink their wine,
and they shall make gardens and eat their fruit.
I will plant them upon their land,
and they shall never again be plucked up
out of the land that I have given them. Amos 9:13-15

The prophets spoke of a coming great 'day of the LORD,' when Is 2:12-17
all the proud would be humbled, and God alone would be exalted.
But even Amos realized that if the people were going to hope for Amos 8:9-10
'the day of the LORD,' they would have to change their lives.

2. *A New Covenant*

Prophetic hope for a messianic era was not confined to the expectation of a great new king to arise from the family of David. Jeremiah used the beautiful traditional concept of covenant to say that in the age of the Messiah, God would establish a new covenant with people, and implant it in their hearts.

I will make a new covenant with the house of Israel and
the house of Judah…
I will put my law within them,
and I will write it on their hearts;
and I will be their God, and they shall be my people…
I will forgive their iniquity,
and remember their sin no more. Jer 31:31-34

3. *A Prophet Like Moses*

The story of the death of Moses at the end of the book of Deuteronomy (written 700 years after Moses lived) ends with
the wistful comment that "never since has there arisen a prophet Deut 34:10
in Israel like Moses." The people began to hope that someday God would send a new great prophet like Moses. (In many ways, the Gospel according to Matthew expresses the Christian belief that Jesus was the fulfillment of this Jewish hope – Jesus is presented as "the new Moses," proclaiming a fulfilled new Law, and creating a new covenant for a new Israel.)

But the most romantic, most galvanizing hope of the Jewish people, one that sustained them through the depths of despair and became more and more prominent in their national dream, was the hope for a leader who would overthrow their oppressors and re-establish the freedom and pride and faithfulness of the people of Israel – a king like David, the anointed one.

4. A New David

In Jewish tradition, the major symbolic ritual at the enthronement of a king was not putting on a crown, but anointing the king's head with oil – abundantly, poured down over his head, dripping down his beard. The king was thus 'the anointed one,' in Hebrew *meshiach,* which we transliterate as 'messiah.' (The Greek word for 'anointed' is *christos*; in the New Testament, the title 'Christ' is the equivalent of the Hebrew concept 'Messiah.')

Fuelled by their disgust for the corruption of their contemporary kings, the prophets encouraged people to hope for the day when God would anoint a good king, someone who, like the legendary David, would be honest and God-fearing, would establish a kingdom based on the rule of God (theocracy), and would lead the nation back to faithfulness.

Their confident hope that God would indeed send them a great new king sustained the people through the difficult centuries of political decline, and inspired them to revolutionary fervour when they were convinced that the Messiah's coming was imminent.

Much of the hopeful poetry about the coming of the great king was written by the prophet Isaiah (the one whose name we do know), more than 700 years before Jesus was born. Since then, Isaiah's imagery has thrilled Christian readers every Advent, as we re-experience the images of hope that inspired the Jewish people.

a) Emmanuel

The original context of the memorable lines of the Emmanuel prophecy was a confrontation between Isaiah and his king, Ahaz. Isaiah considered his society and his king to be corrupt. Ahaz had little interest in the prophet's message, being much more concerned with the threat of invasion by the powerful Assyrian empire. But Isaiah was relentless, and continued to admonish the king to repent and be faithful.

On a certain day that has been remembered for almost 3,000 years, Isaiah tried to persuade the king to listen, inviting him to ask God for anything at all: "Whatever you ask for, God will give you, as a sign that God is real and that you should be faithful." The king demurred, saying, "I will not put God to the test," but meaning, "Go away, Isaiah, you're bothering me."

"Very well, then," said Isaiah, "God will give you a sign whether you ask for one or not." The sign turns out to be a baby: "The young woman is with child, and shall bear a son, and shall name him Immanuel." (*Imma* = 'with'; *nu* = 'us'; *el* = 'God': Is 7:10-17
Immanuel means "God is with us.")

In the original setting, the young woman in question was probably the king's wife. The implication of the 'sign' is this: "Ahaz, you are going to be replaced. Your wife is pregnant; you are going to die some day, and your son will take your place. He will be God's gift to the people because he will be a better king than you are." Thus the original meaning of the Emmanuel prophecy was a warning, a reminder to the king of his own mortality, a claim that God is still in charge of the world, no matter how powerful kings may think they are.

Indeed, in due time, his son Hezekiah did succeed Ahaz, and was a more faithful king than his father had been. But somehow the people realized that, though Isaiah's prophecy had meaning in its original sense, there was more to it. They believed that, though Hezekiah's reign was a partial fulfillment of the prophecy, God had more wonderful gifts in store for the people. And so the Emmanuel prophecy took on an evolved meaning, and became part of a deeper hope for a truly great Anointed One who would be God's definitive gift to the people.

There is one further pre-Christian step in the process of expectation surrounding this text. Five hundred years later, after Alexander of Macedon had conquered an extensive empire, Jewish people settled throughout most of the eastern Mediterranean world. The language of the Empire was Greek, and in time, some Jewish people could no longer understand the Scriptures written in classical Hebrew. For their benefit, a Greek translation of the Scriptures was developed in Alexandria, Egypt, and the translators replaced the Hebrew word for 'young woman' with the Greek word *parthenos*, which means 'maiden' or 'virgin.'

A few hundred years later, to make the point that Jesus is the Anointed One, God's presence among us, and the fulfillment of the Emmanuel prophecy, the writer of the Gospel of Matthew, writing in Greek, and using a Greek copy of the Hebrew Scriptures, reported that Jesus was born of a virgin, to fulfill what was written in the Scriptures:

"Look, the virgin shall conceive and bear a son,
Mt 1:23 *and they shall name him Emmanuel."*

We can see that the work of the prophets was not simply to give us predictions of a variety of details of the life of Jesus centuries before he lived. Rather, they have given us a poetry of faith and hope, a sense that God is faithful and has new gifts in store for people, gifts beyond their greatest imaginings.

Every expression of hope is fulfilled in unexpected ways, and every fulfillment is perceived to be only partial: even after a prophecy is seen to be fulfilled, a new hope arises for further fulfillment. This can even be seen as true about Jesus: though we understand him to have been the fulfillment of the Hebrew Scriptures, and though we believe that in the life of Jesus the reign of God came into being in a definitive way, we continue to realize that there is more to come. In many ways the reign of God has not yet come in fullness (we still pray "thy kingdom come"), and we wait for Jesus to return in glory to establish the definitive reign of God.

The dynamic of prophecy looks to the future – to partial fulfillment and constantly renewed hope.

b) The Prince of Peace

One of the images connected with the anointing of a king was that of new birth. Psalm 2, for example, was originally a coronation psalm, proclaimed at the inaugurals of the kings. There, God announces to the newly crowned monarch, "You are my son; today I have begotten you." The day of coronation was considered to
Ps 2:7 be the day of the king's 'birth' as God's son in a special way (without the sense of divinity that Christians ascribe to Jesus as Son of God).

Chapter 9 of the book of the prophet Isaiah begins with a glowing hymn of praise and thanks. The prophet imagines himself present at the coronation of the Messiah-King. He speaks of a great light shining on people who had walked in darkness for so long; he feels the joy that people feel when there is a plentiful harvest. Using a poetic 'close-up' technique that we associate with films, he focuses on a warrior's boot and blood-soaked robe
Is 9:2-5 dragging in the mud, and says, "Throw them in the fire! We won't be fighting anymore. We are free of our oppressors!"

Why this great feeling of rejoicing? "For a child has been born for us, a son given to us" – meaning, today the new king is crowned. Today a new king will hear the glorious words "You are my son; today I have begotten you." But this will be no ordinary king:

Authority rests upon his shoulders;
and he is named Wonderful Counsellor, Mighty God,
Everlasting Father, Prince of Peace.
His authority shall grow continually,
and there shall be endless peace
for the throne of David and his kingdom.
He will establish and uphold it
with justice and with righteousness
from this time onward and forevermore. Is 9:6-7

No wonder the followers of Jesus, though he had never been crowned as king, believed that he had fulfilled these words of hope in a way unimagined by their author, but prepared for by God.

c) The Jesse Tree and the Era of the Messiah

Jesse was David's father. According to the prophet, the family tree of Jesse had become so rotten that nothing remained but a stump. But hope remained. A new shoot would grow out of the roots of this family tree. God would send a great new king, David, who would reign in peace and justice and faithfulness. Is 11:1

"The spirit of the LORD shall rest on him, the spirit of wisdom and understanding, the spirit of counsel and might…." What we have taught to our children as the seven gifts of the Holy Spirit Is 11:2 was originally a poetic description of the characteristics of the Messiah. Today our prayer is that the Spirit of God will do the same for each of us – make us wise, help us to understand, give us right judgment, inspire us with the courage to be faithful.

The great king will be honest, unlike the kings who have ruled us of late, says Isaiah. He will not judge simply by appearances, but will get to the heart of the matter. Is 11:3-4

His decisions will be equitable, even for people who can't afford a bribe. He will be faithful to the Law of God, the God of widows and orphans.

Isaiah's most memorable images of the era of the Messiah describe a world where natural enemies live together in peace:

The wolf shall live with the lamb,
the leopard shall lie down with the kid,
the calf and the lion and the fatling together,
and a little child shall lead them.
The cow and the bear shall graze,
their young shall lie down together;
and the lion shall eat straw like the ox…
They will not hurt or destroy
on all my holy mountain;
for the earth will be full of the knowledge of the LORD
Is 11:6-9 *as the waters cover the sea.*

How will we know when the Messiah has come? Society will be so transformed into an age of peace, said one rabbi, that all you will have to do is look out the window.

5. *The Servant of God*

Another theme in the prophetic writings throws light on the ministry of Jesus. Second Isaiah wrote a series of poems that talk about a beloved servant of God who is oppressed, afflicted and killed despite being faithful and obedient to God. Somehow through the servant's suffering, people realize that God has been with the servant all along, and that through the servant's death, the people have been made whole. Christians see these poems as foreshadowing the redemptive death of Jesus.

A fascinating anomaly in the history of the interpretation of these texts is that in the Jewish tradition they were never understood to refer to the Messiah. Most likely they were seen to refer to the people themselves, or at least the faithful remnant among the people. At the time of writing, the Israelites had been totally crushed; their land was in ruins. The poems were composed in exile, where the Israelites lived far away from their home.

The poet comforted the people by reminding them that they were God's beloved servants, that God had remained faithful, and that somehow through their suffering God would bring great things for them and for all people.

As this chapter comes to a close with a few readings from Second Isaiah's "Songs of the Suffering Servant of God," we try to keep both understandings in mind – the Jewish tradition about the redemptive suffering of the people, and the Christian interpretation about the redemptive suffering of Jesus.

This text became the foundation for the Christian narrative of the baptism of Jesus, with its voice from heaven identifying him as God's beloved, accompanied by the visible presence of God's Spirit. It is God who speaks:

Here is my servant, whom I uphold,
my chosen, in whom my soul delights;
I have put my spirit upon him;
he will bring forth justice to the nations…
A bruised reed he will not break;
and a dimly burning wick he will not quench;
he will faithfully bring forth justice. Is 42:1-3

Those are beautiful images of protecting the weak: the compassionate servant doesn't snap off a bent reed, nor stifle a smouldering candlewick. Then God goes on, speaking to the Servant:

I have given you as a covenant…
a light to the nations,
to open the eyes that are blind,
to bring out the prisoners from the dungeon,
and from the prison those who sit in darkness. Is 42:6-7

The most famous passage in this vein for Christian believers Is 49:1-7
has been read in the liturgy every Good Friday for centuries: Is 50:4-9

He was despised and rejected by others;
a man of suffering and acquainted with infirmity;
and as one from whom others hid their faces
he was despised, and we held him of no account.

Surely he has borne our infirmities
and carried our diseases;
yet we accounted him stricken,
struck down by God and afflicted…
All we like sheep have gone astray;
we have all turned to our own way,
and the LORD *has laid on him the iniquity of us all.*

Like a lamb that is led to the slaughter,
and like a sheep before its shearers is silent,
so he did not open his mouth.

The righteous one, my servant, shall make many righteous,
and he shall bear their iniquities…
because he poured out himself to death,
and was numbered with the transgressors;
yet he bore the sins of many,
and made intercession for the transgressors.

Is 53:3-4, 6-7, 11-12

11

THE WISDOM OF THE SAGES

In the few hundred years that followed the people's return from the Babylonian exile, Jewish religious literature developed in two very different directions.

In the ruins of Jerusalem, as they tried to re-establish their traditions and culture, religious leaders assembled the records of their past and set to work to develop Torah. As mentioned in Chapter 3, they combined two extensive written narratives of their history that had been preserved through five centuries of turmoil. One, written around 950 BCE, and beginning with the story of Adam and Eve, used the sacred Name of God (YHWH) through the stories of Abraham and Sarah and their generations of descendants. We now call it the Yahwist account. A second narrative was likely developed in the northern kingdom more than a century later. It used the generic Hebrew word for God, *Elohim*, so it is known as the Elohist. In the process of unifying the records of their people's history into one epic narrative, this 'editorial team,' composed of priests who were trying to restore traditional worship in a makeshift temple amid the ruins of Jerusalem, added their own version of events to many of the narratives.

There were at least two versions of the Law of Moses and related narratives. One of them is found in the books of Exodus and Leviticus, the other in the book of Deuteronomy.

Torah was developed to remember the past in the decades after the exile. Soon, Torah was seen as the core of the Word of God, sacred Scripture, reliable guidance about God's enduring love for people. Before long, the scrolls of the prophets were given the same status, and so sacred Scripture included "the Law and the Prophets."

During this time, other insightful believers – the sages of Israel – were reflecting on the present and the future. They reflected on God's involvement in daily life, family relationships, marriage, tragedy, hope, reputation and politics. Their thought never achieved the passionate, radical quality that made the prophets so unforgettable, but their contribution is important.

Their writings were not deemed to be sacred Scripture then, but many of them later would be – some when the Jewish leaders set the list of books in the Hebrew Scriptures after the destruction of the second Temple in 70 CE, and others when the Catholic bishops set the canon of the New Testament and added some Jewish books to the Old Testament more than a millennium later.

In this chapter, we will consider the wide variety of Wisdom literature, beginning with a book that confronts the most difficult question for believers: How is God involved in human suffering?

A. The Book of Job

Misery was everywhere 2,500 years ago, even when there was no war. A majority of children died before puberty, and their mothers often died with them. Illnesses that we now treat with antibiotics were often fatal. Winters were rainy, and the long summers were stiflingly hot and dry. Food had to be coaxed out of a hostile environment; meat (generally from goats or sheep) was a rare luxury, since the animals were needed for other purposes, and their meat spoiled soon after slaughter. When war came, the population of men, needed in society as workers and as mates and fathers, seriously declined. Survivors of war, mostly the elderly, the women and children, had to struggle to live in even harsher conditions in the dusty ruins of their lands and villages.

From the beginning, believers had wondered why a loving God could let life be so consistently terrible. Today we continue to ask that question with deep distress whenever tragedy strikes.

Scripture said that God is loving and faithful, but also just.
Gen 6–9 All the pain people suffered was seen to be punishment for their
Gen 11:1-9 sins or the sins of their ancestors or of all humanity. That theology
Gen 18:20–19:29 is the foundation of the story of the Flood, the tower of Babel and
the destruction of Sodom and Gomorrah. It is the basis of the cosmic myth of the original sin: human suffering is the just consequence of human sinfulness.

The stories in the book of Genesis were developed early in Jewish history, and their theology was still accepted when the stories were included in Torah centuries later. The same understanding is found throughout Jewish tradition, in the history books, the prayers and the writings of the prophets.

But one Jewish thinker begged to differ.

The nameless author of the book of Job, writing during or after the people's exile in Babylon, did not agree with this view. While he firmly believed in the faithful love of God, he could not accept that every bad thing that happens is a punishment from God.

To present his challenge to traditional thinking, the author developed a philosophical situation. In a test designed by God (with the help of the Satan, who is one of the angels in heaven at this stage of Jewish belief), an entirely just man loses his family, his property and his health. Job ends up covered with sores, sitting on a pile of ashes – and still does not accuse God of acting unfairly.

"The LORD gave, and the LORD has taken away; Job 1:21
blessed be the name of the LORD."

By the beginning of Chapter 3, however, Job has lost patience. He complains bitterly about his fate, even cursing the fact that he was ever born. He begins to ask the eternal question: "Why?"

"Why did I not die at birth?...
Why...were there breasts for me to suck?
Why is...life (given) to the bitter in soul,
who long for death but it does not come?" Job 3:11, 12, 20-21

Three representatives of the traditional teaching, who have been remembered ironically as 'Job's comforters,' arrive on the scene. In long passages of thoughtful poetry, they provide no comfort, but instead demand that Job give in and accept the doctrine of just punishment. Job refuses, and challenges God to provide a better explanation for the pain he has suffered.

Finally, God enters the scene. In brilliant sarcastic phrases, God asks Job a few questions.

"Where were you when I laid the foundation of the earth?
Tell me, if you have understanding.

"Or who shut in the sea...and prescribed bounds for it...
and said, "Thus far shall you come and no farther,
and here shall your proud waves be stopped"?

"Where is the way to the dwelling of light,
and where is the place of darkness?...
Surely you know, for you were born then...

"Do you give the horse its might?...
Its majestic snorting is terrible.
It paws violently, exults mightily...

"Is it by your wisdom that the hawk soars...?
Is it at your command that the eagle mounts up
Job 38: 4-11, 19-21–39:19-20, 26-27 *and makes its nest on high?"*

God continues in that vein for four chapters, inviting Job to reflect on the wonders of creation. Job is reduced to silence.

Job 40:4 *"I am of small account; what shall I answer you?"*

"I have uttered what I did not understand,
things too wonderful for me....
Job 42:3, 6 *therefore I despise myself, and repent in dust and ashes."*

Here Job is expressing the humility felt by the author of the book. He has challenged the traditional teaching about God's role in human suffering, but he can offer no other explanation that he finds more satisfactory. He can only admit that God is far greater than any human can imagine, and that humans really don't have an adequate understanding of the meaning of suffering.

The author's objection to the traditional teaching is so thoughtful that his book was recognized as the Word of God and included in the Scriptures. But Job's powerful questions did not win over the popular mind of his day, and some believers continue instinctively to accept the traditional teaching. They believe that God's punishment for sin is a valid explanation for everything from natural disasters to AIDS.

Jn 9:2

Jesus, however, agreed with the author of Job. When his disciples asked him, "Who sinned...that [this blind man] was born blind?" Jesus responded that the blindness was not the result of sin; rather, the greatness of God was about to be revealed as a result of the man's limitation.

The questions of Job endure. Most people today do not blame God for the tribulations of life, but we all wonder what they mean. We feel sure that there must be a reason, but like the author of Job, we are unable to express a satisfactory understanding.

And still we try to believe that God is with us in our pain, always loving us faithfully, no matter what happens to us.

B. Qoheleth/ Ecclesiastes

The book of Ecclesiastes (meaning 'member of the assembly), recently also known by its Hebrew name *Qoheleth* (meaning 'the one who gathers or collects'), is another unusual candidate for a collection of sacred writings.

This Qoheleth sounds like the original beatnik poet. His repeated theme is that "Everything is vanity; everything is useless, and a chasing after wind."

What do people gain from all the toil
at which they toil under the sun?
A generation goes, and a generation comes,
but the earth remains forever…

All streams run to the sea, but the sea is not full.…

What has been is what will be,
and what has been done is what will be done;
there is nothing new under the sun. Eccl 1:3, 7, 9

Qoheleth considers all the efforts that people undertake – hard work, the pursuit of pleasure, even the pursuit of wisdom – and finds no lasting value in any of them. This is the thinker who gave us the motto "Eat, drink, and be merry," urging us to enjoy good things if God gives them to us, precisely because they are gifts from God. We are to enjoy them while we can, for someday we will all die. (Eccl 2:24, 3:12-13)

For the fate of humans and the fate of animals is the same;
as one dies, so dies the other…
All go to one place: all are from the dust, Eccl 3:19-20
and all turn to dust again.

The famous verses beginning with "For everything there is a season, and a time for every matter under heaven" (Eccl 3:1-8) have been taken as inspirational, but are in fact fatalistic and despairing. The poet is grumbling because "there is a time to be born and a time to die," and there's nothing you can do about either one.

The book of Qoheleth goes on to present several chapters of more conventional wisdom in the style of the books of Wisdom and Proverbs, but always with the overriding sense that "this, too, is vanity." At the end of the book, someone has added a tribute to the author, and a warning that some of these ideas are dangerous and should be read with caution.

Jewish religious leaders debated about the value of this troubling document, but ultimately recognized that it is permissible to wonder and doubt, and that God inspires even our questioning and our distress. The book of Qoheleth recognizes that honest searching, and even doubting, can be as important as getting the right answer.

C. The Song of Songs

The Song of Solomon, or Song of Songs, is a love poem set as a drama, with the prospective bride and groom expressing their love and anticipation in the most sensuous of imagery.

Unlike the printed versions of plays we can read today, however, there is nothing in the Song of Songs to indicate who is speaking, though most modern translations give us clues by inserting headings.

Most couples today would find the imagery of the Song of Songs amusing if they read the text aloud, but the biblical couple is clearly in a state of romantic bliss.

The Bride:

Let him kiss me with the kisses of his mouth!
Song 1:2 *For your love is better than wine…*

The Groom:

I compare you, my love,
Song 2:9 *to a mare among Pharaoh's chariots.*

The Bride:

Look, he comes,
leaping upon the mountains,
bounding over the hills…
Look, there he stands
behind our wall,
gazing in at the windows…
Song 2:8-9

And then these memorable lines, every bit as eloquent as any Romantic poet's:

"Arise, my love, my fair one,
and come away;
for now the winter is past,
the rain is over and gone.

The flowers appear on the earth;
the time of singing has come,
and the voice of the turtledove
is heard in our land.
The fig tree puts forth its figs,
and the vines are in blossom;
they give forth fragrance.
Arise, my love, my fair one,
and come away. Song 2:10-13

The Bible is much more accepting of sexuality than Christian Europe proved to be under the influence of Greek philosophy. The Bible portrays sexual relationships as part of life, in all their joy and pain. It often honestly expresses the great harm that is done by the ruthless and powerful use of sex, and it also at times portrays the beauty of sexual attraction.

The name of God never appears in the Song of Songs, and yet the tradition recognized that the joys of young love are to be relished as both profoundly human and profoundly sacred, and so this extended love song was included in the collection of sacred books. As time went on, the tradition came to perceive this rhapsodic poetry as a symbol of God's love for the people.

D. The Books of Wisdom

The Book of Proverbs
The Book of Sirach [= Ecclesiasticus]
The Wisdom of Solomon [= The Book of Wisdom]

The three books listed under the heading above are quite similar to each other, though they were written several hundred years apart. Proverbs was written in the late 400s BCE, Sirach around the year 180 BCE, and the Wisdom of Solomon within 100 years before the birth of Jesus. The Wisdom of solomon was written in Greek, probably in Egypt, for Jewish people who had migrated to various locations around the Mediterranean, many of whom were unable to understand Hebrew.

The Lessons of Experience

Some of the wisdom of the sages seems directed to the more educated people who were connected to the centre of power in Jerusalem, while other lists of maxims seem to represent the opinions of the patriarchs of ordinary peasant families.

These revered sages may sound very much like a grandfather – the paterfamilias and a respected citizen – who gathers the younger generation around his chair and rambles on about the secrets of his success. It's not clear how much God matters to these authors, since the sage talks about what he has learned from his experiences. (Proverbs doesn't mention the history of the Jewish people, their covenant with God, the Law of Moses, or the hope for the Messiah, but the others do.) Or, to express the point in a more positive light, the sages knew that God is involved in every aspect of human life, whether God is mentioned or not. Their attitude is surprisingly similar to that of many people of our time who spend little time in prayer or at church, but still
Prov 1:7 consider themselves to be believers and good people. The one
Prov 9:10 religious phrase that appears from time to time is "The fear of the
Sir 1:11-13 LORD is the beginning of wisdom." 'Fear' in this context may best
be understood as profound respect, the kind of 'awe' that is at the root of the English word 'awful.'

Many of their aphorisms are presented in lists of observations and instructions – as many as 375 consecutively in one section of
Prov 10:1–22:16 the book of Proverbs. Sometimes the proverbs contradict each
other, but they are so general that both may be true in a way.

Predictably, in those times, the sages stood for strong discipline, the importance of a good reputation, respect for your elders (i.e., themselves), patriarchal values, scorn for everyone they considered to be fools, and the naive expectation that riches will be God's reward for those who act wisely.

The last chapter of the book of Proverbs is a tribute to the qualities of a 'capable wife.' Some modern women find this tribute acceptable, but others object to it because the woman is praised primarily for actions that benefit her husband and enhance his reputation. The woman praised is more than a subservient housewife, however. Besides managing her household staff (the family was obviously prosperous), she is respected in the community for her enterprise in the economic sphere.

She considers a field and buys it;
with the fruit of her hands she plants a vineyard.
She perceives that her merchandise is profitable…
She opens her hand to the poor
and reaches out her hands to the needy…
She makes linen garments and sells them…
Strength and dignity are her clothing…
She opens her mouth with wisdom,
and the teaching of kindness is on her tongue…
let her works praise her in the city gates. Prov 31:10-31

Who Is Wisdom?

These three books offer several hymns in praise of Wisdom, at first almost as an attribute of these elders themselves, for the accomplishment of their years of thoughtful reflection. Their wisdom is what enables them to understand the world and to instruct others about the proper way to live.

While I was still young…
I sought wisdom openly in my prayer.
…I will search for her until the end.
For I resolved to live according to wisdom,
and I was zealous for the good…
My soul grappled with wisdom,
and in my conduct I was strict…
I directed my soul to her, and in purity I found her. Sir 51:13-20

She made among human beings an eternal foundation,
and among their descendants she will abide faithfully…
She inebriates mortals with her fruits;
She fills their whole house with desirable goods… Sir 1:14-17

There is in her a spirit that is intelligent, holy,
unique, manifold, subtle…
For she is a breath of the power of God, and a pure
emanation of the glory of the Almighty…
She reaches mightily from one end of the earth to the other, Wis 7:22,
and she orders all things well. 25; 8:1

Scholars speak of the personification of Wisdom in passages like these; and modern translations use feminine pronouns for Wisdom, perhaps because the Hebrew and Greek words for wisdom are feminine. Later in the Wisdom tradition, Wisdom was perceived almost as an attribute of God that is especially visible, in the benign view of the sages, in the created world and in the Jewish people.

Wisdom praises herself…
"I came forth from the mouth of the Most High,
and covered the earth like a mist…

Sir 24:1-3, 9-12 *"Before the ages, in the beginning, [God] created me,*
and for all the ages I shall not cease to be.
I took root in an honoured people, …(God's) heritage."

"O God of my ancestors and Lord of mercy,
who have made all things by your word,
and by your wisdom have formed humankind
to have dominion over the creatures you have made…
Wis 9:1-4 *give me the wisdom that sits by your throne."*

Life Beyond Death

The book of Wisdom is included in the Christian Old Testament, though it was not part of the Jewish Scriptures. One important reason for the Christian endorsement is the book of Wisdom's expectation of life beyond death.

Since it was written in Greek for a Jewish community away from its homeland, the book of Wisdom uses some Greek ideas that were not familiar to traditional Jewish thought, nor later to Jesus. The Greek concept that humans are composed of body and soul was unknown to the Hebrew tradition; the Greek idea of immortality is not the same as the Jewish hope for resurrection. These distinctions will be discussed in more detail in Chapters 14 (on resurrection) and 26 (on life everlasting).

Originally, Jewish faith did not include hope for life beyond death. God's just reward for living well and God's retribution for sin were thought to take place on earth – if not during a person's lifetime, then in the lives of later generations. The book of Job took issue with that concept, but did not propose life beyond death as the solution.

Hope for resurrection came into Jewish faith through the influence of the Persians in the last few hundred years before Jesus, but was not accepted by everyone. Hope for immortality was added when Greek civilization was exported to the whole

Mediterranean world. It is as a result of that development that we often read at funerals from the most recent book of the Old Testament:

The souls of the righteous are in the hand of God,
and no torment will ever touch them.
In the eyes of the foolish they seemed to have died…
but they are at peace.
For though in the sight of others they were punished,
their hope is full of immortality…
because God tested them and found them worthy… Wis 3:1-5©145

12

THE PEOPLE'S PRAYERBOOK

The Book of Psalms

Themes of the Psalms

Because we believe that God is involved in our lives, we pray. Our prayers express our hopes and fears, our thankfulness and trust, our insecurity and our need for forgiveness. Sometimes we let slip what we really wish for, even if it is petty or vicious or unworthy of ourselves at our best.

What we know about how people prayed before Jesus lived we learn mostly from poetry. The book of Psalms is a collection of 150 prayers written by a variety of poets (some of whose names appear in the heading of their prayers) over a period of a thousand years. Most of them were intended to be sung as part of worship. The sentiments that are expressed in the psalms represent what most of us pray about today – at our best and at our worst.

This chapter will give examples of some of the more important themes found in these ancient prayers. None of these headings should be taken as exclusive – some psalms could appear under several headings. Many other psalms that could have been used as examples under each heading are not mentioned.

1. In Praise of the Creator

One of the best ways for us to gain perspective about our place in the universe is to reflect on the magnificence of creation. People long ago did not have the benefit of the Hubble telescope. Nor were they aware of the microscopic complexity of bacteria, or of recent revelations of the human genome project.

But they were wise enough – as so many of us are not – to be awestruck by nature as they knew it, and to pray in wonder to the Creator God.

When I look at your heavens, the work of your fingers,
the moon and the stars that you have established;
what are human beings that you are mindful of them,
mortals that you care for them? Ps 8:3-4

The heavens are telling the glory of God;
the firmament proclaims [God's] handiwork...
There is no speech, nor are there words;
their voice is not heard;
yet their voice goes out through all the earth,
and their words to the end of the world.

Ps 19:1-4

One psalm is a reflection on a thunderstorm. The storm progresses across the water and goes up into the hills with devastating effect. In each of seven frightening claps of thunder, the poet hears the voice of God.

The voice of the LORD is over the waters;
the glory of God thunders...
The voice of the LORD flashes forth flames of fire.
The voice of the LORD shakes the wilderness...
The voice of the LORD causes the oaks to whirl,
and strips the forest bare;
May the LORD give strength to [the] people!
May the LORD bless [the] people with peace!

Ps 29

Psalm 104 is an inspiring reflection on the glory of God as revealed in things great and small in the world around us – a world that the author imagined in very much the same way as the author of the first chapter of the book of Genesis.

O LORD my God, you are very great...
You stretch out the heavens like a tent,
you set the beams of your chambers upon the waters.
you make the clouds your chariot,
you ride on the wings of the wind...

You set the earth on its foundations,
so that it shall never be shaken...

You cause the grass to grow for the cattle,
and plants for the people to use,
to bring forth food from the earth,
Ps 104:1-15 *and wine to gladden the human heart...*

2. *The God Who Changes History*

a) The Story of a People

The Jewish people saw the hand of God in all that happened to their community – the wanderings of their ancestors, the escape from Egypt at the time of Moses, the arrival in a land they hoped to call their own, the monarchy, the disasters of division and defeat. They reflected on their history, and decided that God had been part of it ever since the creation of the world.

Psalm 114 is a short lyrical burst of enthusiasm proclaiming that

When Israel went out from Egypt...
the sea looked and fled...
the mountains skipped like rams, the hills like lambs.

Tremble, O earth, at the presence of the LORD*...*
who turns the rock into a pool of water...

Ps 114:1, 3-4, 7 Many of their prayers were epic poems of thanksgiving for God's accompanying them on their journey. Psalm 136 is a litany; the worship-leader would proclaim a verse, and the congregation would shout back its response:

V. O give thanks to the LORD*, for [God] is good*
R. For [God's] steadfast love endures forever.

V. O give thanks to the God of gods,
Ps 136:1-2 *R. For [God's] steadfast love endures forever.*

In this manner, the whole history of the people was recalled and rehearsed as part of community prayer.

Psalm 78 brings together themes from the prophets and the sages, recounting what God has done and challenging the people for their unfaithfulness.

Give ear, O my people, to my teaching...
We will tell to the coming generation
the glorious deeds of the LORD*...*

and the wonders [God] has done…
In the sight of their ancestors [God] worked marvels
in the land of Egypt…
[God] divided the sea and let them pass through it…
Yet they sinned still more against [God], Ps 78:1, 4, 12,
rebelling against the Most High in the desert. 13, 17

It is a long poem, interpreting the entire journey of the people through prophetic eyes. Psalms 105 and 106 explore a similar theme.

Prayer also dealt with defeat.

O God, the nations have come into your inheritance;
they have defiled your holy temple;
they have laid Jerusalem in ruins.
They have given the bodies of your servants
to the birds of the air for food…
They have poured out their blood like water
all around Jerusalem, Ps 79:1-3
and there was no one to bury them.

One of the more poignant psalms is the lament of the troubadours, written in exile in Babylon after the destruction of Jerusalem. Their captors asked them to sing of their homeland, but they could not.

By the rivers of Babylon –
there we sat down and there we wept
when we remembered Zion.
On the willows there we hung up our harps… Ps 137:1-2, 4
How could we sing the LORD's song in a foreign land?

Psalm 137 became the basis of a popular rock song ("By the Rivers of Babylon") in the late twentieth century, two and a half millennia after it was written. The psalm also expresses the lust for revenge, rather than peace:

O daughter Babylon, you devastator!
Happy shall they be who pay you back
what you have done to us!
Happy shall they be who take your little ones Ps 137:8-9
and dash them against the rock!

b) The Royal Psalms

Kings were seen as God's gift to the nation, charged with defending the people, caring for the poor, judging honestly and nurturing the flock as God's shepherd. The prophets were fiercely critical of corrupt monarchs, but several psalms are the hopeful prayers of the people for beneficent rulers.

Give the king your justice, O God,
and your righteousness to a king's son.
May he judge your people with righteousness,
and your poor with justice...
In his days may righteousness flourish
and peace abound, until the moon is no more.
May he have dominion from sea to sea,
Ps 72:1-2, 7-8 *and from the River to the ends of the earth.*

(Canadians will recognize the phrase in the first line of that last couplet as the motto found on the national coat of arms: *A mari usque ad mare* – "From sea to sea.")

Ps 45:10-11 Psalm 45 was written on the occasion of a royal wedding between Israel and Sidon, a city-kingdom that still exists on the Mediterranean coast in Lebanon. The poet advises the foreign princess to "forget your people and your father's house," and "since [your new husband] is your lord, bow to him." If this poem was written for the marriage of King Ahab to Jezebel, Elijah reminds us that the foreign-born queen paid no attention to the God of Israel, and was far from subservient to her husband.

In discussing Isaiah's prophecies about the coming of the Messiah, we looked at Psalm 2, which was written for the coronation of the kings of Israel. Christians later referred to Psalm 2 in their efforts to express their faith that Jesus was both the Anointed One and the Son of God in a way that went beyond what the phrase meant when it was used to describe earthly kings.

Why do the nations conspire...?
The kings of the earth set themselves...
against the LORD *and his anointed...?*

I will tell of the decree of the LORD [says the new king]:
[God] said to me, "You are my son:
today I have begotten you.
Ask of me, and I will make the nations your heritage,
Ps 2:1-2, 7-8 *and the ends of the earth your possession."*

3. *The Songs of Ascents, the Ceremonies*

Devout Jews were expected to make pilgrimage to the holy city of Jerusalem and its Temple as often as they could for the high holy days. Several of the psalms were developed to be sung on the road or around the campfires during the laborious journey up through the desert hills to Jerusalem; 15 short "songs of ascents" are collected as Psalms 120–134. They evoke images not only of travel but also of life at home that must have aroused feelings of longing in the hearts of tired pilgrims. They still speak affectingly today as pilgrims pray for peace in the holy city.

I lift up my eyes to the hills –
from where will my help come?
My help comes from the LORD
who made heaven and earth…
The LORD is your keeper;
the LORD is your shade at your right hand.
The sun shall not strike you by day,
nor the moon by night. Ps 121:1-2, 5-6

Happy is everyone who fears the LORD,
who walks in [God's] ways.
You shall eat the fruit of the labour of your hands;
you shall be happy, and it shall go well with you.
Your wife will be like a fruitful vine within your house;
your children will be like olive shoots around your table. Ps 128:1-3

Restore our fortunes, O LORD,
like the watercourses in the Negeb [the southern desert].
May those who sow in tears reap with shouts of joy.
Those who go out weeping, bearing the seed for sowing,
shall come home with shouts of joy, carrying their sheaves. Ps 126:4-6

I was glad when they said to me,
"Let us go to the house of the LORD!"
Our feet are standing within your gates, O Jerusalem…
Pray for the peace of Jerusalem:
"May they prosper who love you.
Peace be within your walls,
and security within your towers." Ps 122:1-2, 6-7

Once they arrived in Jerusalem, the pilgrims would take part in various religious ceremonies, including processions through the streets and outside the city gates with the ark of the covenant, the wooden chest containing the stone tablets of the Ten Commandments. The ark was thought to be the earthly throne of God; one can imagine the "King of Glory" being praised at the gates of Jerusalem.

Lift up your heads, O gates!
and be lifted up, O ancient doors!
Ps 24:7 *that the King of glory may come in.*

Let God rise up, let [God's] enemies be scattered…
Your solemn processions are seen, O God,
the processions of my God, my King, into the sanctuary –
the singers in front, the musicians last,
Ps 68:1, 24-25 *between them girls playing tambourines…*

Clap your hands, all you peoples;
shout to God with loud songs of joy…
God has gone up with a shout,
the LORD *with the sound of a trumpet…*
God is king over the nations;
Ps 47:1, 5, 8 *God sits on his holy throne.*

4. *Life Prayers*

The Psalms are full of sentiments that people like us have felt in their hearts for thousands of years – prayers for guidance and well-being, laments, prayers for deliverance from fearful situations, humble prayers for forgiveness, prayers of thanksgiving and trust. They can also bring us consolation as we search for God amidst our worries and fears.

a) Wisdom and Guidance

The sages of Israel firmly believed in God's faithfulness and loving-kindness. They found God in every aspect of human life and saw God's laws as a gift, a light for our path, a guide for our journey. Naively, they promised that all would be well for people who were faithful to God's laws. Some of the wisdom of the sages comes to us in poetic prayer.

To you, O LORD*, I lift up my soul;*
O my God, in you I trust;
do not let me be put to shame…

Make me to know your ways, O LORD;
teach me your paths.
Lead me in your truth, and teach me,
for you are the God of my salvation... Ps 25:1-5

Rejoice in the LORD, O you righteous...
For the word of the LORD is upright,
and all [God's] work is done in faithfulness.
[God] loves righteousness and justice;
the earth is full of the steadfast love of the LORD.

Truly the eye of the LORD is on those who fear [God],
on those who hope in [God's] steadfast love,
to deliver their soul from death,
and to keep them alive in famine. Ps 33:1, 4-5, 18-19

Trust in the LORD and do good;
so you will live in the land and enjoy security.
Take delight in the LORD, and [God] will give you the desires of your heart. Ps 37:3-4

Psalm 119 is a long artificial prayer. It is an acrostic poem: each verse in Hebrew begins with a successive letter of the alphabet. As well, each verse contains the word 'law' or a synonym for law. It has several memorable verses.

Your word is a lamp to my feet and a light to my path...
Let my supplication come before you;
deliver me according to your promise.
My lips will pour forth praise,
because you teach me your statutes.
My tongue will sing of your promise,
for all your commandments are right.
I long for your salvation, O LORD,
and your law is my delight. Ps 119:105, 170-2, 174

b) Laments and Prayers for Deliverance

A significant number of the prayers in the book of Psalms express the feelings of people in distress who beg God to set them free from the threats of their enemies and from life's pain. Believers have shared this grief and hope down through the centuries.

Give ear to my words, O LORD;
Give heed to my sighing.

Listen to the sound of my cry,
my King and my God, for to you I pray…
You destroy those who speak lies;
the Lord abhors the bloodthirsty and deceitful.
But I, through the abundance of your steadfast love…
I will bow down toward your holy temple in awe of you.

For there is no truth in their mouths…;
their throats are open graves;
they flatter with their tongues.
But let all who take refuge in you rejoice…
Ps 5:1-11 *Spread your protection over them…*

How long, O Lord? Will you forget me forever?
How long must I bear pain in my soul,
and have sorrow in my heart all day long?
Ps 13:1-2 *How long shall my enemy be exalted over me?*

Vindicate me, O God,
and defend my cause against an ungodly people;
from those who are deceitful and unjust, deliver me!
For you are the God in whom I take refuge;
Ps 43:1-2 *why have you cast me off?*

God is our refuge and strength,
a very present help in trouble.
Therefore we will not fear,
though the earth should change,
though the mountains shake in the heart of the sea…
Ps 46:1-2, 5 *God is in the midst of the city; it shall not be moved.*

Save me, O God, for the waters have come up to my neck.
Ps 69:1-2 *I sink in deep mire, where there is no foothold.*

One psalm written in this spirit of distress and hope was used by Jesus to express his feelings as he was dying. While Jesus spoke only the first line of the psalm, it is reasonable to assume he knew the entire prayer. The psalm offers a remarkable glimpse into the humanity that Jesus shares with us, and consolation for any who despair.

My God, my God, why have you forsaken me?
Why are you so far from helping me,
from the words of my groaning?

But I am a worm, and not human;
scorned by others, and despised by the people.
All who see me mock at me...

Yet it was you who took me from the womb;
you kept me safe on my mother's breast...
Do not be far from me, for trouble is near,
and there is no one to help.

You who fear the LORD, praise him!...
For God did not despise or abhor
the affliction of the afflicted...
but heard when I cried to him...

Future generations will be told about the LORD,
and proclaim [God's] deliverance to a people yet unborn... Ps 22:1, 6-7, 9, 24, 30-31

c) Prayers for Forgiveness

God's willingness to forgive us when we have sinned is central in our faith tradition. It was a key component of Old Testament faith, and Jesus emphasized it in his teaching. Yet Christians have tended to doubt God's generosity, and to emphasize retributive justice rather than the gratuitous forgiveness revealed to us in the Scriptures. We must convince ourselves that God loves us no matter what we do; as repentant believers we need not torture ourselves about the past, but can look forward with hope to completing our journey nurtured by the faithful love of our God. Many of the psalms speak of our need for forgiveness and God's willingness to forgive us.

Happy are those whose transgression is forgiven,
whose sin is covered...
While I kept silence, my body wasted away
through my groaning all day long...
Then I acknowledged my sin to you,
and I did not hide my iniquity...
Many are the torments of the wicked,
but steadfast love surrounds those who trust in the LORD. Ps 32:1, 3, 5, 10

Have mercy on me, O God, according to your steadfast love;
according to your abundant mercy
blot out my transgressions...

For I know my transgressions, and my sin is ever before me.
Against you, you alone, have I sinned,
and done what is evil in your sight…
Create in me a clean heart, O God,
and put a new and right spirit within me…
Ps 51:1, 3-4, *The sacrifice acceptable to God is a broken spirit;*
10, 17 *a broken and contrite spirit, O God, you will not despise.*

Bless the L*ORD*, *O my soul,*
and do not forget all [God's] benefits –
who forgives all your iniquity…
who crowns you with steadfast love and mercy.
The L*ORD* *is merciful and gracious,*
slow to anger and abounding in steadfast love…
[God] does not deal with us according to our sins,
nor repay us according to our iniquities.
For as the heavens are high above the earth,
so great is God's steadfast love
toward those who fear [God];
as far as the east is from the west,
so far [God] removes our transgressions from us.
Ps 103:2-4, *As a father has compassion for his children,*
8, 10-13 *so the* L*ORD* *has compassion for those who fear him.*

Out of the depths I cry to you, O L*ORD*.
If you, O L*ORD*, *should mark iniquities,*
L*ORD*, *who could stand?*
But there is forgiveness with you,
Ps 130:1, 3-4 *so that you may be revered.*

d) Thanksgiving

Several of the psalms we have looked at could be classified as thanksgiving psalms; many more see the good things of life as gifts from God.

I waited patiently for the L*ORD*;
[God] inclined to me and heard my cry.
[God] put a new song in my mouth,
a song of praise to our God…
I have told the glad news of deliverance
in the great congregation;
Ps 40:1, 3, 9 *see, I have not restrained my lips.*

Make a joyful noise to God, all the earth;
sing the glory of [God's] name…
Say to God, "How awesome are your deeds!"…
Come and hear, all you who fear God,
and I will tell what [God] has done for me…
Blessed be God, because he has not rejected my prayer
or removed his steadfast love from me. Ps 66:1-2,16, 20

I give you thanks, O Lord, *with my whole heart;*
before the gods I sing your praise…
and give thanks to your name
for your steadfast love and your faithfulness…
On the day I called, you answered me,
you increased my strength of soul. Ps 138:1-3

e) Prayers of Trust

Ultimately, believers are called to trust in God. Through all the turmoil of life, through all the questions and confusion in our search for understanding, we try to believe that God's love for us is enduring, and it is God's faithful love that gives meaning and fulfillment to our lives. That conviction was repeated frequently by the psalmists, in words that have become familiar to us through modern hymns. The first is now sung as "On Eagles' Wings":

You who live in the shelter of the Most High,
who abide in the shadow of the Almighty,
will say to the Lord, *"My refuge…*
my God, in whom I trust…"
Under [God's] wings you will find refuge;
[God's] faithfulness is a shield.
You will not fear the terror of the night,
nor the arrow that flies by day… Ps 91:1-2, 4-5

The Lord *is my shepherd, I shall not want…*
Even though I walk through the darkest valley,
I fear no evil; for you are with me;
your rod and staff – they comfort me.
Surely goodness and mercy shall follow me
all the days of my life,
and I shall dwell in the house of the Lord
my whole life long. Ps 23: 1, 4, 6

13

JESUS

Some Background Impressions

Jesus seems to have been an ordinary craftsman who lived in a backwoods village in Palestine for most of his life. He was not a rabbi by profession; he was not a priest; he was a simple lay person, a working man.

None of the gospels offers us a physical description of Jesus. We know only that he was Jewish, a native of the district of Galilee, so most likely he resembled people who are native to north Africa and the east coast of the Mediterranean Sea. Thus he was probably short in stature, perhaps stocky, with black hair, dark eyes and dark skin. Since wood in a desert country was an expensive commodity, it is likely that his work involved building stone houses and laying roof beams rather than crafting delicate cabinets. That he may have earned his living in construction work could indicate a measure of physical strength.

The gospels do not suggest that he was a frail ascetic; on the
Mk 2:18-19 contrary, some accused him of not fasting as much as they thought
he should. During his years as a travelling preacher, he accepted
hospitality wherever he went, probably discussing his teachings
around the table long into the night: "The Son of Man came eating
Mt 11:19 and drinking," he says of himself.

Jesus in His Homeland

The district of Galilee, where Jesus lived, was in the hill country. It was few days' journey (about 100 km) north of the great city of Jerusalem, but it was light years away culturally. Jerusalem was the centre of Jewish civilization and religion. Although there were synagogues where rabbis led worship in the towns, there was only one Temple in the whole country, in Jerusalem; it was impressive and undergoing renovations that were still unfinished at the time of his death. There priests offered sacrifices and led the celebration of the high holy days. The Temple Mount dominated the city of Jerusalem, and in a way it dominated the whole country. Political and religious leaders in Jerusalem collaborated with their Roman overlords, and had grown accustomed to a fairly privileged lifestyle. They gave orders and expected the people to obey.

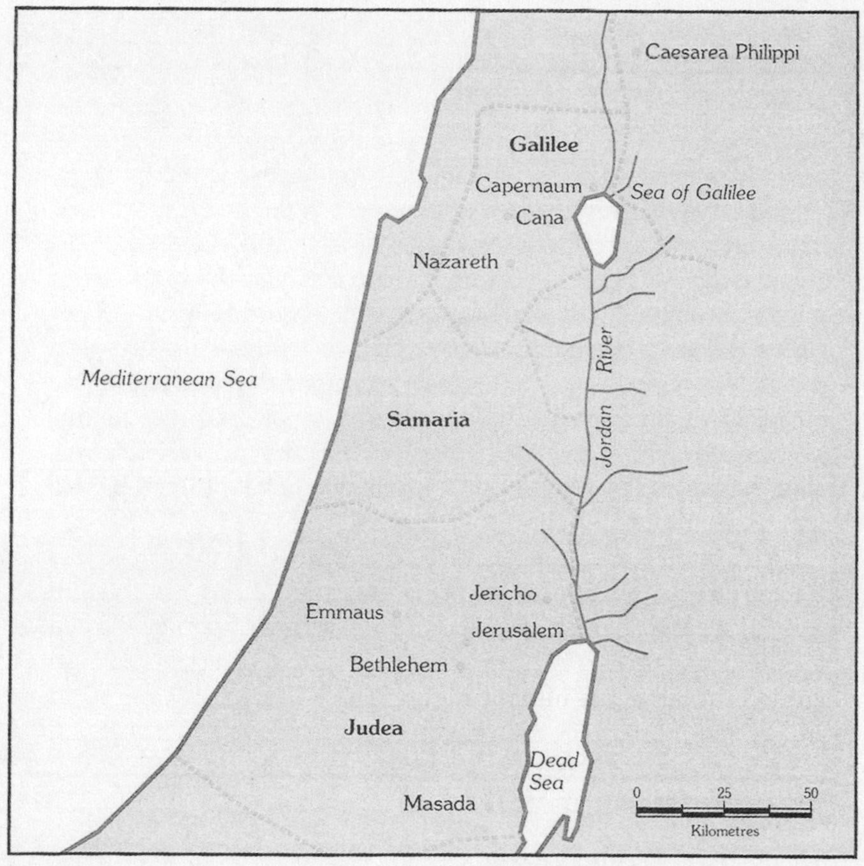

The people of Galilee, on the other hand, were poor. They were not well-educated; they spoke in a dialect, with a distinctive accent. After Jesus was arrested, when Peter tried to claim that he
Mt 26:73 didn't even know Jesus to a group loitering in the high priest's courtyard, Jerusalem servant-girls remarked on his backwoods style of speaking: "Your accent betrays you."

As a citizen of Galilee, Jesus' first language was Aramaic. Apparently he could read Hebrew (the language of the Scriptures), which would be taught to young males by the rabbis in the local synagogues; no doubt he spoke it with the same accent as Peter. Because the language of the Roman Empire was Greek, Jesus may have spoken a little of that language as well. There is no evidence that Jesus could write; that skill was for professional scribes, not construction workers.

Mt 4:15 Over the years, many Galileans had assimilated with a series
quoting Is 9:1 of conquerors (Assyrian, Babylonian, Greek and Roman) and in some ways had become more gentile than Jewish – "Galilee of the nations." Though they attended services in local synagogues, they rarely travelled to the capital city for Temple worship. Strict orthodox Jewish authorities – the leaders in Jerusalem – scorned the Galileans as irreligious and ignorant.

Average life expectancy was 22 years, due to the high rate of infant mortality. People lived short and miserable lives; 95 per cent were dead by the age of 45. They married at puberty and started their families immediately in the hope that one out of five offspring might live to adulthood and help support the family. Jesus, who was about 30 years old when he began to preach, was already an elder in his community. The people he grew up with were becoming grandparents at that age.

Then Jesus, after 30 unexceptional years of smalltown life, stepped out of his craftsman's role and announced that his life was to be the turning point of human history. He claimed that he lived in intimate friendship with God, and that he spoke for God more reliably than the traditional religious leaders did.

Jesus and His Family

Mk 3:21 His family was seriously concerned, "for [the people] were saying,
'He has gone out of his mind.'" The townspeople were dubious,
Mk 6:2-3 even hostile, asking, "Is this not the carpenter, the son of Mary
MT 13: 54-56 and brother of James and Joses and Judas and Simon? …Where
did this man get all this?"

These words about Jesus' family can cause some anxiety among believers, but the questions must be faced.

Did Jesus Have Brothers and Sisters?

Even the Gospel of Matthew, whose narrative of Jesus' birth clearly teaches that he was born of a virgin, refers to his brothers and sisters, as does Mark. Elsewhere in the New Testament, James, the brother of the Lord, is mentioned by Paul as a leader of the Jerusalem community after the resurrection.

Mt 1:18-25

Gal 1:19

The New Testament does not claim that Jesus was Mary's only child; indeed, by giving the names of four brothers and referring to his sisters, the gospels seem to be indicating that Mary was fortunate enough to have at least seven children grow to adulthood.

Still, the belief that Mary was 'ever virgin' (that she never had sexual intercourse, and had no other children than Jesus) has been a long-standing tradition in the Catholic Church. The tradition depends on deciding that the people listed in Mark 6:3 are members of Jesus' extended family: cousins rather than blood brothers. And yet, in other places the gospel writers use the proper word for 'cousin' or 'relative'– for example, in identifying Elizabeth, the mother of John the Baptist, as Mary's 'relative' in the Gospel of Luke.

Lk 1:36

Didn't His Mother Know of His Greatness?

Most scholars agree that the Gospel of Mark was the first to be written. Although it has a strong theological understanding of Jesus as the Son of God, it gives us a down-to-earth picture of him as he was remembered four decades after the Resurrection.

see Mk 1:1 and 15:39

Mark gives us no stories of Jesus' childhood. The well-known Christmas stories are part of the Gospels of Matthew and Luke, which were written at least 10 years after Mark. (The Christmas stories will be discussed in some detail in Chapter 25.) Mark's community was not aware that Mary had special knowledge about the greatness of Jesus. Mark reports instead what his community remembered: that there was significant tension between Jesus and his family. They do not come across as being among his early supporters; for some people, his refusal to see them when they try to talk with him – "Who are my mother and my brothers?" – seems rude and harsh.

Mk 3:32-33

Even Matthew and Luke, who do speak of Mary's role in the early childhood of Jesus, report his refusal to speak to her in that situation; it is a significant comment expressing Jesus' conviction that the bond with one's family in faith should be deeper than that with one's biological family. Mark never mentions Mary again
Mk 6:3 after the townspeople express amazement at how different Jesus
Mt 27:55// has become after a long life as an ordinary citizen. Matthew, Mark
Mk 15:40// and Luke do not report that Mary was present at Jesus' death,
Lk 23:49 though they name other women who were. Our tradition about
Jn 19:25 Mary's presence at the death of Jesus depends solely on the Gospel
of John.

The Christmas stories were developed long after the resurrection, primarily to assure believers about the greatness of Jesus. Their depiction of Mary as having received special revelations about her son may be theologically useful, but they are historically questionable.

The Religious and Political Background

Jesus was a Jew, as were his friends and most of his enemies. There were many factions in Jewish religious society, and they often disagreed with each other. Jesus occasionally agreed with some of them, perhaps more often than we have been led to believe.

The Priests

All Jewish priests were members of the tribe of Levi, but only a select few enjoyed the hereditary privilege of working at the Temple in Jerusalem. At that one location only, such priests offered grain and animal sacrifices on behalf of worshippers, made declarations regarding the Law of Moses, and presided at the annual festivals. The council of Temple priests was known as the Sanhedrin; at the time of Jesus the president of the council, the High Priest, was Caiaphas.

To consolidate their position, the priests co-operated with the Roman occupying force, which had established its headquarters in the Fortress Antonia, adjoining the Temple area. The priests enjoyed the trappings of power, and did not take kindly to opposition from an upstart Galilean working man, especially when he invaded the seat of their authority and challenged them directly in front of their subjects. All the gospels blame the Temple priests

(rather than the Roman governor) for causing the death of Jesus; as a result, no follower of Jesus was ever called a 'priest' in the New Testament, though the community was called 'a royal
priesthood.' Interestingly enough, the Acts of the Apostles reports Acts 6:7
that many Jewish priests later became Christians.

The Letter to the Hebrews speaks of Jesus as the great High Heb 4:14-15
Priest of the New Covenant who "offered for all time a single Heb 10:12
sacrifice for sins." In later centuries, the term 'priest' was restored to honour among Christians, as they realized that the leaders of the Christian community were carrying on the ministry of Jesus, the great High Priest.

The Scribes or Rabbis

The scribes (so called because of their ability to write) were scholars who knew and taught about the Jewish Scriptures and traditions. Their disciples called them 'rabbi,' a title of respect meaning 'master' or 'teacher.' (Sometimes people called Jesus 'rabbi' to honour his teaching, but he was not a rabbi by profession.) The rabbis taught in the synagogues in every town where Jewish people lived.

In general, the scribes were opponents of Jesus (and later of
the early Christian community); they were involved in his trial Mk 12:38-40
and supported his execution. He responded to their attacks in Mt 23
kind, with fervour. And yet, the New Testament reports that some Mt 8:19
individual scribes wanted to follow Jesus, and asked for and Mk 12:28-34
respected his opinion. Lk 20:39

The Pharisees

The Pharisees were scholars united by a point of view; they were one school of thought within the Jewish community. They studied the Law of Moses with great care, offering interpretations about exactly what was required by the Law. Most of the scribes (or rabbis) belonged to the Pharisees' school; that is why the two terms are lumped together in some of Jesus' more vitriolic denunciations.

The Pharisees were not entirely closed to new thought and new traditions. After Jerusalem and the Temple were destroyed by the Romans in 70 CE, it was primarily the Pharisees who took charge, reorganized the community, and initiated 'Judaism,' a new form of Jewish tradition that has endured for 2,000 years.

Jn 3:1-8 We tend to see all the Pharisees as being against Jesus, but
Jn 7:50 this is not true. The Gospel of John describes a Pharisee named
Jn 19:39-40 Nicodemus who sought enlightenment from Jesus, defended him
from attacks by religious authorities and, loyal even after Jesus'
execution, participated in his burial. Paul, who also adhered to
Acts 23:6 the Pharisees' point of view, became a Christian and a great early
missionary.

The Sadducees

Most priests were Sadducees, a much more conservative school than the Pharisees. They refused to accept any teaching that was not in Torah, even if it was found in the prophets or other scriptural writings.

For example, they considered the belief in a future resurrection
of the dead to be an unacceptable teaching. Many Jews, including
Mt 22:23-32 Pharisees (and Jesus), had accepted this belief, which had become
popular only in the previous few centuries (and therefore was
not found in Torah).

The Essenes

The Essenes, a sect within the Jewish community, were devout and faithful people who abhorred the compromises that most people made in their social and political lives and tried to live with integrity under near-monastic conditions. At times they were given to ferocious self-righteousness, calling on God to bring victory to their cause and destruction to the compromisers.

The preaching of John the Baptist may have been influenced by Essene thought. Qumran, which is perched on a plateau overlooking the Dead Sea, was probably an Essene community. That 150-year-old village was demolished during the uprising of 70 CE, but not before the inhabitants had hidden their treasured library in caves in the nearby cliffs. Almost 2,000 years later, in 1947, a shepherd boy discovered what became known as the Dead Sea scrolls. As a result of that discovery, we are able to read, in Hebrew, documents that people were reading when Jesus was alive.

The Zealots

The Zealots were a revolutionary political faction that called for armed rebellion against the Roman occupying force. They were responsible for repeated uprisings, and eventually for the protracted rebellion in the late 60s CE, which led to the destruction of Jerusalem and the eviction of the Jewish people from Palestine.

One of Jesus' inner circle of twelve was known as Simon the
Zealot. His relationship with Levi the tax collector (who had Lk 6:15
collaborated with the Romans to earn his daily bread) must have
been carefully monitored. Barabbas, who was imprisoned for
having committed murder during the insurrection, was probably Mk 15:7
a Zealot, as were the brigands who were crucified at the same Mk 15:27
time as Jesus.

The Herodians

King Herod the Great was a self-appointed ruler who persuaded the Romans to install him in power as a puppet king. He was not a descendant of the royal family of David, and in fact was ethnically different from his Jewish subjects, being a member of a desert tribe from Idumea, in southern Palestine. He was cruel and unpopular, but managed to hold power with Roman assistance until his death in 4 BCE.

His four sons divided his kingdom into tetrarchies (four
kingdoms); one son, also named Herod, was tetrarch of Galilee
in the late 20s CE, and therefore nominally the ruler responsible
for Jesus of Nazareth. Herod happened to be in Jerusalem at the
time of Jesus' trial, and according to Luke's gospel, was given the
opportunity by Pontius Pilate to pass judgment on Jesus. Lk 23:6-12

The Herodian party took the opposite approach from the Zealots: their comfort was based on collaborating with their Roman overlords.

Jesus' Ministry in Galilee

When Jesus began his ministry of teaching and healing, many
people rejected him. According to Luke, Jesus' townspeople Lk 4:28-29
attempted to kill him (a common treatment for insanity with
religious overtones), and drove him out of his hometown
permanently. Jesus left his own village and established a base in
the fishing community of Capernaum, by the shore of the Sea of
Galilee, some 20 kilometres east.

The Sea of Galilee is a small lake in the northern part of Jesus' homeland. Though it is below sea level, it is a freshwater body; the Jordan River flows into it from the north, and out of it towards the south on its way to the Dead Sea. In the gospels, this same lake is called Lake Tiberias (so named by the Romans to honour one of their emperors) and Lake Gennesareth (named after the area to the east of the lake). Today it is called Kinneret, and vacationers waterski and sailboard on its surface. It is not really a sea as it is no more than 10 kilometres wide; you can always see the other shore, wherever you stand. Peter and his friends would catch the sort of small fish that could live in such a confined area; today, you can order "St. Peter's fish" (tilapia) at local restaurants and buy it in North American grocery stores.

Mk 2:1 With Capernaum as his base, Jesus became a travelling
Mk 1:38-39 preacher and healer, moving mostly within a 20-kilometre circle from village to village among the poor of Galilee. People were enthralled with his proclamation of good news, his wonderful healings, and his claim that through him, God was acting to free poor people from sin and oppression and to begin an era of everlasting love.

Mk 3:6 While the authorities in Jerusalem had heard of his ministry and had sent agents to observe his activities, they probably would have let him continue to proclaim his message to the poor of Galilee indefinitely if Jesus had stayed within the area around the shores of the lake and in the surrounding hills.

Lk 9:53 But Jesus was more radical and more daring than that. After many months of ministry in his home district, "his face was set toward Jerusalem."

Climax in Jerusalem

According to Mark, Matthew and Luke, Jesus' ministry took place entirely in Galilee, until he went to Jerusalem for the first time in his adult life the week before Passover. (John reports several earlier trips to Jerusalem.)

Mk 11:9-10 Jesus arrived in the capital with a little band of followers who were shouting messianic slogans ("Hosanna to the Son of David"). One can imagine the big-city crowds watching this little procession of hill people and asking each other, "What is going on here?" "Who does this person think he is?" Jesus entered the city riding a donkey, recalling the prophet Zechariah's poetic description of
Zech 9:9 the humility of the Anointed One. Jesus was symbolically acting out the role of the Messiah taking possession of his capital city.

Five days later, he was dead.

A brief narration of his activities in the last week of his life makes it clear that he was attacking the power structure of his society, and that he knew exactly the effect that such radical political action would have.

The day of his arrival, according to Mark, Jesus rode
purposefully into the Temple area, silently inspected the scene, Mk 11:11
and then left the city to spend the night in Bethany, a village just
a few kilometres east of Jerusalem.

The next day, Jesus came back into the city and started a riot
in the Temple area. There was a market in the outer courtyard of
the Temple, where merchants sold doves, goats, sheep and
bullocks to be used in the sacrifices. Jesus freed the animals and
knocked over the sellers' tables. As Jeremiah had done 600 years
earlier, Jesus shouted that they were defiling the sacredness of Jer 7:11
the house of God and turning it into a house of robbers. He wasn't Mk 11:15-18
just challenging corrupt money-changers; he was attacking the
whole Temple system: the role of the high priests, their political
collaboration with the Romans and their position of power in
Jewish society. The Temple priests knew it, too. They saw him as
being very dangerous to them.

On subsequent days, Jesus taught in the Temple area and Mt 21:23-46
attracted some followers. The authorities challenged him with Mt 22:15-22
questions that they intended to be confounding, but Jesus
responded brilliantly. He denounced the Temple authorities with Mt 23
unexpectedly forthright and vicious accusations.

Within a few days of his arrival in Jerusalem, the Temple
authorities had Jesus in custody. The arresting agents are identified Mt 26:47//
as "a crowd" or "the Temple guard" or (only in John) a detachment Mk 14:43//
of soldiers together with police from the chief priests. The Temple Lk 22:47
priests held a trial; they thought Jesus was wrong, for they believed Jn 18:3
their power to be God-given. When Jesus claimed to be God's Mk 14:61-64
favoured son, they considered his claim blasphemy – an offence
that called for the death penalty.

The religious leaders had to convince the Roman authorities that Jesus was also dangerous to the state. For that purpose, the claim that he aspired to kingship was more appropriate.

The gospels don't primarily blame the Romans for the death of Jesus; for one thing, the Romans were still in command when the gospels were written, and the Christian community did not wish to give them any reason for increasing persecution.

The gospels don't blame the Jewish people, either, for Jesus and all his friends were Jewish. Even the cry of the Jerusalem crowds was understandable, since Jesus was an almost-unknown agitator from the back country. Barabbas, whom the crowd chose to be freed rather than Jesus, may have been a local hero, since he
Mk 15:7 was "in prison with the rebels who had committed murder during the insurrection" – in other words, he was a revolutionary who had fought against the Romans.

The gospels clearly blame the Temple priests for Jesus' death. The hereditary high priesthood that ruled from the Temple was a powerful elite that ensured its continued state of privilege by co-operating with the conquerors; for this reason, many Jewish people hated them.

The next moment in the Christian story was Jesus' resurrection. Resurrection transformed the disciples' understanding of Jesus' life and ministry. The New Testament is, in many ways, a narrative of the decades of development of Christian understanding about the meaning of the life of Jesus. Every word of the New Testament is a reflection on the ministry of Jesus, seen through the lens of resurrection. In the next chapter, we will explore the New Testament's teaching about resurrection, as a prelude to a discussion of the development of the New Testament. Following those two chapters, we will begin a detailed presentation of the life and teachings of Jesus.

14

THE RESURRECTION OF JESUS

Everything the gospels tell us about Jesus has come to us in the light of decades of reflection on his ministry after the resurrection. The resurrection was the foundation of early Christian belief in Jesus. His followers realized that by raising Jesus to new life, God had put the 'stamp of approval' on Jesus' teaching and ministry; through him, God was offering to transform the lives of all believers. Therefore, early Christian faith in the resurrection of Jesus is the basis of the scriptural understanding of Jesus' teaching, the accounts of his miracles, and particularly the gospels' portrayal of Jesus' identity as Son of God.

This chapter will deal with the narratives of the disciples' shocked recognition that Jesus had conquered death and risen to new life. We will begin with some background information comparing Hebrew and European philosophies of humanity, and therefore understandings about death. In that light, we will explore New Testament expressions about the resurrection (and ascension) of Jesus. Our own hope for life everlasting will be discussed in Chapter 26.

Philosophical Understanding About Humanity

Dualistic vs. Unitary

Most Christians (including those of Asian and African heritage, whose faith can be traced to the teaching of European missionaries) are heirs of a European tradition of belief, and have grown up with an understanding about humanity that originated in pre-Christian Greek philosophy. This Greek philosophical understanding is fundamentally dualistic: it sees humans as being composed of two almost opposite elements – a material body and a spiritual soul. The soul is seen as the life-principle, in which reside all the more exalted human abilities – to think, to decide, to pray. The body, at best, is seen as a vehicle by which the soul can live in this world, learn through the senses and communicate with others. At worst, the body is seen as a trap, overwhelming the mind with emotion and deluding the soul by pursuing attractions that are unworthy of it.

Such a philosophy can imply negative attitudes towards human bodiliness, towards emotion, and in particular towards sexuality. Especially in northern Europe, Christianity has suffered from such attitudes for centuries, and as a result some aspects of Christian tradition can be described as cold, legalistic and intellectual.

With regard to death, European Christianity developed an understanding, based on Greek dualism, that only the body dies. The soul is immortal; it cannot die but lives forever, either in a heaven of souls, in purgatory for a time, or in hell. In Greek thought, and at times in Christian thought, death was something to be desired, since it meant liberation: freed from its bodily prison, the soul can live in a spirit-world where it is truly at home. Hope for resurrection 'on the last day' became hope for a further stage of life beyond death, the reunion of body and soul in a transformed state to participate in an everlasting kingdom of God.

Many Christians are surprised to learn that Jesus was unfamiliar with this European understanding of humanity, since he was the heir to a very different 'unitary' understanding about humanity. In the biblical tradition, humans are body-beings capable of spirituality – they can think and love and hug and kiss and know God and pray and make decisions and dance and sing. Humans are units, rather than composites made up of two opposite elements.

This unitary way of looking at humanity seems compatible with modern scientific findings, which describe much of human activity in physical terms. Thinking, choosing, feeling emotion, sensing pain and pursuing various 'spiritual' activities are described as the function of our brains (rather than our souls). The difference between humans and animals is seen as a difference in brain complexity; the decisive distinction is thought by many to be the human brain's ability to reflect on events and to find meaning in behaviour. Death is defined in terms of cessation of brain activity. Our contemporary understanding of humanity is instinctively unitary, and in that way compatible with the Bible.

As a result of its unitary philosophy of humanity, the biblical tradition has a more balanced view of bodiliness, emotion and sexuality than the Greek philosophical tradition does. The Bible
accepts and revels in human bodiliness while realistically por- Song
traying the many ways that humans harm each other through
misusing emotion, sexuality and physical strength. Both sensual Is 54:1-5
and sexual imagery is used for God in the Bible: God is portrayed
as the male sexual partner of Israel, wooing her enthusiastically Ezek 16:8
and giving her offspring, and also as the mother, giving birth to Is 66:13
the people, caring for them and nursing them at the breast.

In the Hebrew understanding, the life-principle in a human
being resides not in a soul that can live independently, but in the Lev 17:11
creature's breath or blood. Thus, God breathed life into the first human. A person who is not breathing has died. "The life of the flesh is in its blood," as Leviticus puts it. According to kosher rules, meat should have the blood drained out of it; humans should not eat the life of the animal, because the life is God's gift. That is why an animal's blood was used in rituals and sacrifices, because blood is a form of direct contact with God.

That unitary understanding of humanity explains why Jesus gave us his body and blood in the Eucharist, rather than his body and soul: for a Hebrew, 'body and blood' means the whole living person.

Body and Soul, Flesh and Spirit

When the Bible uses the terms body and soul, flesh and spirit, the Hebrew rather than the Greek understanding is usually meant.

In Hebrew, 'body' means the whole person – an individual, a human person, a body-being. We have much the same sense in English when we use the word 'somebody,' or when teachers say, "There are 35 bodies in this small classroom." In this sense, when
Paul writes that we should "present your bodies as a living Rom 12:1
sacrifice," he means we should offer our whole lives. Thus, as we shall see shortly, 'resurrection of the body' means resurrection of the whole person.

'Soul' in Hebrew also refers to the whole person, with emphasis on the inwardness of humanity. "My soul is troubled" means "I am distressed." In English, we speak of a town being home to 3,000 souls, or we might say that "there wasn't a soul in the place." The term 'soul music' is a fascinating phrase to express the blend of inwardness and bodiliness in a single human being.

'Flesh' and 'spirit' are not dualistic terms in the Scriptures; they describe a person's relationship with God. 'Flesh' refers to the whole person, unaided by the saving action of God. If we try to live without God's help, according to the Bible, we are doomed to failure and sinfulness. But 'flesh' does not refer exclusively to carnal or sexual sinfulness: pride and envy are sins of the flesh, though they are inward human activities. 'Flesh' refers to the whole person, left to one's own devices, unredeemed.

'Spirit' refers to the whole person acting under the influence of God. When we live in love, joy, peace and patience, says Paul,
Gal 5:22 we know that the Spirit of God is active in our lives. Living in the Spirit can involve all kinds of bodily activity: a married couple expressing their faithful love through sexual intercourse is 'living in the Spirit,' in the biblical sense. Spirit refers to the whole person living under the reign of God.

Death

For people with a unitary understanding of humanity, death is the end of life. The Israelites had a sense that the human life-principle is unkillable, so they spoke of an underworld ("The Pit," *She'ol*) in which the life-principles of the dead continued to exist. To be in *She'ol* was not really to be alive, because human beings are body-beings; it was not a place of reward or punishment;
Ps 115:17 it was a shadowy underworld. "The dead do not praise the Lord, nor do any that go down into silence," says the psalmist. For centuries, the Israelites' only hope for life beyond death was that they would live on in the memories of their descendants. "The
Ps 112:6 righteous…will be remembered forever." The worst thing that could happen would be if all one's descendants were to die, for if a person's name was wiped off the face of the earth, the person was irredeemably dead – unremembered.

In the few centuries before Jesus' time, some Jewish people came to hope for resurrection and life beyond death. Resurrection did not mean "immortality of the soul" (a Greek idea based on a dualistic philosophy), or "coming back to life as it was before" (resuscitation), or "living another life" (reincarnation).

Their hope was that God would raise them – as a whole person – to new life in a transformed state, so that they could participate in the glorious kingdom established by the Messiah.

It is that hope for resurrection – new life in a transformed state – that the early Christians believed was realized first in Jesus.

The Resurrection of Jesus

On the basis of a unitary philosophy about humanity, the resurrection of Jesus is proclaimed in the New Testament – not as a reunion of body and soul, not as a coming back to life, but as a resurrection to new life in a transformed state. The person Jesus lives in a new way beyond death.

Two conceptual terms provide a counterpoint that must be maintained in trying to be faithful to the New Testament proclamation: *continuity* and *transformation*. In very simple language, "It's the same Jesus, but he's totally changed." He is really alive after his death – but so different that even his best friends didn't recognize him.

Some of the narratives about the risen Jesus emphasize *continuity*: "It's really Jesus, whom we knew." Those are the narratives in which he shows his disciples that he is Jesus by eating broiled fish, or inviting Thomas to put a finger into his wounds, or cooking breakfast for his friends. Lk 24:41-43 Jn 20:24-29 Jn 21:9

Other narratives emphasize *transformation*: the body of Jesus is missing from the tomb; he appears in locked rooms without entering through the door; his friends look right at him – even walk with him for hours – without recognizing him. Lk 24:13-35

Let us look briefly at a few New Testament accounts that testify to the resurrection of Jesus.

1. *The First Letter to the Corinthians*

The earliest extended testimony to the resurrection is found in a letter written by Paul some 25 years after the event, and more than ten years before the first gospel was written.

In a short early-Christian 'creed,' Paul reminds his readers of what he had already preached to them: "that Christ died for our sins in accordance with the scriptures, and that he was buried, and that he was raised on the third day in accordance with the scriptures." 1 Cor 15:3-4

Without ever mentioning the empty tomb, Paul goes on to
enumerate several appearances of the Risen Lord, some of which
are not recounted in any gospel (e.g., an appearance to “500
1 Cor 15:6 brothers and sisters at one time, most of whom are still alive”).
The list ends with reference to an appearance of Jesus to Paul
himself some years after the resurrection – another event that is
not mentioned in any of the gospels.

In the rest of the chapter, Paul goes on to defend the
importance of the resurrection in Christian belief. He is writing
to a predominantly Greek community that has a dualistic
understanding of humanity. For them, resurrection of the body is
not something to be desired. They have been taught to hope for
immortality of the soul in a spirit-world. Paul insists that he is
indeed talking about resurrection of the body (which according
to his background means the whole person/body-being), and that
1 Cor 15:17 “If Christ has not been raised, your faith is futile and you are still
in your sins.” His further effort to express what he understands
about life beyond death for believers will be discussed in Chapter
26.

2. *The Empty Tomb*

Mt 28 The disciples' initial awareness of the resurrection, as remembered
Mk 16 in all four gospels, took place during a visit to Jesus' grave by one
Lk 24 or more of his women friends, who were going to perform funeral
Jn 20 observances. The women were shocked to find the tomb open
and empty.

In Matthew, Mark and Luke, the explanation of what has happened is provided for the women by an angel or by one or two young men dressed in dazzling white robes – characters who may best be understood as artistic devices developed by the tradition to express in words what the community had come to believe about the resurrection.

But perhaps the women simply found the tomb empty and,
Mk 16:8 as Mark phrases it, fled from the tomb in trembling and astonishment, “for they were afraid.”

By itself, the empty tomb proves nothing about the resurrection; there could be any number of explanations for an empty tomb other than an unprecedented resurrection. It is the narratives of Jesus' appearances to his friends that pour content into the mysterious fact of an empty grave, and express what the disciples came to believe about Jesus' transformed life beyond death.

But the empty grave remained as one detail in the framework of support for the faith of the early Christians. There is no doubt that the disciples really believed that the tomb was empty, that they were shocked by the discovery, and that their explanation of the evidence was that Jesus had risen to new life. They maintained that conviction even when threatened with death for their beliefs. And no one has ever produced the body of Jesus as the ultimate disproof of the Christians' claims that Jesus had risen.

3. *The Road to Emmaus: A Narrative of Transformation*

The longest gospel account about an appearance of Jesus after his resurrection is Luke's narrative of two disciples walking away from Jerusalem towards a village named Emmaus. As the pair proceeds, a stranger joins them and enters their conversation. The two travellers explain about their shattered hopes for Jesus of Nazareth, his devastating death, and the rumours of the empty tomb. In response, the stranger offers a long interpretation of the Hebrew Scriptures to show that it was necessary for the Messiah to undergo such sufferings in order to enter into his glory.

Lk 24:13-53

At suppertime, the two disciples prevail upon the stranger to dine with them. In the course of the meal, the stranger takes bread, blesses it and breaks it. With that, they recognize who he is – and instantly he vanishes.

This narrative wonderfully expresses the transformation side of our belief in the resurrection of Jesus: he is alive, but he has been transformed so much that his best friends fail to recognize him.

The narrative was intended to reassure believers in Luke's community who, like us, had never seen the risen Jesus. Like us, they believed, but they asked, "How can we be sure? How can we find the risen Jesus in our world and know that he really is alive?"

To those first readers, and to us, the narrative proposes three ways to recognize the living Jesus in our world.

He can be found in the community, living in the hearts of his followers. Jesus walked miles with his friends, and they didn't realize that it was he. "Open your eyes," says the story. "He's walking right beside you, working at the next desk, sitting at your dinner table – and you don't even recognize him! But Jesus is with us all the time, alive in a new way. Be aware! Believe!"

The risen Jesus can also be found in the word of God, the Scriptures, if only we can perceive the value of the interpretations offered in the community of believers. The stranger explained the Scriptures to his companions, but they apparently didn't catch on. Jesus lives today, among us, in his word. The word of God can transform our lives and give them purpose and meaning – but we have to listen. Jesus' word to the heart responds to our deepest searching and hopes. Our hearts, too, "burn within us"
Lk 24:32 when we realize that the word of God is good news that will lead us to wholeness.

Most importantly, the risen Jesus can be recognized "in the
Lk 24:35 breaking of the bread." He comes to us, as he came to the first readers of Luke's gospel, in the Eucharist. He lives, but he lives in a new way, and there is a danger that we will fail to recognize him. If we do recognize Jesus in the breaking of the bread, he will feed us; our inner lives will be nourished, our bonds of love with each other will be enhanced, and we will continue to grow towards that wholeness that is God's ultimate gift of love.

Where can we find the risen, transformed Jesus? He lives with us now, says Luke, walking with us in the journey of life, helping us through his word to perceive and accept God's faithful love in our lives, nourishing us inwardly and pulling us together into a community of love. No one can prove that resurrection happened, but for those who recognize the living presence of the risen Lord in our lives, faith is more reliable than proof.

4. *The Transforming Power of the Resurrection*

Christian faith in the resurrection of Jesus is not simply about something that happened to Jesus long ago. It is not only a matter of accepting historical facts or believing in a creed. We don't simply proclaim that Jesus is alive beyond his death, and therefore we can be sure that he is the Son of God.

Christian faith in the resurrection is not only about Jesus; it is also about us. We believe that through the resurrection of Jesus, a huge tide of divine power surged into the world – a power that can transform people's lives, overcome our sinfulness, set us free, give meaning and purpose to our lives, help us to be true to ourselves and be fully human, and enable us to love in a way that we could not do without God's help. Thus the resurrection is good news for us: by the power of the resurrection, we are led to wholeness – a wholeness that will not end with death.

5. *The Ascension: Overcoming the Feeling that Jesus Has Left Us Behind*

The ascension forms another aspect of our understanding of the resurrection.

First-century Christians believed that Jesus rose to new life but, like us, they had not witnessed an appearance of the risen Saviour. Then as now, many people felt the absence of Jesus more than his presence. Their faith needed to be supported, especially when their very lives were threatened if they continued to proclaim that Jesus had risen.

The resurrection narratives helped believers to recognize in our world the living presence of Jesus in the Scriptures, in the Eucharist, and in the lives of believers. The ascension narratives expressed the resurrection faith from a different viewpoint: Jesus lives with God and sends the Spirit to give us strength.

The Gospel of John reflects at some length on the disciples' Jn 16:16
feelings about the loss of Jesus' presence. At the Last Supper, Jesus Jn 14:18
admits that he will be leaving his friends behind, but he assures Jn 14:2-3
them that he will not leave them as orphans: he will prepare a Jn 16:7
place for them in his Father's house. Jesus also says that he must
ascend to the Father so that he can send his Spirit – the divine Jn 14:25-26
power of truth and love – to strengthen his followers.

When he meets Mary Magdalene in the garden, Jesus tells Jn 20:17
her not to hold on to him, because he is ascending to the Father.
Later that same evening, Jesus appears in a locked room, and
breathes Holy Spirit into the disciples. Thus the Gospel of John
presents the teachings about ascension (Jesus has returned to the
Father) and Pentecost (Jesus has sent the Holy Spirit to his Jn 20:22
followers) all within the narratives of Easter Sunday.

In the Acts of the Apostles, written by the author of Luke, we
find the more familiar account of Jesus' ascension from the Mount Acts 1–2
of Olives (just outside Jerusalem) 40 days after Easter, followed
by Pentecost ten days later. But the themes are very similar: the
disciples will not see Jesus anymore; they must believe. They
should not stand there on the hilltop looking up to heaven and Acts 1:11
bemoaning his absence, but should await the coming of the Spirit
and then become missionaries for Jesus to the ends of the earth. Acts 1:8
The admonition to believe and to spread the good news is
addressed not only to the little band of Jesus' followers, but to
every reader of the New Testament through the ages.

The Gospel of Matthew contains a slightly different response to the believers' feeling that Jesus is absent from them. In Matthew, there is no ascension. Jesus never leaves his friends at all! In a scene set on a mountain in Galilee, Jesus commissions his followers to "make disciples of all nations," and closes with the ringing assurance, "Remember, I am with you always, to the end
Mt 28:18-20 of the age."

What we have explored in this chapter is the foundational faith of the Christian community in the resurrection of Jesus. On the basis of that belief, the community reflected on Jesus' life and teaching for decades, and came to understand who Jesus was in terms that no one had used before his death. The New Testament came into existence in the process of that reflection. In the next chapter, we'll look at how the New Testament took shape.

15

HOW THE NEW TESTAMENT CAME TO BE

Memories about Jesus, and reflections on the meaning of his life, were proclaimed in a living, evolving oral tradition in little communities of Christian disciples for several decades after the resurrection. Because most people at that time were illiterate, and most Christians expected Jesus to return soon and establish the reign of God in glory, there was little reason to commit the tradition to writing at that time. As the communities began to spread around the Mediterranean world, and their distance from the eyewitnesses began to be measured in generations of believers, a need for a written account emerged.

In due time, under various circumstances, such documents appeared. They give us a snapshot of the tradition about Jesus at different times in different communities, and indeed stopped the evolution of the oral tradition. The New Testament is a collection of what were once separate books written by several different authors, many of them anonymous, within the first 100 years after the resurrection of Jesus. Several different types of literary art are represented: gospels, letters, sermons, prayers, hymns, liturgical formulas, creeds and apocalyptic writing are included among the books of the New Testament.

The Letters of Paul

The most significant event of the first ten years after the resurrection was the conversion of Saul, a well-educated, zealous member of the Pharisees, to Christianity. He had never met Jesus, and at first violently persecuted the movement being spread by his followers.

Gal 1:11-24 But eventually, as Saul, who was now called Paul, tells the story, "God was pleased to reveal his Son to me," and Paul became Christian.

At first, he was treated with caution by the followers of Jesus, who suspected he was trying to infiltrate their groups for purposes of further violence. Later, the friends of Jesus resisted his work because Paul had a different sense of the meaning of the gospel than did the little band of poor hill-people who had known Jesus personally.

In some ways, Paul seems to have understood Jesus' greatness better than the earliest disciples did. When Paul proposed bringing the gospel to the non-Jewish people of Asia Minor, the friends of Jesus had misgivings. They still saw themselves as faithful Jews, and they felt that if the good news of Jesus were to be brought to the Gentiles, the neophytes must be persuaded to become Jews first, and then be told that Jesus was the fulfillment for which the Jewish tradition had been hoping. The predominantly Jewish Christian communities wanted Paul to insist that any male Gentiles who wished to become Christian would have to undergo the traditional Jewish initiation rite of circumcision first, and be baptized later.

Paul was vociferously unwilling to require his recruits to submit to the Jewish initiation rite, claiming that Jesus was not merely the fulfillment of Jewish hopes, but Saviour of the world in his own right. In time, Paul convinced the original Christians of the merits of his case, and went on to become the greatest Christian preacher of the first – or any – century.

It was Paul who crossed the Hellespont and brought the gospel to Western Europe. As a result, almost every follower of Jesus today (including those in Africa and Asia) is an heir of Christianity as moderated by European culture. One wonders how Christianity might have been different if Paul had turned right towards Asia instead of left towards Europe when he came to an unknown crossroads one day almost 2,000 years ago.

Paul's method in each town was systematic. As a well-educated Jew, he would go first to the synagogue and proclaim to the faithful his conviction that Jesus of Nazareth was the Anointed One. They would likely throw him out of the place, but one or two believers might follow him to hear more. Paul would proceed to the town square, and begin to preach there, forming a small community with those who were interested, staying with them a few months to tell all that he knew about the good news of Jesus, then leaving someone in charge of the group, and travelling down the road to the next town to begin the process all over again.

We can only imagine what an effective preacher Paul must Acts 17:16-34
have been. The Acts of the Apostles paints a verbal picture of him standing in the Areopagus in Athens, surrounded by the magnificent white marble temples whose ruins still dominate the city, speaking to the heirs of the civilization that gave us the *Iliad* and the *Odyssey*, Plato and Aristotle, and a tradition of unforgettable mythology. Paul was trying to convince the citizens of Athens that a poor Jewish craftsman who had been executed by the Romans 20 years before on the other side of the Mediterranean was the Saviour of the world and the answer to their deepest questions about the meaning of life. "Some scoffed; but others said, 'We will hear you again about this.'" He must have been a convincing speaker.

After Paul had left one village and begun to evangelize in a new one, problems would inevitably arise in the first community, and messengers would arrive with questions for the apostle to answer. Paul's written responses took the form of letters to his 'faithful brothers and sisters in Christ.'

These letters became the earliest written documents of the Christian tradition. All of Paul's letters were written before Mark, the first of the gospels. Paul was killed in the mid-60s of the first Christian century; the Gospel according to Mark was composed somewhere near the year 70. The dateline that follows lists the letters, in the order in which they likely were written. There is debate about the authorship of some other New Testament letters; these letters do not appear on the dateline. Many scholars believe that Colossians, Ephesians, the letters to Timothy and Titus, and Hebrews were written more or less 'in the spirit of Paul' by unknown authors after his death.

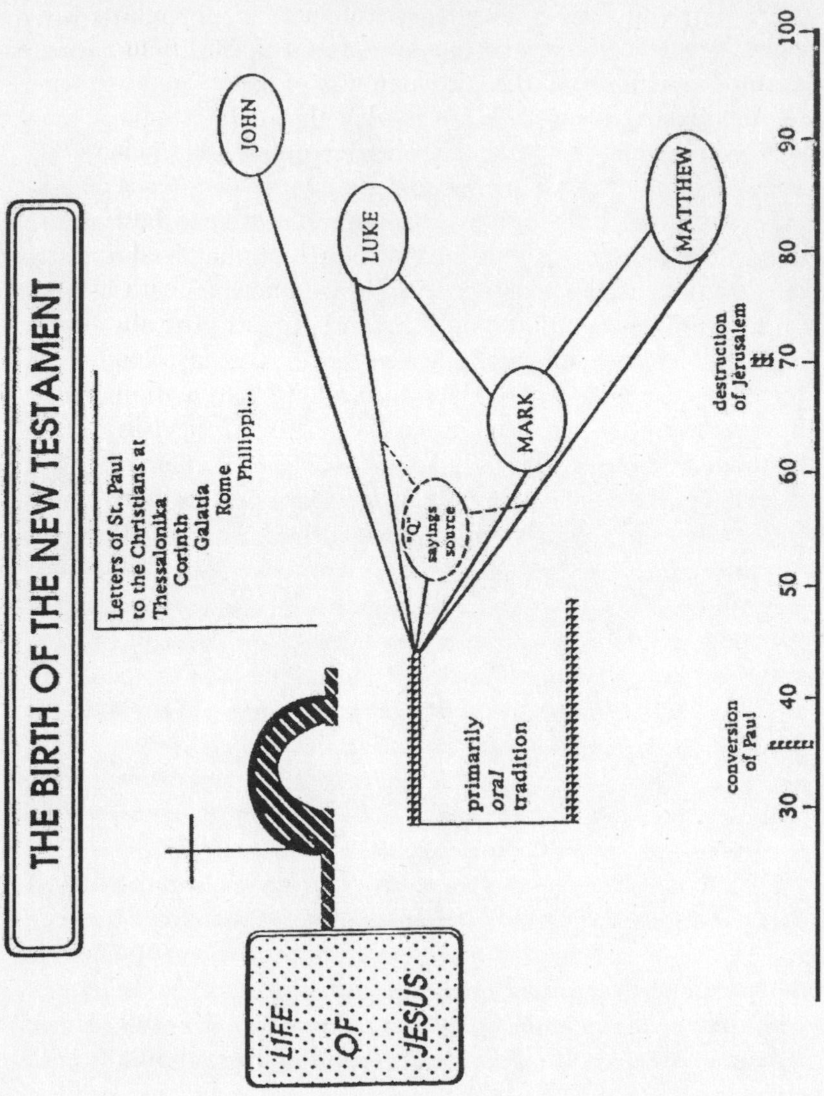

Paul's letters give us little historical information about the life of Jesus. Presumably, during the months that he was setting the foundations of the community in a certain town Paul told the people all he knew about what Jesus had done. The letters, on the other hand, give us a picture of early Christian community life and the problems that arose when unexpected events or disagreements upset a formerly peaceful group of believers.

Invariably, Paul used those problems as springboards to remind people of what he had taught and to call them back to faithful observance of the Christian way of life.

Whenever we want to learn what the first Christians were saying about Jesus, or about the resurrection, or the Eucharist, or the Church, we search the letters of Paul for our earliest available evidence. His letters give us a glimpse of Christian faith in the 50s and 60s; the gospels tell us what Christians believed at a later date, in the 70s, 80s and 90s, some years after the death of Paul.

A significant event took place in Palestine shortly after Paul's death at the hands of the Roman authorities. Many elements of Jewish society were outraged at the continuing occupation of their homeland by the 'infidel' Empire. Unsuccessful uprisings were commonplace. In the late 60s, the forces of rebellion came together in one final burst of energy against the strongest military power in their world. They were doomed to defeat. Around 70 CE, the Romans, under the general Titus, demolished Jerusalem, the recently renovated second Temple and numerous Jewish villages. Jewish presence in Palestine was effectively reduced to nothing for the next 1,900 years.

The Jewish tradition became the responsibility of the religious leaders (primarily the Pharisees), who made the necessary decisions to preserve their religious and cultural identity on the basis of Scripture rather than priesthood and Temple.

For the Christian community, the destruction of Jerusalem signalled the termination of the Old Covenant. Christians believed that the demolition of the Temple had been foretold by Jesus as a signal that a New Covenant had been initiated. The gospels (with the possible exception of Mark, which may have been written before the fateful events of the year 70) are written with a sense of liberation and exultation: we, the disciples of Jesus, are the new chosen people of God.

The Synoptic Tradition

The relationship among the gospels has been the subject of speculation for centuries. The Gospel according to John is highly distinctive, and seems to be the product of a rather independent community and a brilliant creative author. Matthew, Mark and Luke, on the other hand, can be compared with each other episode by episode to discover similarities and differences. Thus they are known as the synoptic gospels. (In Greek, *syn* = with, together; *optic* = related to the eye: the three gospels can be seen together.)

In the past hundred years, scholars have almost come to consensus about the relationship among the synoptic gospels as it is shown in the diagram on page 180. Mark was likely the first to be written. It seems that the authors of both Matthew and Luke knew the Gospel of Mark, and copied it, with some slight changes, into their own versions of the gospel. Seven-eighths of the content of Mark is found in Matthew and Luke, often almost word for word. There would have been no thought that such a practice was inappropriate; the authors were honouring and expanding the influence of Mark's gospel by using almost all of it for their own audience. In the process they added their own interpretation and materials that had not been available to Mark.

Mark reported relatively few of the sayings of Jesus. Matthew and Luke have a great many more, again clearly copied from a written source. We are confident that the authors of Matthew and Luke did not copy from each other, because so many sayings are reported verbatim, while the contexts in which they are set are completely different. Scholars have decided that there must have been a collection of sayings of Jesus, with no story surrounding them, that both Matthew and Luke had but Mark did not. Because the scholars who first conceived of this theory were German, they called this hypothetical document *das Quelle* or The Source. Ever since, scholars discussing the synoptic gospels have referred to the collection of sayings of Jesus as 'Q.'

Matthew and Luke also used some material that was in no other gospel. Some of that material may have remained in oral form until they recorded it; some of it may have been written by someone else and included by these authors.

One classic example of pre-written source material known to only one gospel writer may be Luke's version of the Christmas stories. The author begins the gospel with an introduction, written in flowing, elegant Greek, with complex subordinate clauses. Then follows the story of the birth of John the Baptist, in language of a very different, almost childish style, in which many of the sentences begin with the simple conjunction 'and.' It seems likely that the stories about the birth of Jesus were written by someone else and incorporated into the gospel by the author who wrote that elegant introduction.

Imagine the desk on which the author of Luke wrote his gospel. On it are the Gospel according to Mark, another scroll with collected sayings of Jesus, and some other written material (including the Christmas story) preserved only in Luke's community. Also at the author's disposal is his familiarity with the oral tradition – the way the stories of Jesus have been retold in his community, at eucharistic celebrations, week after week, for years. Finally, the author has his own genius, his own artistic talent, his own faith and understanding about the meaning of Jesus for the people of his community. With all those resources at hand, the author sets out to write an "orderly account of the events Lk 1:1
that have been fulfilled among us."

Somewhere, perhaps not too far away in place or time, the author of the Gospel according to Matthew is undertaking the same kind of project. How each of them expressed their understanding of the good news of Jesus is the topic of Chapter 17.

The Gospel According to John

A decade or more later, a brilliant writer living in another Christian community somewhere in Asia Minor created a vastly different version of the good news of Jesus. The author of the fourth gospel apparently was not familiar with the letters of Paul or the interactive tradition that gave us the synoptic gospels. The Gospel according to John does not report most of the events and teachings of Jesus that we find in the synoptic gospels. On the other hand, it does report several events in the life of Jesus with which the synoptic narrators were not familiar, and includes a vast repertoire of teaching that was unheard of in the synoptics. John's community had evolved tremendously in its insight about who Jesus was and in the vocabulary it used to express that insight. John was so different from the first three gospels that there was serious doubt for centuries within the Christian community about whether it should be accepted as an authentic expression of the good news of Jesus.

Eventually, its authenticity and greatness could not be denied, and the Gospel according to John took its place as the fourth gospel.

We will discuss the Gospel of John in some detail in Chapters 22 and 23.

Other Christian Writings

Several other early Christian writings came into existence in the first century after the resurrection of Jesus. Many of them claimed to be written by friends of Jesus or by influential early Christians. Some early letters, purportedly written by Peter, John, James and Jude, eventually were accepted as worthy components of the New Testament. The book of Revelation was written on the Mediterranean island of Patmos by an author who identifies himself as 'John,' but does not claim to have been a friend of Jesus.

Other early Christian writings that were not accepted as Scripture included letters attributed to Paul's friend Barnabas, and gospels alleged to have been written by Peter and Thomas, among others. Authorship and reliability of content were prime criteria for accepting writings as the Word of God. Gospels that were rejected portray Jesus as warlike, cruel, doing miracles to take revenge after childhood conflicts, and having negative attitudes towards women. Still, they report many familiar teachings of Jesus, as well as a few deeds and teachings that are not reported in the New Testament and that may be accurate records of some aspects of his thought. Scholars study them with care, always seeking better insight into what early Christians believed about Jesus and, perhaps, fuller understanding of what Jesus said and did. For interested readers, those early Christian writings can be found in university libraries and religious bookstores.

Conclusion

Each of the four gospels of the New Testament, in its own way, presents Jesus to the thoughtful, searching reader. We no longer pretend that the gospels are all saying the same thing. Instead, we cherish their differences and try to learn more about Jesus by exploring the meaning of the variations among the gospels.

The gospels are like four spotlights focused on one individual. Each one illuminates from a different angle. If one of the spotlights were missing, some aspect of the person's identity would be in darkness.

We can appreciate the differences among the gospels because we know that faith in Jesus does not depend only on facts. When they hear that the tradition about Jesus evolved for more than 50 years before being written down, some people feel that we can't trust the gospels to give us the facts about Jesus. It's true: the gospels differ on many details about his life.

But the gospels are not simply books of facts. They do report real events from the life of Jesus; they do have a historical basis. But they are primarily documents of faith; their purpose is to bring readers to believe that Jesus is the answer to the yearning of every heart about the meaning of life; that Jesus is God's gift to us; that through Jesus, God will lead all of us – individually and together – to live in a way that is true to our deepest selves; and that through Jesus, God will make us whole.

The next eight chapters will examine several aspects of how the four gospels express the greatness of Jesus and the value of the reign of God for each of us.

16

MARK

Jesus, the Messiah, the Son of God, in the Gospel According to Mark

The Gospel according to Mark was likely written some 40 years after the resurrection, far away from Jesus' homeland, during the ill-advised revolution which, in the year 70, led to the destruction of the Temple, the city of Jerusalem, and Jewish society in Palestine. The community that gave us this gospel was probably the Christian community of Rome, where both Peter and Paul had lived for a time before being killed in Nero's persecution in the mid-60s CE. We shall see that the community's understanding of the meaning of Jesus' life was profound and paradoxical, born of 40 years of reflection, fear and suffering. The fact that so many in their community had shared Jesus' experience of being persecuted and killed for their beliefs gave immense poignancy and immediacy to their reflections on the reign of God that Jesus had proclaimed.

The best way to begin would be to read the Gospel according to Mark all the way through, like a novel. Try to forget what you know from having heard the gospels read at church, or from having learned about Jesus in religious studies courses. In those settings, the unique characteristics of each gospel are rarely mentioned. Let Mark, the gospel writer, tell you the story of Jesus in his distinctive way. Prepare to be a little surprised. Then read this chapter.

Using the following headings, we will attempt to articulate the distinctive style of Mark's presentation of the good news of Jesus:

A. The Title
B. Part 1: The Ministry of Jesus
C. The Mid-Point of the Gospel: Assessment and Adjustment
D. Part 2: Jesus Clarifies His Mission
E. The Culminating Revelation: The Death of Jesus

A. The Title

The beginning of the good news of Jesus Christ, the Son of God. Mk 1:1

We don't know the names of most of the people who wrote the many books collected in our Scriptures, including the authors of the gospels. The first verse of the gospel was apparently a heading or title written by the author, but it does not mention the author's name. The title that now begins the gospel was not part of the original text, but was added more than a century later. It is impossible to establish for certain the author's name or to know whether he is the same person as the John Mark who was a companion of Paul. For convenience, we will use the names Matthew, Mark, Luke and John for the authors of the gospels. (Acts 12:12)

Interestingly, the brief heading that is the first verse of the Gospel of Mark presents no fewer than four significant concepts whose meaning should be explored as an introduction to the gospel.

1. *Gospel*

With this term, the author identifies the purpose of the document – what kind of literary art form he considers it to be. It is not a history book, not a biography, not a newspaper report – it is a gospel, a Greek word meaning 'good news.' A gospel is not trying simply to report selected facts as a newspaper or history book might claim to do. A gospel is a document of faith; it is biased by design. It is written to persuade the reader to accept the author's conviction that Jesus is the answer to everyone's deepest questions about life, that his life was indeed good news for everyone. A gospel depends on its historical basis for credibility, but it provides a careful interpretation of the events it reports; that interpretation is the decisive purpose of the writing.

The author of Mark announces with his first phrase that he is setting out to convince us that Jesus is good news for us, to invite us to share the author's faith and to find in Jesus the answer to our deepest searching. The gospel is intended to speak to our hearts.

2. *Jesus*

The English name 'Jesus' derives from the Greek version (*Iesous*) of a very common Hebrew name that we know as Joshua. (In Jesus' dialect it may have been pronounced more like Yeshua.) Many people in his time, as in ours, were called Joshua.

This name, like many Hebrew names, has a religious meaning. Yeho-shua means 'God saves.' The first syllables are recognizable as a form of the sacred Name of God; the second half of the name
Mt 1:21 is a form of the verb 'to save.' Christians perceived significance in the name of Jesus, "for he will save his people from their sins."

Jesus' family name probably changed at least three times during his life. When he was growing up in Nazareth, Jesus was probably known as his father's son: Jesus ben Joseph. Thus, in English, his name would be Joshua Josephson. After Joseph's death, Jesus continued to work as an artisan for a number of years,
Mk 6:3 and would probably have been known as "the carpenter." One curious aspect of the speculative name Joshua Carpenter for Jesus is that wood was rare and expensive; he may be better called an 'artisan' or even 'smith.'

When, in time, Jesus left his home town and became a travelling preacher, he was known as Jesus of Nazareth, the name under which he was crucified. Jesus undoubtedly did have a family name, perhaps even three different names in the course of his life. No one, however, used Christ as his family name.

3. *Christ*

In Chapter 10, where we explored the prophets' hope for the coming of the Anointed One, we saw that *christos* is the Greek word for the Hebrew *meshiach*, meaning 'the anointed one.' This was a term used for the great political and religious leader, the new David whom the Jewish people expected God to send, to free them from oppression and to establish a society based on faithfulness to God.

By the time the Gospel according to Mark was written, Christians were confidently making the claim that Jesus was the fulfillment of this aspect of Jewish hope in a way that the Jewish tradition had not foreseen. The title became so familiar to Jesus' followers that they repeatedly called him Jesus the Messiah, *ho christos*. Eventually they left out the definite article and called him simply Jesus Christ (as in Mark 1:1).

There is an unmistakable sense throughout the gospels, however, that Jesus had misgivings about being called the Messiah, probably because the title was too political for his sense of his mission. If he had clearly claimed the mantle of the Anointed One, the people of his time would have understood it to involve political revolution against the Roman Empire. According to the Gospel of John, after Jesus fed 5,000 people with a few loaves of bread and some fish, he perceived that "they were about to come Jn 6:15
and take him by force to make him king," and he fled.

Jesus doubtless understood himself to be the fulfillment of Jewish hopes, but he preferred other ways of expressing that understanding, since he wasn't interested in being a political leader. This makes one wonder why the title 'Christ' became so popular among his followers after the resurrection.

In our study of the gospel, we will differentiate among the various titles people have used to honour Jesus. 'Rabbi' or 'teacher' is less reverent than 'Lord.' 'Son of David' and 'Christ' mean specifically a religious and political leader. There were many other titles by which people have honoured Jesus, but perhaps the greatest, most succinct expression of New Testament faith is found in the phrase 'Son of God.'

4. *Son of God*

All people were called children of God in the scriptural tradition. Kings were called sons of God in a special way; the day of their anointing was seen as the day of their birth as God's sons. That Ps 2:7
use of language continued in the time of Jesus; because of what he did, he may have been called a son of God during his life.

But never in the Jewish tradition was a human being called a Son of God in the same sense that Mark uses it in the first line of his gospel. In the decades after the resurrection, Christians came to believe that Jesus was not simply a small-town craftsman who had been sent by God. They struggled to find words to express what they had come to believe: that in Jesus, the great God who spoke to Moses had lived a human life, one of us, and yet so much more than the greatest of human beings.

The followers of Jesus knew that in his godliness he had prayed to God, and therefore was not identical with the Creator. Because he had so often spoken of God as his Father, eventually Christians began to express the divinity of Jesus by calling him Son of God, in a way that meant much more than the title had meant when it was used for the kings of Israel and Judah.

The process of trying to express the Christian faith about Jesus was to continue for four centuries, until it culminated in the Creed accepted in 325 CE at the council of Nicaea. The Nicene Creed is a statement of faith in the divinity of Jesus that uses language of philosophy and symbolism, some of which was unknown to the biblical authors: "God from God, Light from Light, true God from true God, begotten not made, one in being with the Father, from whom all things were made...."

At the time of the writing of the Gospel of Mark, however, Christian reflection could be encapsulated in the simple but profound phrase 'Son of God.' It is the greatest early-Christian expression of the divinity of Jesus.

The first verse of the gospel is like the author's table of contents. He advises that he intends to convince the reader that the life of Jesus will provide welcome answers to life's deepest questions (good news), that Jesus is the fulfillment of Jewish hopes (Messiah), and that Jesus is the living presence of God on earth (Son of God). "This is the good news of Jesus Christ, the Son of God."

Then, the author sets out to show us the Son of God in action.

B. Part One: The Ministry of Jesus

From the beginning of his gospel, the author of Mark works quickly, briefly reporting one event after another. For the first eight chapters, he shows us Jesus at work, and invites us to put ourselves into the minds of the onlookers, to ask with them, "Who is this man? What does he think he is doing?" At the end of Chapter 8 of the gospel, the reader, like the disciples who knew Jesus, is asked for an assessment: "Who do you say that I am?"

As you will have seen from your reading of the gospel, Mark portrays Jesus in a surprisingly gutsy, warts-and-all, human way. Clearly, Jesus' ministry would upset many good, faithful Jewish people, as well as the religious authorities whom he challenged. And yet many people stayed with him. They wanted to see and hear more. He was attractive; his preaching made sense. Let us look at these two opposing perceptions of his ministry, as Mark presents it.

1. *The Disturbing Radical*

The style of Jesus' ministry must have challenged the 'respectable,' simple believers of his community.

For one thing, he kept unusual company. One of his friends, Levi, was a tax collector. Tax collectors were despised because
they made deals with the Romans to deliver a specified amount Mk 2:13-17
of tax money, and then used intimidation and violence against the citizens to extort a much larger amount for their own benefit. A comparable figure in today's society might be a drug dealer with gang connections. Jesus invited Levi to follow him, and dined at Levi's home with other disreputable characters. He was hoping to change their hearts, to be sure, but what would people think?

A man identified as Simon the Cananaean was part of Jesus' inner circle. Because he was a member of a minority group in
Galilee, faithful Jewish people likely objected to his being a friend Mk 3:18
of this preacher who claimed to speak for the God of Abraham.

A number of women were also welcome as Jesus' friends and companions – a surprising practice in such a strict patriarchal
society. Mark gives the names of three women who stayed with Mk 15:40
Jesus until his death, and who were the first to find his tomb Mk 16:1
empty on Easter morning. And Jesus defended a woman who Mk 14:3-9
took an unexpected initiative and poured ointment over his head during the last week of his life.

But perhaps the most distressing aspect of Jesus' ministry for ordinary believers was his attitude towards the Law of Moses. While it is true to say that Jesus was an observant Jew, he interpreted the Law differently than Jewish religious leaders did.

In some instances, it seems that he felt free to change or repeal some of God's laws – a claim that could only be seen as outrageous by any faithful believer. An example is his comments about the kosher laws, which are still observed by many faithful Jews, and are enshrined in the laws of contemporary Israel.

Mk 7:14-15 "Listen to me, all of you, and understand: there is nothing
Mk 7:19 outside a person that by going in can defile, but the things that
come out are what defile." With these words, comments the gospel writer, "Jesus declared all foods clean." On what grounds could one justify these words of a former small-town artisan who had been exiled from his home village because people thought he was out of his mind?

One dramatic episode that illustrates Jesus' attitude towards Jewish tradition is narrated at the beginning of Chapter 3 of Mark. Jesus had been building quite a reputation as a healer. When he was worshipping in the synagogue in the fishing village of Capernaum, his new home base on the shore of the Sea of Galilee, a man with a disabled hand was among the crowd.

The law forbade work of any kind during the sabbath. The
Num 15:32-36 law was interpreted very strictly in Jewish tradition; the death
Exod 35:2 penalty was imposed on a man for gathering wood on the sabbath.
Yet the tradition was not inflexible: it was understood that a matter of life and death could override the law.

But this man's problem was only a crippled hand. He had presumably lived with it for some time; he could wait until tomorrow to be healed.

The scene is skillfully portrayed by Mark with great economy of words. Jesus invites the man to come forward in the crowded synagogue, and he throws out a riddle to the onlookers:

Mk 3:4 *"Is it lawful to do good or to do harm on the sabbath,*
to save life, or to kill?"

Taking the second half of the conundrum first, Jesus is reminding the people that according to their law, it is permitted to work on the sabbath when someone's life is in danger; in fact, according to traditional interpretation, if you have a chance to save someone's life on the sabbath, and you refuse, you are to blame if the person dies, as if you have killed that person. "To save life, or to kill?" The law would say "save life."

But Jesus extends the interpretation exponentially with the other half of his riddle: if you have a chance to do good on the sabbath, and you don't do it, you have done evil. Jesus is offering his own interpretation of God's real intention in creating the sabbath law: to give working people a weekly day of rest, not to tie them up in knots of guilt. Jesus' view is that on the sabbath a faithful believer should do good, rather than do nothing.

No one in the synagogue responds to his challenge. One can Mk 3:5
sense the electricity in the room as Jesus scans the congregation with fire in his eyes and sadness in his heart. Mark is wonderful at portraying Jesus as passionately involved in every situation. Jesus heals the man, and the religious authorities recognize that this is sedition: with such actions Jesus is usurping their role as Mk 3:6
God's spokesmen. They immediately begin to plot his death.

Nor would their fears be allayed by his saying that the sabbath was made for the benefit of people; people were not made to serve the sabbath. "So the Son of Man is lord even of the sabbath." ..."Who does this fellow think he is?" they wonder. Mk 2:28

That is the question that Mark wants every reader to consider.

2. *The Attractive Healer*

In spite of the upsetting aspects of Jesus' style, throngs of people were attracted to him, listening to every word and watching every deed. A list of what attracted them could be easily developed by any Christian; here are four ways of saying why people resisted the admonitions of their religious leaders and followed Jesus around the countryside.

a) Jesus announced that the reign of God had arrived, and the people hoped he was right.

The reign of God was the predominant theme of Jesus' teaching. Mk 1:15
Even without knowing exactly what he meant by that phrase, the people knew that if Jesus was right, it was good news for all of them. They expected God to act radically to change the course of history – to set them free from foreign oppression and also from the sickly, hungry, brutal, brief and miserable life that was the unavoidable lot of poor people. Jesus announced that the time they were hoping for, the time described in Isaiah's 'poetry of paradise,' had finally arrived. Everything he did was intended to illustrate the reign of God in action. Somehow, almost wordlessly, the good news was dawning in the minds of the poor.

b) Jesus healed people in a way that no one could explain.

Jesus lived in a world where death hung like a noxious cloud over every family. Children died from illnesses that in our society are almost forgotten. Women died in childbirth. Behaviour that we would attribute to mental illness frightened people and was attributed to the work of demons. Nutrition varied with the seasons: when the plenty of harvest season had been exhausted, months of hunger followed. Sanitation was desperately primitive; infection raged; times of good health were rare.

In such an atmosphere, healing brought freedom. Healing was a sign of God's action to overcome human misery and lead people to wholeness. Jesus used healing to support the authenticity of his teaching.

His opponents never claimed that he did not heal people, but they did allege that he was doing it by evil power rather than by the power of God. Jesus was furious at their accusations; he called their attacks unforgivable – sin against the Holy Spirit. The people
Mk 3:22-30 sensed that Jesus was right. They stayed with him; they hoped for more.

c) Jesus' ideas about how people should live were beautiful.

We know more about the moral teaching of Jesus from the other three gospels than we do from Mark. Yet Mark does tell us of Jesus' freeing attitude towards the letter of the Law, of his vision
Mk 10:1-31 of lifelong marriage, his concern about the desensitizing effects of wealth, and his endorsement of childlike faith.

People who heard Jesus teach about a truly saved, truly human, truly faithful way of life must have felt exhilaration and inner freedom when they realized that they were listening to profound moral wisdom – even though it challenged their traditional values in some ways.

d) When Jesus talked about God, people could tell he knew God.

Jesus taught people what God is like, but his teaching was not conceptual. Mark, in fact, sees the significant actions of Jesus as
Mk 1:27 the heart of his teaching: Jesus used works to show people what God is like. He did not urge them to recite a creed or to affirm a theology. Instead, he urged them to pray.

Mk 14:36 Mark reports that Jesus prayed to God as *abba,* the Hebrew word for father that children used, the evening before his death. It is the poignant prayer of a child in the most frightening and vulnerable moment of his life. Jesus may not have explicitly taught people to feel a similar sense of childlike intimacy with God in prayer, but his followers must have noticed that he had a comfortable, loving relationship with God. When he spoke in the name of God, they sensed that God was indeed with him, and that his teaching was the word of God for them.

While we will discuss the reign of God and the miracles in greater detail in Chapter 18, this concludes our summary of the themes of the first eight chapters of the Gospel according to Mark. Mark shows Jesus in action; he is both disturbing and attractive. Mark portrays the reaction of opponents and disciples, and invites the reader to consider the value of what Jesus offers. At the mid-point of the gospel, Mark offers readers an opportunity for personal evaluation.

C. The Mid-point of the Gospel: Assessment and Adjustment

1. *The People's Opinion*

"People have seen me in action now for some time," Jesus might have said to his close friends as they were heading north, away from central Galilee towards the Roman resort town of Caesarea Mk 8:27
Philippi. "What are they saying? Who do people think I am?"

"Some say, John the Baptist; others, Elijah; and still others, one of the prophets," came the response. The answers are a little puzzling, but generally, the consensus is that Jesus is from God, and not, as the religious authorities would say, from the side of evil. "Jesus speaks for God as the prophets did" is the theme of the people's reaction to his work.

Why anyone would think he was John the Baptist is odd, especially since the gospel has already reported the death of the Mk 6:14-29
Baptist. Remember that John's ministry took place near the Dead Sea, many days' journey away from their Galilean home; most of the people of Galilee would never have seen John, although they would have heard of him. Perhaps they had not yet been told of his death.

The legend of Elijah's return is a little more understandable. According to Jewish tradition, the prophet Elijah had never died, 2 Kings
but had been taken up to God's heaven in a fiery chariot. In the 2:11-13
closing verses of Malachi, the final prophetic book of the Hebrew Mal 4:5-6
Scriptures, there is a promise that Elijah will return before the final 'day of the LORD.' People combined that hope with the expectation of the Anointed One, and came to believe that Elijah

would return to prepare the way for the Messiah. To this day, an extra place is set in every Jewish home at the Passover supper in the hope that Elijah will join the family that evening.

So according to Mark, some people think Jesus may be the Elijah figure – the one who comes to prepare the way for the Messiah.

Jn 1:19-23 The Elijah theme is mentioned elsewhere in the New Testament. In the Gospel of John, agents from Jerusalem ask John the Baptist whether he is the Messiah (he denies it), and then whether he is Elijah. He denies that, too, claiming to be nothing but Isaiah's "voice crying in the wilderness." But in the Gospel according to Matthew, it is reported that Jesus, in talking about
Mt 11:14 the ministry of John the Baptist, declares that the latter is "Elijah who is to come." Christians, of course, have always considered John the Baptist as the forerunner of the Messiah. We may not have realized that some people thought that Jesus was the forerunner, and that the early Jewish Christians believed John the Baptist to be the expected Elijah figure.

In assessing Jesus, his friends report that the people of Galilee believe he is a prophet sent by God. Despite the scornful attacks of religious leaders, the people think of Jesus as good, not evil.

2. *The Disciples' Opinion*

"Very well," Jesus presses his friends. "Now I've heard your report about what the people are saying. They think that I have been sent by God. How about you? Who do you say that I am?"

According to Mark, Peter's response is brief: "You are the Messiah." Jesus' rejoinder is unexpectedly emotional. He sternly
Mk 8:30 orders them, "Don't you dare tell anybody that!"

Mark's version of this episode is surprising to anyone who remembers Jesus' response in the Gospel according to Matthew:
Mt 16:17 "Blessed are you, Simon… For flesh and blood has not revealed this to you, but my Father in heaven." Matthew, writing ten years after Mark, wants to give a different impression of that pivotal moment.

In Mark, Jesus does not deny that he is the Anointed One, but he is clearly hesitant about making a public claim of messiahship, perhaps because the popular hope for the messiah involved more political and military implications than Jesus was prepared to accept.

3. *Jesus Begins to Clarify His Sense of Messiahship*

Rather than endorsing Peter's declaration of his messiahship, Jesus responds by using a different title for himself, then shocks the disciples by telling them he expects to be killed for his activities.

'Son of Man' is the only title Jesus ever uses to refer to himself in the synoptic gospels. Even when the council of priests at his trial demand to know whether he thinks he is the messiah and Son of God, Jesus answers, "I am," and then goes on to describe his future coming as the Son of Man. Since 'Son of Man' was so important to Jesus, we should try to understand what the phrase meant to him. Mk 14:62

In the Hebrew Scriptures, *ben adam* is simply a human being, a 'mortal,' as the New Revised Standard Version (NRSV) translation frequently puts it. Jesus uses the phrase 'Son of Man' repeatedly in the gospels to refer to his humanness, with an emphasis on his mortality – as in the episode we are studying, where he makes it clear that he expects to be killed.

An almost opposite meaning of the phrase is also found in the gospels, when Jesus speaks of returning in glory on the clouds of heaven, "seated at the right hand of the Power." Upon hearing this, many of his hearers would recall the same image used in the Book of Daniel:

> *I saw one like a human being*
> *coming with the clouds of heaven…*
> *To him was given dominion and glory and kingship,*
> *that all peoples, nations, and languages should serve him.* Dan 7:13-14

'Son of Man' has a rich depth of meaning, implying both the frailty of the human experience that Jesus shares with us, and his future heavenly glory.

4. *The Last Temptation of Christ*

One can only imagine Peter's confusion as this scene draws to a close. He has been travelling with Jesus and has come to recognize his greatness so much that he is ready to call Jesus 'messiah' – the fulfillment of centuries of hope. But no sooner does Peter declare his allegiance than Jesus orders him to tell no one, and promptly shatters the disciples' hope with a prediction of his own death.

Peter, naturally enough, expresses his dismay and tries to reassure Jesus that his mission is not doomed. When Jesus

Mk 8:33 explodes at Peter, calling him 'Satan,' Mark's portrait of Jesus as a profoundly emotional, even volatile person, emerges. We may think that such strong expressions of feeling are inappropriate, but Mark has no such inhibitions. This episode may give us a better sense of what kind of person Jesus was, and perhaps even a new sense of what it means to be human.

If we take Jesus' humanness seriously, we must abandon our impressions that he was a superman, or that he was God pretending to be human, that he knew everything, that it was easy for him to make good decisions, that he never doubted or exploded or struggled. Jesus was apparently normal enough that his townspeople lived alongside him for 30 years without thinking that he was superman. Jesus grew to become an exceptional person, with wonderful insight into human nature and a profound togetherness with God, but he had to learn like any other child. He had to struggle to make good choices in life, just as all of us must do. New Testament writers, labouring to express their
Heb 4:15 awareness of his ordinariness as well as his extraordinary qualities, stated that he was "as we are, yet without sin," and that

Though he was in the form of God…
emptied himself, taking the form of a slave,
Phil 2:6-7 *being born in human likeness.*

Jesus was completely human. If he had not been, he could not fully share our experiences.

Why would Jesus react so fiercely to Peter's reassertion of his hope that Jesus was the messiah? Peter's hope was a kind of temptation, similar to the temptations that are reported in some detail in the Gospels of Matthew and Luke. The theme of all the
Mt 4:1-11// temptation narratives is that Jesus felt pressured, not only by
Lk 4:1-13 public expectations but also within himself, to be the wrong kind of messiah. Peter expects him to fulfill people's hope for a messiah who will be a political and religious leader, to drive out the Romans and to establish a political kingdom of God. Instead, Jesus knows that he must live in a way that is true for him – a way that will lead inevitably to death rather than power.

The temptation narratives are based on the recognition that Jesus – like all of us – had to struggle to be true to himself and to God. He was not the serene, placid, calmly decisive type of person that we have (wrongly) come to equate with a saint. He was more like us. He was attracted to ways of living that he knew would not be true for him. He had to decide, over and over again, to do what is right. When Peter insists that people want Jesus to be the messiah they have been hoping for, Jesus is vulnerable and feels threatened by this expectation. His violent reaction reveals how tempting it was to be the wrong kind of messiah.

This scene brings the first half of the gospel to a close with a moment of reflective evaluation. Immediately, the author begins the second half of the gospel, in which Jesus tries to revolutionize the expectations of his followers by telling and showing them his understanding of the real purpose of his life.

D. Part Two: Jesus Clarifies His Mission

In the brief two chapters leading to Jesus' triumphant arrival in Jerusalem and the extended narrative of the last days of Jesus' life, he is portrayed as extending his ministry of teaching and healing, knowing that his integrity will lead to his death. His friends, unfortunately, were not able to adjust their hopes and thoughts as well as Jesus must have wished.

Two of his fisherman friends, James and John, who have earlier
been nicknamed 'the sons of thunder,' come to him quietly and Mk 3:17
make the request that every parent has heard from crafty little Mk 10:35
children: "Will you do for us whatever we ask of you?"

Jesus, like any wise adult, responds with a question: "What
do you want?" And the two men say, "When you come into power, Mk 10:37
can we be right beside you?"

One can see Jesus sadly shaking his head as he says, "You
have no idea what you're asking for. Do you think you can survive Mk 10:38
what we are going to have to go through together?"

"Sure!" is the naive reply.

Jesus simply says, "Well, you will indeed face some difficult experiences with me, but what I'm doing is not about power. Not at all."

When the other ten members of the inner circle find out what the sons of thunder have been doing, they show that their faith is no deeper than James and John's, and complain that *they* deserve the leadership roles rather than the sons of Zebedee.

In this setting of desperate stupidity and ambition among his friends, Jesus makes one of his greatest declarations about the heart of his teaching and about his understanding of his own mission. “All over the world,” says Jesus, “political authority involves power and domination. But that is not what Christianity is all about....”

It is not so among you;
but whoever wishes to be great among you
must be your servant,
Mk 10:43-44 *and whoever wishes to be first among you*
must be slave of all.

This is a profound statement about the meaning of authority in the Christian community. With a few brief words, Jesus challenges everyone in authority to understand leadership as an opportunity for self-giving service. His statement applies to everyone in authority in the Church, but also to Christians in government, to administrators in business, to teachers in classrooms, to parents in families. Everyone on that list knows that those roles give endless opportunities for service and self-giving, and contain plenty of potential for self-serving and domination. Not everyone fills those roles in the spirit of Jesus, but everyone in authority must reflect on the implications of this magnificent statement about Christian leadership.

Then Jesus goes on to describe the meaning of his life in one sentence, here presented in an adapted translation:

Mk 10:45 *The Son of Man came not to be served but to be Servant,*
and to give his life as a ransom for many.

The word ‘ransom’ had been used for a thousand years by the Jewish people to describe what God had done for them. They spoke consistently of God as their redeemer who had set them free from oppression at the time of Moses, and who had continued to set them free in many ways through the centuries. Earlier in this book, in our discussion of the fundamental faith of the Jewish people, we connected the word ‘salvation’ with this action of God, who forms a covenant bond with us human beings, offers people love and invites love in return, teaches us how to live as faithful people of God, and leads us towards wholeness whereby we are true to ourselves and to our Creator.

Jesus understands the gift of his life – not just his death, but his whole life – to be continuing the redeeming action of God, leading us to wholeness, saving us by the power of love. He truly intends to give his life to set people free.

There is one other word that must be explored in this great self-declaration of Jesus: servant. We can't understand that term unless we are familiar with the great poems about the servant of God in the book of the prophet Isaiah. Those poems describe a servant, chosen and loved by God, who is scorned and persecuted and even killed – and then vindicated, as people realize that God was always with the servant, and that somehow, through the servant's suffering, the people are made whole. Is 52:13–53:12

The poems in Isaiah had not been part of the messianic hope in the Jewish tradition, but one can imagine Jesus sitting down with his closest friends and saying to them, "If you really want to know how I understand my mission, don't read only the prophecies about a great new king from the line of David. Read also the poems about the servant of God in the book of Isaiah.... For the Son of Man has come not to be served, but to be servant, and to give his life to set people free."

E. The Culminating Revelation: The Death of Jesus

Five long chapters in the Gospel of Mark are devoted to a detailed account of the last week of Jesus' life. The importance of these narratives for the early Christians is clear: if they were going to claim that Jesus is good news for the world, they would have to explain why his mission had led to such an untimely and paradoxical conclusion. They were proud to proclaim that the death of Jesus expressed the meaning of his life, and gives meaning to ours.

The details of the extended narrative are familiar to most Christians. It might be of value to point out the subdued style of the accounts. Even in reporting this particularly brutal form of execution, there is no morbid emphasis in the gospels on pain and blood. In this respect, the gospels are much more dignified than the medieval stations of the cross. It is true that the gospels tell of the customary flogging, and of the crowning with thorns, but nowhere in the gospels is it reported that Jesus fell while he was carrying the cross through the city. The story of Simon, a visitor from North Africa who was yanked out of the crowd to help Jesus, is part of the gospel narrative, but there is no story of a woman who wipes Jesus' face and whose cloth then reveals his picture. There is no mention that he met his mother on the way

to Calvary. In fact, the gospel accounts don't even state that Jesus was nailed to the cross, except that this (quite plausible) detail
Jn 20:25 appears in a resurrection narrative in the Gospel of John. (Pope John Paul II proposed a new series of Stations of the Cross, based exclusively on the gospel narratives.)

Each episode in every gospel deserves careful reflection, but our brief discussion here will focus only on the climactic scene of the death of Jesus – the most important moment in the Gospel according to Mark.

1. *Jesus' Cry from the Cross*

Mk 15:25-35 According to Mark, Jesus hung on the cross for six hours, wordlessly accepting the taunts of his fellow victims and of the scornful citizens of Jerusalem. As he neared death, he spoke only one line, which was so disturbing that the gospel writer recorded it in Jesus' native Aramaic, and then translated it into Greek for his readers:

Mk 15:34 *"Eloi, Eloi, lema sabachthani?"*
"My God, my God, why have you forsaken me?"

It must have been an unforgettable moment for people who would later continue to be followers of Jesus. As he was dying, he cried out that he felt abandoned by God, that he could not get in touch with God, that he felt alone. Far from the peaceful picture
Lk 23:27-43 Luke paints of Jesus dying while dispensing blessings from the cross, Mark's portrayal of the death of Jesus depicts a frightening moment of abandonment and horror. And yet, as we saw in Chapter 12, we must consider these words in the context of the entire Psalm 22:

My heart is like wax; it is melted within my breast;
my mouth is dried up like a potsherd,
Ps 22:14-15 *and my tongue sticks to my jaws…*

With some impatience, the poet prays for God to set him free from his tormentors:

Why are you so far from helping me?…
Ps 22:1-2 *I cry by day, but you do not answer…*

Towards the end of the psalm, a kind of peace and confidence returns, along with the sense that God is in control of history, and that

Future generations will be told about the Lord,
and proclaim his deliverance to a people yet unborn… Ps 22:30-31

No doubt the whole psalm, including the closing lines of hope, was in Jesus' mind when he spoke his dying words.

2. *"Truly This Man Was God's Son!"*

The culminating moment in the Gospel according to Mark is found Mk 15:39
in the words of a Roman soldier who had witnessed Jesus' final hours, and had heard his final cry. (He could not, however, have seen the curtain of the Temple torn in two, as it was far away on Mk 15:38
the other side of Jerusalem. The Christian writer is showing that the Old Covenant is over; the New Covenant has begun.)

Seeing Jesus die in that horrifying way, the Roman soldier, who was presumably a pagan and not a Jew, makes the profound act of faith that forms the triumphant conclusion of Mark's gospel.

For Mark, this statement expresses the Christian community's faith in Jesus 40 years after his death. The gospel began with a Mk 1:1
table of contents: the author declared that he would convince the reader that Jesus is good news, the one Anointed to fulfill Jewish hopes, and the Son of God – the presence of God among us, living a single human life. With the declaration of the Roman soldier, the author rests his case: "Now you know what I mean. Jesus is truly God's Son."

This climactic statement is a challenge to the modern reader. How could anyone looking at Jesus dying in such a fashion perceive his divinity?

Children confronted with that question often give very thoughtful answers: "Maybe the soldier could tell that Jesus gave his life for us." "Because Jesus died for what he believed in." "Because Jesus loved us and his death showed it." Such answers come very close to the intention of the author of Mark. People in his community, facing persecution and living in fear, wanted God to be the wonder-worker, to act with power to rescue them from the grief of their lives. But God's role is not wish-fulfillment, says Mark. God is not going to take away the hard things in your life. Look at Jesus. We believe that Jesus was the living presence of God among us, but you can perceive Jesus' divinity not only in his healings, but in his death. The God whom Jesus taught us to know is not like Santa Claus, the kind of god whom we might invent for ourselves. Rather, God is truly revealed in the integrity and self-giving love of the dying Jesus. For Mark, Jesus showed us what God is really like more by the way he died than by his miracles or even his resurrection.

The resurrection narrative in Mark is anti-climactic. One brief narrative describes three women who find the tomb empty on Sunday morning, are told that Jesus is risen, and are given the mission to tell his disciples to go back to Galilee and await his appearance.

Mk 16:8 *They went out and fled from the tomb,*
for terror and amazement had seized them;
and they said nothing to anyone, for they were afraid.

Most biblical scholars agree that verses 9 to 20 of the last chapter were added to the original manuscript of Mark because it felt incomplete. It seems quite possible that the author of this paradoxical gospel intended to conclude with the troubling scene of the women who were the first to know that Jesus had risen.

17

MATTHEW AND LUKE

Distinctive Gospels in the Synoptic Tradition

Chapter 16 examined the good news of Jesus as it was presented in the Gospel according to Mark. This chapter will introduce Matthew and Luke, the other two synoptic gospels. Both used Mark as a source, adding materials and insights of their own.

The purpose of this chapter is briefly to indicate the distinctive characteristics of Matthew and Luke, so that readers may begin to notice the differences in each gospel when reading or listening to them.

The Gospel According to Matthew

Authorship

Most mainstream scholars agree that the author of the 'first gospel' Mt 9:9
was not the former tax collector who is known as Levi in the Mk 2:14
other gospels, and who is identified as Matthew only in this gospel. Instead, this gospel likely records the faith of a Christian community more than 50 years after the resurrection of Jesus, in an era when very few people lived to be more than 50 years old. If the author had been an eyewitness and a friend of Jesus', why would he have copied the Gospel of Mark as the basis of his accounts of the life of Jesus instead of using his own memories?

So who was the author, then? And how did the names of certain disciples (Matthew, Mark, Luke, John) become attached to the four gospels?

Perhaps, in the first decades after the resurrection, a friend of Jesus' named Matthew came to preach in a certain town, and began to build a Christian community. The disciple recounted as much as he could about the memorable events in Jesus' life, nurtured the community and responded to questions. When he left for another village, that community had the Gospel according to Matthew in oral form.

The neophyte Christian community would have treasured the good news, retold the stories time after time for decades, orally reshaped the Gospel according to Matthew to the needs of their members, and grown in their understanding of the meaning of Jesus' ministry. Over the years, some members of the community may have written down some of these stories of Jesus. After the year 70, a copy of the Gospel according to Mark may have come into the community; also circulating among the Christian churches was a written collection of the sayings of Jesus, most of which Mark had not reported.

Eventually, perhaps 50 years after Matthew's first preaching of the gospel in that town, an educated member of the community may have decided to write a gospel using Mark, the sayings from Q, and some other written material, as well as the oral tradition that had developed in that community. Drawing on his own faith and skill as a writer, he produced the Gospel according to Matthew as we know it today.

The Community in Which the Gospel Was Created

Matthew's community seems to have included many Christians of Jewish heritage, as well as Gentiles. Jesus' relationship to the Jewish tradition is a major theme throughout the gospel: he is portrayed as a new Moses – greater than Moses himself. Jesus comes out of Egypt, escaping from a powerful ruler who tried to kill him as a child. In the Sermon on the Mount (which is found only in Matthew), Jesus proclaims the new law from a new mountain to a new people of God. His teachings are gathered into five collections, probably to match the five books of Torah; Jesus' role is repeatedly described as "to fulfill what was written in the prophets."

While the community is deeply concerned about establishing that Jesus is the fulfillment of Jewish hopes, it is also open-minded enough to realize that the reign of God is not confined to people
Mt 2:1-12 of Jewish heritage. That recognition is expressed in the story of the sages who travelled from far away to pay their respects to the infant Jesus, in Jesus' remark about the Roman centurion ("Truly,

in no one in Israel have I found such faith"), and in the great Mt 8:10
commission that concludes the gospel: "Go and make disciples Mt 28:18-20
of all nations...."

The Flow of the Gospel of Matthew

After two chapters about the childhood of Jesus, the main body of the gospel is divided into five sections. In each section, a few chapters of narrative lead to a collection of sayings of Jesus. The gospel concludes with a detailed narrative of the last week of Jesus' life and the stories of the resurrection. Let's look at the five great discourses or collections of sayings found in the Gospel of Matthew.

a) The Sermon on the Mount (Chapters 5–7)

This famous series of teachings is a beautiful description of the Christian way of life, proclaimed by Jesus as the Law of the new covenant. No one thinks it is a record of a sermon Jesus preached one afternoon; instead, it is a collection of some of his teachings on the theme of morality – the Christian way of life. It begins
with the beatitudes, in which Jesus pronounces blessings on the Mt 5:3-12
poor in spirit, the mourners, the meek and the merciful. Then follows a strong exploration of the relationship between Jesus' teaching and the Law of Moses, a discussion that emphasizes both that the Law is still to be revered and that Jesus' authoritative
teaching goes beyond it and fulfills it. (We will discuss the 'six Mt 5:17-48
antitheses,' in which Jesus contrasts his teaching with six traditional laws, in Chapter 20, on the moral wisdom of Jesus.)

Chapter 6 of Matthew's gospel deals with sincerity in prayer Mt 6:9-13
and piety; his version of the Lord's Prayer is the centrepiece of the chapter. Chapter 7 includes a number of loosely connected
moral teachings, among which the most famous has become Mt 7:12
known as 'the golden rule.' The sermon concludes with the challenge to be doers of the word, and not just hearers.

b) The Disciple as Missionary (Chapter 10)

After two chapters in which Jesus shows the kingdom of God in action by healing a number of people, he chooses his inner circle of twelve disciples and sends them forth to preach the good news. His advice to the missionaries is found in Chapter 10. While some

of what he says is reassuring, most of it is based on the realization that their preaching will cause conflict and tension, in their own families and among the people they meet. "I am sending you out
Mt 10:16 like sheep into the midst of wolves," he says.

c) The Parables of the Kingdom (Chapter 13)

As we shall see in more detail in Chapter 19, on parables, the predominant theme of the parables collected here is that the reign of God is an initiative taken by God. It will inevitably bring great results; nothing can stop it. While we must seize the opportunity and accept the gift of God and live in its spirit, the overwhelming feeling is one of great joy.

d) The Charter of the New Community (Chapter 18)

The Gospel of Matthew places more emphasis on community life than the other gospels. The word 'church' is used only three times in all the gospels, and only in Matthew. Most familiar to Roman
Mt 16:18 Catholic readers may be Jesus' saying to Peter that "on this rock I will build my church," but the extended collection of sayings in Chapter 18 is an insightful reflection on community life.

The chapter begins by saying that a truly Christian community will be characterized by its concern for its weakest members. It is here that Matthew has placed sayings about the need for everyone to become like little children, and to avoid scandalizing the 'little
Mt 18:12-14 ones.' Here, too, we find the parable about the shepherd who leaves 99 sheep in search of the one that is lost.

The middle section of the chapter deals with conflict in the community. The earliest Christian communities were not perfect: the first followers of Jesus had disagreements just as we do. The Gospel of Matthew proposes a rather structured series of steps by
Mt 18:15-20 which the community can handle conflict, and recognizes that if the process fails, a disruptive member may need to be ejected from the group.

The concluding third section of the charter of the new community is a brilliant antidote to the sober realism of the previous paragraphs. The gospel tells us that what holds every community together is forgiveness. Here we find Jesus' great saying
Mt 18:21-22 in response to Peter's request for a limit: "How often should I forgive?" Jesus' ideal answer is that there is no limit. While we

can't always live up to his ideals – an issue we will discuss in Chapter 20, on the moral wisdom of Jesus – we need to try. Jesus supports his words with a forceful parable making the point that
God cannot forgive any of us "if you do not forgive your brother Mt 18:35
or sister from your heart."

e) The End-Time (Chapters 24–25)

As Jesus moves inexorably towards his death, Matthew portrays him in conflict with the religious leaders of Jerusalem in a series of sayings and actions, culminating in the ferocious diatribe against the hypocrisy of the scribes and Pharisees in Chapter 23. Chapters 24 and 25 are sometimes called the synoptic apocalypse – a collection of sayings about the future. It is unclear whether the sayings refer to the destruction of the Temple and the city (which had already happened when Matthew was written), the return of the Son of Man (was the destruction of Jerusalem a partial fulfillment of that expectation?), or the end of human history. We have a different perspective on the final fulfillment now, after 20 centuries of waiting, and see such sayings of Jesus about the future as poetic rather than literal.

The section concludes with "the last judgment" – a symbolic scene found nowhere else in the New Testament – when Jesus' great moral teaching about concern for the poor and the disadvantaged is outlined through a scene of judgment. Jesus accepts one group of people into the reign of God and rejects
another, because "just as you did not do it to one of the least of Mt 25:45
these, you did not do it to me." This chapter (combined with other sayings in the gospel) led Christian Europeans to see salvation as an earned reward rather than as a gift of God, and played on believers' fear and guilt. It instilled profound fear in the hearts of guilt-ridden believers for centuries; it also inspired some of the great art of western Europe, from Dante's *Inferno* to Michelangelo's magnificent fresco on the front wall of the Sistine Chapel. It is certainly a profound and challenging expression of one aspect of the teaching of Jesus, but it should be seen in the balancing perspective of Jesus' equally strong teaching about God's saving and forgiving love for all.

The Gospel According to Luke

The Gospel according to Luke has remarkably different preoccupations than Mark and Matthew.

Authorship

There has never been any suggestion that the author of Luke ever met Jesus. Even the traditional theories about authorship acknowledged that Luke was at best a second- or third-generation Christian (i.e., the eyewitnesses are the first generation of Christians; the people they spoke to are the second generation; the people the second generation told are the third generation. Neither Luke, Mark nor Paul were eyewitnesses of the ministry of Jesus.)

Scholars agree that the author of Luke also wrote the Acts of the Apostles, the fifth book of the New Testament, which portrays the history of the early Christian communities and the great missionary career of Paul. There is significantly more debate, however, about whether the author was the friend of Paul's
Philem 1:24 identified as Luke in the brief letter to Philemon (and mentioned
Col 4:14 in two other letters that may have been written after Paul's death).
2 Tim 4:11 The author of Luke and Acts shows no knowledge of any of the letters of Paul, and portrays Paul's thought in a way that doesn't fit with what we know of Paul from his letters. Most likely, Luke and Acts were written in the 80s (or later), 20 years after Paul's death, by someone who knew Jesus and Paul in a community of faith, but not in person.

Like the author of Matthew, Luke used the Gospel of Mark as a source, along with a collection of sayings of Jesus (Q), some other written material (e.g., the stories about Jesus' birth and childhood), and traditions preserved orally in that community.

The Community in Which the Gospel Was Created

The author of Luke was apparently familiar with Jewish tradition, but his community was not Jewish. The author had to explain Jewish customs to his readers repeatedly. His sense of Jesus' greatness is much more attuned to a philosophical ideal of humanity than to the fulfillment of the hopes of Judaism. Most likely the community was predominantly Gentile; the author's central purpose is to proclaim that Jesus is the saviour of all the world.

The Flow of the Gospel of Luke

Many observers perceive a geographical structure in Luke-Acts,
with Jerusalem being the focal point to which the good news was
addressed at first, and from which it burst out into all the nations
of the world. According to Luke, Jesus visited Jerusalem twice as
a child. His adult ministry began in Galilee. Halfway through his
ministry, "he set his face to go to Jerusalem," where the climactic Lk 9:51
events of his life were to occur.

Acts of the Apostles begins in Jerusalem, where the risen Jesus
tells the disciples, "You will be my witnesses in Jerusalem, in all Acts 1:8
Judea and Samaria, and to the ends of the earth." The Spirit of
God transforms the disciples in Jerusalem, and Acts tells of their
years of missionary work, concluding with the scene of Paul
preaching "with all boldness and without hindrance" in Rome, Acts 28:31
the capital of the Empire. There is no mention that Paul would
soon be executed there.

The Portrait of Jesus in Luke

Luke's portrait of Jesus has heavily influenced popular ideas of what kind of person Jesus was. Through the ages, many people have not been attracted by Mark's volatile, emotional portrait of Jesus. Others weren't interested in Matthew's picture of Jesus in dialogue with Jewish hopes. But people of all times have cherished Luke's portrait of Jesus as the compassionate, calm, gentle, forgiving, philosophically ideal human.

To begin near the end, only in Luke does Jesus heal the ear of Lk 22:51
one of the people who came to arrest him; only in Luke does
Jesus forgive his killers while he is dying on the cross; only in Lk 23:34
Luke does he promise paradise to one of his fellow victims; only Lk 23:43
in Luke does he end his life not with the cry that God has
abandoned him, but with a prayer: "Father, into your hands I Lk 23:46
commend my spirit."

Those examples are consistent with Luke's portrayal of Jesus. Lk 10:30-37
Only Luke includes the parables of the Good Samaritan, the Lk 15:11-32
Prodigal Son, and the Pharisee and the Tax Collector, three Lk 18:9-14
magnificent statements about the Christian way of life and the
compassion of God.

Jesus is presented in Luke as a prayerful person. He prays at
his baptism before setting out on his ministry; he prays before Lk 3:21-23
choosing his inner circle of twelve; he prays before moments of Lk 6:12-13

Lk 9:18-20 self-revelation; he prays before he is arrested, and he prays while
Lk 9:28-31 dying. The prayer of Jesus is often linked to the influence of the
Lk 22:41-43 Holy Spirit: when Jesus prays, things happen. Prayer results in
Lk 23:46 action.

Luke portrays Jesus' friendship with women, which was revolutionary in his patriarchal society. The gospel begins by giving Mary the central role in the stories of Jesus' childhood, with attention also given to Elizabeth (the mother of John the Baptist) and the prophet Anna. Later, Jesus brings back to life the only
Lk 7:11-17 son of a widow, defends a woman who has entered without
Lk 7:36-50 invitation a Pharisee's house where Jesus was dining and debating,
Lk 10:38-42 and supports his friend Mary, who preferred to think about
religious questions rather than do housework. Only in Luke is
Lk 15:8-9 the parable of the woman who searches for her lost coin told
alongside the parable of the shepherd who searches for his single
Lk 8:1-3 lost lamb. Women are the friends and financial supporters of Jesus;
Lk 23:27 they grieve while he carries his cross through the city and they
Lk 23:55 stay with him until his death. Women are also the first witnesses
Lk 24:10-11 to the resurrection.

One final important theme in Luke is Jesus' concern for the poor and marginalized, and his demanding challenge to everyone to break free of the grip of money.

> *"Blessed are you who are poor,*
> *for yours is the kingdom of God.*
> *Blessed are you who are hungry now,*
> *for you will be filled…*
> *But woe to you who are rich,*
> *for you have received your consolation.*
> Lk 6:20-26 *Woe to you who are full now, for you will be hungry."*

In Luke, the beatitudes are not about poverty in spirit. Luke portrays Jesus as announcing that the reign of God has come to people who are literally poor and hungry: this is the promised time that they have been waiting for. And he pronounces woes against people who are rich and satisfied. Every time Luke records Jesus telling people to sell everything or give up everything for the reign of God, Luke's quotation is invariably harder and more demanding than the same saying in other gospels. Many think that in this regard, Luke has captured the spirit of Jesus more accurately than the other gospel writers:

"If you lend to those from whom you hope to receive,
what credit is that to you?
But love your enemies, do good, and lend,
expecting nothing in return." Lk 6:34-35

Only in Luke do we find the parable of the rich fool who built bigger and bigger storehouses, only to die that very night. And only Luke has recorded the parable of Lazarus and the Rich Man who lives a sumptuous life without even noticing Lazarus lying at his gates – until their roles are reversed in the great hereafter. Lk 12:16-21 Lk 16:19-31

Luke's version of the good news of Jesus is distinctive from Mark's and Matthew's, even though the three share a great deal of material. The differences in theme and spirit in the gospels are all rich sources of inspiration for us. Each has interpreted the message of Jesus in its own way. Each is faithful to our Saviour, but no one gospel exhausts the amazing depth and wealth of his teaching.

18

THE REIGN OF GOD AND THE MIRACLES OF JESUS

The Reign of God

Mk 1:14 *"The kingdom of God has come near."*

Lk 17:21 *"The kingdom of God is among you."*

Mt 12:28 *"If it is by the Spirit of God that I cast out demons,*
then the kingdom of God has come to you."

Lk 6:20 *"Blessed are you who are poor,*
for yours is the kingdom of God."

Mt 13:44 *"The kingdom of heaven is like treasure hidden in a field…"*

Which teaching of Jesus was most important to Jesus himself?

Many people might respond that Jesus' moral instruction was the heart of his teaching – the importance of love, or "Do unto others…." But a brief study of the gospels will quickly convince any perceptive reader that Jesus devoted most of his teaching and ministry to describing the kingdom of God. He announced the
Mk 1:14 coming of God's kingdom at the beginning of his ministry. Numerous parables were specifically directed to explaining the meaning of the phrase. Most importantly, Jesus taught people to understand his miracles as examples of God's kingdom in action.

Yet the phrase 'kingdom of God' has regrettably little impact on the modern reader. If the concept was so important to Jesus, we need to try to understand it better.

1. *The Reign of God: God's Action in Our Lives*

The reign of God is God's loving initiative to make us whole.

Even though it may be more abstract, commentators have been using the term 'reign' in recent years, rather than 'kingdom,' to describe Jesus' most common proclamation. 'Reign' expresses the meaning of Jesus' teaching more accurately; it speaks of God's influence in people's lives. 'Reign' also sounds less political than 'kingdom' and is gender-inclusive.

The reign of God is the action of God in our lives. Jesus proclaimed that God offers to take over our lives: to reign in our hearts, to transform us, to enable us to grow into wholeness and to love generously and to be true to ourselves – and in that way to be faithful to God. A parallel term for the reign of God is salvation: "God saves us" means "God makes us whole." The reign of God is something God does for us. This is truly good news. It is not something we accomplish on our own or something we earn; it is God's gift.

As we shape our lives by our decisions, as we seek to be free and happy and loving and fully human, Jesus offers us the power of God's love working within us, leading us to wholeness. What we must do, essentially, is accept the offer: open our lives to the transforming action of God and allow God to reign in our hearts.

Such an understanding of life is religious rather than scientific; it is to be believed rather than proven or measured.

2. *The Reign of God Is Communal*

In order to understand how God acts among us, we must recognize that no one grows to wholeness alone. All of us are indispensable to each other's salvation. To be true to ourselves involves seeing the needs of others, giving ourselves in love, acting together to bring the reign of God to others. In that sense, the reign of God exists not in a collection of individuals, but in the community of believers.

Friendship is thus a privileged vehicle of the reign of God. People who marry become part of each other's story of salvation. Whether they stay married forever or not, they are forever part of each other's journey towards wholeness. Parents bring the reign of God into the lives of their children, and children bring the reign of God into the lives of their parents.

Every believer depends on the community for support on the journey. We are the Church, and we all help each other to grow by expressing our faith, by seeking deeper understanding in the context of a supportive tradition, by praying together, by challenging each other to live in a way worthy of disciples, by mourning and rejoicing together, and by forgiving each other. No one journeys alone in the reign of God.

3. *The Reign of God Is Now…and Not Yet*

Most of Jesus' teachings about the reign of God (including those at the beginning of this chapter) speak of God's action in people's lives now. The reign of God is already within us.

Jesus promised that God's love for us will continue beyond our deaths, but did not emphasize life beyond death in his teaching. Many believers associate the phrase 'kingdom of God,' and especially 'kingdom of Heaven,' with life after death. Because of the Jewish tradition's great reverence for the name of God, the word 'Heaven' was often used to replace 'God.' Thus 'kingdom of Heaven' means 'the kingdom that comes to us from heaven' – the reign of God in our hearts now.

Mt 25:31 We look forward with hope to a future fulfillment that is
Jn 6:44 described by a variety of images other than 'kingdom of Heaven':
Rev 21:1-4 "The Son of Man will come in glory"; "I will raise you up on the
last day"; there will be "a new heaven and a new earth." (Chapter 26 will discuss our hope for life everlasting in more detail.)

Jesus taught us how to live, not how to get ready to die. His proclamation of the reign of God emphasized the powerful, generous, saving action of God in our lives. Jesus invites us to open our hearts to the reign of God…right now.

The Miracles of Jesus

What should be our central focus when we reflect on the miracles of Jesus? When we were growing up, most of us were taught to focus on the greatness of Jesus himself – that he was kind and helpful to people who were suffering, and that he had amazing powers, unlike anyone in our world. Regrettably, such a focus caused many of us to think of Jesus as a superhero, very different from us and from anyone we know.

Jesus himself declared that he healed people not to draw attention to himself, but to show everyone that "the reign of God is at hand." The miracles are to be seen as signals that God is at work, as examples of the reign of God in action. In a visible way, they show what happens to people when God takes over in their lives: people become whole.

1. *What Is a Miracle?*

When two lonely people meet and discover that they were meant for each other, could that be a miracle? When a life is unexpectedly saved, could that be a miracle? Is it a miracle when people escape across the sea from oppression into freedom, whether by sailing across the South China Sea with 25 people in a leaky rowboat, or by walking across a 'Sea of Reeds' where the pursuing chariots cannot follow?

The significant point about miracles isn't that only God could do it, or that it is an event that goes beyond nature (as we understand nature), but rather that these events give new meaning to people's lives.

When people interpret events in a religious way, they perceive the presence of God in their lives: God who loves us as we are; God who enables us to find meaning in our lives and grow towards wholeness, no matter what happens to us. If someone enters the next phase of her life after a heart bypass with a new outlook, sees her additional years of life as a gift, seeks to devote more of life to the most important human endeavours, surely she is right to say, "That operation was a miracle!" What happened is not beyond the boundaries of nature; it was done by a skilled team of medical professionals, not by the action of God.

Events can be miracles, even if the causes of the event are explainable. But such events can only be called miraculous if people perceive the hand of God in their lives.

Was Jesus a miraculous healer? There is a great deal of evidence that he healed people in a way that no one could explain. Because there are so many miracle narratives in the gospels, it is hard to believe that they are mere inventions. Some modern observers would claim that Jesus healed people through the power of suggestion, mind power, helping people believe they could heal themselves. If one accepts the point of view expressed above, such explanations pose no problem: we don't have to prove that the healings were beyond what is natural, we don't have to prove that only God could do it. We can easily accept the idea that many other people have been known as healers throughout history, some of them even in the Bible.

The key point about the miracle stories is that people saw the hand of God in their lives as a result of Jesus' interventions. Anyone who sees nothing but the physical results in a miracle story (the blind see, the lame walk) has missed the point. Jesus wanted people to see the depth of the meaning of what he did. He wanted people to realize that the reign of God was bursting into the world to make them whole. When a leper was healed, the miracle was not simply that his skin condition got better; more important, his deep hopelessness and alienation from society were overcome by new hope, self-esteem, friendship and love. The reign of God had taken over his life.

2. *The Healing Miracles: God Acts to Bring Wholeness*

Mk 1:40 If you were diagnosed with leprosy in Jesus' society, you didn't just have a skin disease. Your life was over. Imagine the despair of the man in Mark's gospel on the day he was told he had leprosy: he would have been rushed out of town without even having a chance to say goodbye to his wife and children; he could never work again. He had to live in a camp outside the town, with other people whose only hope was to die. The only way they could get food would be from people who would throw it to them. The day that man was told he had leprosy, his family considered it the day of his death, and lived their lives as if he no longer existed.

Mk 1:40-45 And imagine the feelings of the man when he approached Jesus, who was getting a reputation as a healer in the villages of Galilee. Mark's narrative contains several precious details: Jesus responds with emotion to the man's distress. No cool and distant hero, Jesus reacts to the pain of the people he meets. Further, he knows how to help in a sensitive way: he reaches out and puts his hand on the leper's shoulder. The onlookers gasp and move back. A surge of electric hope passes through the man's body. How long has it been since anyone touched him? And he is made whole.

As well as curing the symptoms of skin disease, Jesus was restoring the man's humanity: he could kiss his wife and children again, return to his job, have friends, go to synagogue. Here is a classic story of a person whose life had been destroyed by illness and social exclusion, and who experienced the true meaning of rebirth. This is what happens when God reigns in a person's life: the person becomes whole.

In another narrative, while Jesus is on his way to restore life Lk 8:43-48
to a girl who has died, a woman in the crowd courageously helps herself by reaching out to touch his cloak. She, too, has been isolated by society's attitudes: because she has been hemorrhaging for years, she and anyone she touches are considered unclean. She breaks the rules, shakes off the shackles of oppression, reaches out for help – and is rewarded. "Take heart," says Jesus; "Your faith has made you well." (or 'whole'; the original Greek says, 'Your faith has saved you.')

Our challenge in reading the miracle narratives is to find ourselves in each story. In some way, *we* are the outcast, *we* are the person in chronic pain, *we* are the person who needs vision, *we* are the bereaved. God offers to bring wholeness into our lives – perhaps not by taking away the pain, but by enabling us to deal with it, to find meaning, to grow towards wholeness as free human beings. In that way, the reign of God is upon us.

3. *Miracles of Vision*

Some blind people today feel doubly disabled when they are taught that the Bible equates their physical condition with darkness of soul or lack of insight. They have no access to a miraculous healer, and know that they must live in physical darkness. Their challenge is to live as fully as possible, to live lives full of wisdom and love, to become truly whole. The reign of God lives in them, though they remain blind.

The stories where Jesus heals blind people are symbolic of all our lives, whether we are sighted or not, as we move from darkness into light, seeing life in a new way, opening our eyes and our hearts to the reign of God. We will look at three remarkable miracles that explore this theme.

The first concludes the first half of the Gospel according to Mark. The episode is set immediately before the mid-gospel scene
of 'assessment,' when Jesus asks the disciples about the crowd's Mk 8:27-33
reaction to him, and then asks, "Who do you say that I am?" Later, he warns them that his ministry will result in his violent death.

Just before that scene in the Gospel of Mark, some people bring a blind man to Jesus. Jesus leads him by the hand outside
Mk 8:22-26 the village, puts saliva on his eyes, lays hands on him, and asks, "Can you see anything?" The man's remarkable response is, "I can see people, but they look like trees walking." Jesus keeps working; this time, the man "saw everything clearly."

Mark is using the story at this point in the gospel for a symbolic purpose: believers will often progress slowly as they grow to recognize and accept the reign of God. The assessment scene that follows this miracle narrative shows the crowds recognizing that Jesus is from God, but not realizing his true greatness; they need better sight. Jesus' friends perceive his role a little more accurately – but they, too, will need further clarification before they can see clearly. Like them, all of us understand our lives to some extent in the light of our faith, but all of us have plenty of growing to do before we see with perfect clarity.

Later in the gospel, we meet Bartimaeus, the blind beggar of
Mk 10:46-52 Jericho. When he heard that Jesus was passing his station, he began to shout for attention. Bystanders urged him to shut up, so he shouted all the louder. When Jesus responded, the irrepressible Bartimaeus threw off his cloak, jumped up and ran towards the healer's voice. Jesus asked him – as Jesus asks all of us – "What do you want me to do for you?" The blind man asked for vision. Jesus remarked that what he had been given was wholeness. And the man "followed Jesus on the way" (an early Christian term for the disciples' way of life).

That story has been artfully situated at the end of the second section of Mark, immediately after Jesus' great declaration about
Mk 10:45 his mission in life: "The Son of Man came not to be served but to serve, and to give his life a ransom for many." "Now, dear reader," Mark implies, "you, too, can see more clearly – but, like Bartimaeus, you must take the initiative. Cry out for God's help!"

One other great narrative of the healing of a blind man, with a reflective exploration of the meaning of the event, occupies Chapter 9 of the Gospel of John. At the end of that chapter, the author uses clever wordplay about seeing and believing to propose that self-righteous people who think they see everything clearly are in fact the blind ones.

"We know that God has spoken to Moses, but as for this man, we do not know where he comes from.... Surely we are not blind, are we?" say the Pharisees.
"Now that you say, 'We see,' your sin remains," responds Jn 9:29, 40-41
Jesus.

The one who is open-minded enough to ask Jesus for insight is rewarded with clear self-revelation.

"Do you believe in the Son of Man?" Jesus asks the newly sighted man.
"Who is he, sir? Tell me, so that I may believe in him."
"You have seen him, and the one speaking with you is he." Jn 9:35-38
"Lord, I believe."

Similar understandings could be developed regarding miracles where Jesus enables people to hear, speak, walk and use their hands.

4. *Good Versus Evil: The Exorcisms*

In many narratives, Jesus demonstrates the coming of the reign of God by casting out demons from afflicted people.

Today, it is very unlikely that demonic possession would be the diagnosis in those cases. Two thousand years ago, when people were confronted with uncontrollable behaviour or a horrifying illness, they blamed evil spirits. When they knew the name of the
illness, they used it. Thus Mark's description of a boy's convulsions Mk 9:18
is called demon possession; Matthew describes similar symptoms Mt 17:14
and calls the illness epilepsy.

The exorcisms portray the coming of the reign of God as a cosmic struggle. The force of evil oppresses people, destroys their freedom, reduces them to a shadow of their true selves. The power of God sets people free, gives them the power to love, leads them
to wholeness. In Jesus' ministry, the power of God always wins. Mk 5:1-20//

Among the exorcism stories in the synoptic gospels is that of Mt 8:28//
a man who probably suffered from what today would be called Lk 8:26
manic behaviour. Treatment at the time involved chaining the man to tombstones, but he was so strong that he kept breaking the chains, and spent the nights and days howling on the mountains and bruising himself. After an interesting debate with the legion of demons, Jesus overpowers them and casts them into a nearby herd of pigs (this was in Gentile country). Soon the man

is in his right mind, sitting on the tombstones to which he used to be chained, chatting with people. Jesus advises him to "go home to your friends." This is a beautiful image of a person going from isolation and persecution to sanity and community: the reign of God has brought wholeness to his life.

Mk 7:24-30 The dramatic story of the Syro-Phoenician woman whose daughter was possessed by a demon may raise uneasy feelings in the reader's heart about one aspect of Jesus' attitudes. At issue is where the healing took place – the region of Tyre on the Mediterranean coast, in what we know as southern Lebanon. Jesus had apparently sought respite from the crowds by leaving his native land; the woman who accosted him was not Jewish, but a member of the great seafaring Phoenician nation. She knew of his fame and begged him to heal her daughter. Apparently Jesus was as yet unprepared to bring the reign of God beyond the Jewish
Mt 15:24 people. Matthew reports him saying, "I was sent only to the lost sheep of the house of Israel."

Both Matthew and Mark also report that Jesus said, "It is not fair to take the children's food and throw it to the dogs." In this sentence, the Jewish people are the children, and the gentiles are the dogs.

The story continues as a triumph for the offended mother. She responds by saying, "Even the dogs under the table eat the children's crumbs." Jesus rewards her persistence by healing her daughter.

This miracle was used in the early Christian community to make the point that Jesus did indeed bring the reign of God to everyone, and not only to Jewish people. In this episode, he not only defeats the power of evil, but does so for the nations – the world at large.

Mt 17:14-21// The story in Matthew of the epileptic boy is remarkable for
Mk 9:14-29// its detailed and accurate description of a convulsion, which people
Lk 9:37-42 saw as demonic possession. Mark tells us of a poignant dialogue between Jesus and the boy's father. One can feel the man's desperation when he says that his son has had convulsions near open fires and near streams – he thinks that the demon is trying to kill the boy. "But if you can do anything, have pity on us and help us," he says to Jesus. The poor father's cry is the cry of us all: "I do believe! Help my unbelief!"

The attention from the famous healer and the crowd causes the boy to have a convulsion; afterwards, he is unconscious, and seems like a corpse. The gospel writer has skillfully turned the reader's mind to death and resurrection.

5. *Miracles of Creative Power and Abundance*

Some of the miracle narratives go beyond the theme of healing as a sign of the wholeness brought by the reign of God. Sometimes called the nature miracles, these accounts portray Jesus as equal in power to the Creator God.

The creation narrative that begins the book of Genesis depicts a stormy sea as a symbol of chaos. By speaking words of creative power, God controls the waters and brings order out of chaos.

In the gospels, Jesus stops a raging storm with a word of Mt 8:26//
rebuke (in fact, an exorcism formula: it was thought that demons Mk 4:39// Lk 8:24
caused thunderstorms). On another occasion, Jesus walks across Mt 14:25//
the waves to join his friends in their fishing boat. Many Mk 6:48//
commentators wonder about the historical reliability of those Jn 6:19
narratives, because they seem to portray Jesus as drawing attention to himself. But as a Christian statement about the greatness of Jesus, their purpose is clear: just as the Creator God controlled the chaotic waters in the beginning, Jesus controls the seas. Jesus shares the creative power of God.

The other famous wonder of creative power and abundance Mt 15:32-38//
is Jesus' feeding of thousands of people with a few loaves and Mk 8:1-8
fish. This is the only miracle of Jesus to be reported in all four Mt 14:13-21// Mk 6:34-44//
gospels, and it appears in six versions. Lk 9:12-17//

This story depicts the greatness of the reign of God as 'the Jn 6:1-13
banquet of the Messiah' – a theme that has continued down through the centuries in the Eucharist.

By feeding his hungry followers, Jesus shows that the reign of God abundantly satisfies our deepest needs. Jesus nourishes people who are hungry for wholeness and hope. The reign of God not only fills our emptiness, it is so magnificently superabundant that baskets full of food are left over, available for anyone who needs to be strengthened.

Are these accounts historically reliable? Those who believe in Jesus know he could do such wonderful deeds. The real question is, would he? Are the nature miracles consistent with the kind of person we know Jesus to be?

Commentators rightly note that people of biblical times would not distinguish healing miracles from nature miracles: everything that Jesus did was seen as a sign of the hand of God, leading people towards wholeness.

Yet this group of miracles raises questions about historicity in many contemporary people's minds. Stopping a thunderstorm with a gesture or walking across the surface of a lake seem to call attention to Jesus himself, rather than to the reign of God.

It is possible that some of these stories developed in the early Christian communities. Jesus had spent his ministry proclaiming the reign of God. The early communities were interested in trying to understand who Jesus was. These narratives show symbolically that Jesus was equal in power to the Creator God; he could control the forces of nature.

Some commentators speculate that the calming of the storm may have developed as a symbolic story to reassure the early Christians as they faced perilous times: the Church, symbolized by the boat full of disciples, seems to be sinking in a storm of persecution. Yet Jesus is there with them; he has not deserted them.

The faith in Jesus expressed in the nature miracles is true faith. For Mark, Jesus' divinity is most clearly visible in the way he gave his life in integrity and love to set people free. The nature miracles express the community's faith in Jesus and the reign of God in a different way.

6. *The Final Enemy: Life Conquers Death*

The reign of God conquers even humanity's greatest fear: death.

In one dramatic scene, Jesus pushes his way through the mourners at a child's funeral, and restores to life the little girl who had died. The gospel writer, in a touch that speaks of authentic memory, gives us Jesus' words in Aramaic: "*Talitha, koum*," then translates, "Little girl, arise!"

Another time, Jesus meets a funeral procession on a road, and raises to life a young man who was his widowed mother's only son.

Perhaps the most famous narrative of Jesus' command over death is found in the Gospel of John, where Jesus restores life to his friend Lazarus, who had been dead for three days. The meaning of the event is expressed in the symbolic language of the gospel:

"Those who believe in me, even though they die, will live,
and everyone who lives and believes in me will never die." Mk 4:35-41//

The resurrection of Jesus is the most profound miracle of life over death, showing all believers that the power of God, the power of love, is stronger than death. That fundamental miracle of Christianity is discussed in more detail in Chapter 14.

Mt 8:23-27//
Lk 8:22-25

The reign of God, described by Jesus in word and in action, transforms our hearts, beginning before we are born and continuing after we die. It leads us towards wholeness and peace and fullness of life, and ultimately towards the complete union with God that is the deepest hope of every human heart.

19

THE PARABLES ABOUT THE REIGN OF GOD

By his healings, Jesus showed people how their lives could become whole when they allowed themselves to be transformed by the reign of God.

He also used stories to explain the reign of God. Parables convey a depth of meaning that cannot be reached by conceptual language. The most effective way to let Jesus speak to our hearts through a parable is to 'get into' the parable itself, and let it challenge us, face to face.

Parables may be broadly defined as any use of figurative
language to convey spiritual truth. Many parables are brief but
Mt 5:14 striking images: "A city built on a hill cannot be hid." Or "No one
Mt 5:15 after lighting a lamp puts it under the bushel basket, but on the
lampstand, and it gives light to all in the house." These two
parabolic sayings, set side by side in the Gospel of Matthew, are
designed to teach believers about their responsibility to proclaim
the reign of God. Another image on the same theme is more
Mt 10:16 sobering: "I am sending you out like sheep into the midst of
wolves." Each of these terse, hard-hitting sayings is an opportunity
to use our imaginations to understand more about the reign of
God in our lives.

Some parables are more extended figurative sayings; others are brief stories with a plot. Most likely Jesus told the parables and left his hearers to figure out the lesson of each one; later preachers have added interpretations of some of the parables in the gospel texts as we have them now.

Look for the Unexpected

The parables are often seen as pious stories, suitable for children, used to illustrate obvious truths that everyone takes for granted. The reality is quite the opposite. The parables, when confronted honestly, are often shocking and paradoxical. They teach something different from what everybody believes and practises – they challenge a comfortable, respectable way of life. In fact, one of the best methods of finding the meaning Jesus intended in a parable is to look for the hook, or focus on the unexpected, surprising element. Far from being easy to understand, the parables are sometimes too complex for children, and extremely challenging for adults.

A classic example is the parable of the labourers in the vineyard: the landowner gives the same pay to the workers Mt 20:1-15 whether they have worked all day or only an hour. Our society is so accustomed to the 'reward for merit' system that when we hear this story we shout, "That's not fair!" When you find yourself disagreeing with Jesus' point, you have indeed found the hook in the parable.

With this story, Jesus is proclaiming that the reign of God is pure gift; it is not about our concept of fairness; it is about God's generosity. We don't earn the gift; we are offered it, and either we accept it or we don't. We have no right to look at others and say that they don't deserve the gift. Jesus was harsh towards self-righteousness, and clear that the reign of God is God's action to lead us to wholeness – a gift that God offers to all.

The same challenge is proposed in the second half of the parable of the prodigal son, or the forgiving father. Many people Lk 15:25-32 would agree with the elder brother in the story, who complains that he never did anything wrong, and it's his irresponsible brother who is getting a big party. Jesus is saying that the older brother is mistaken. His protest is born of self-righteousness; he thinks he deserves a reward and his brother does not. Again, paradoxically, the reign of God is not about fairness; it is about the generous, all-forgiving love of God. No one has the right to protest that God is too generous to someone whom we may consider to be undeserving.

The Parables: Weapons in Controversy

Jesus believed in the persuasive power of parables so much that he used them to argue with his opponents, even when he was being attacked.

One memorable conflict was initiated by some scribes from Jerusalem who came to watch Jesus healing people in his home
Mk 3:22// territory. Afterwards, they announced their verdict: he was healing
Mt 12:22// by black magic. "He has Beelzebul, and by the ruler of the demons
Lk 11:14 he casts out demons," they said. Jesus was furious. He contradicted
the scribes forcefully, using three short parables.

"If a kingdom is divided against itself,
that kingdom cannot stand.
And if a house [i.e., a royal family] is divided against
itself, that house will not be able to stand...
No one can enter a strong man's house
and plunder his property
without first tying up the strong man;
Mk 3:24-27 *then indeed the house can be plundered."*

With those three comparisons, Jesus argues in the style of a rabbi to prove his opponents' accusations ridiculous.

What Jesus means is this: "If Beelzebul is helping me to cast out demons, that means that Satan is fighting Satan, and the kingdom of Satan is doomed. Is that what you think is happening? That's ridiculous. When I cast out demons, I'm plundering Satan's kingdom. A robber can't plunder a strong man's house unless the strong man is incapacitated. If I'm robbing Satan's house, you can be sure that I have defeated Satan."

According to Matthew and Luke, Jesus goes on to make a positive point about what he is doing: "But if it is by the Spirit of God that I cast out demons, *then the kingdom of God has come to*
Mt 12:28 *you.*" That was always the purpose of everything Jesus did: not to prove anything about himself, but to help people recognize the reign of God.

At the end of this episode, Jesus rages that the scribes' accusation is monstrous: they are looking at the action of God and calling it the action of Satan. That, says Jesus, is blasphemy against the Holy Spirit, and the speaker "will not be forgiven,
Mt 12:34 either in this age or in the age to come." Was he angry? That's when he used a parable!

Descriptions of the Action of God

Perhaps the most common misconception about the purpose of the parables is thinking of them as primarily directed towards moral teaching. Preachers and teachers often insist on drawing a moral out of the parables, but this isn't always what they're for. Most of the parables are intended to explain the reign of God – to show us what God is like, rather than tell us what we must do.

The beloved parable of the prodigal son, for example, is not intended to teach us that we must forgive. It is to teach us that God is always ready to forgive, like the father in the story.

That parable is found in Chapter 15 of the Gospel of Luke, Lk 15:11-24
again amidst a controversy. The religious establishment demands that Jesus justify his association with the outcasts of society. Jesus answers by telling three stories.

The first describes a shepherd who leaves 99 sheep to fend
for themselves to search for one stray animal. God is like the Lk 15:4-6
shepherd, says Jesus, and that is why I act as I do: like God, I reach out to the weakest ones, to help those who need it most. (In reading the parables in the Bible, try to notice exactly where the parable ends. Many scholars think that a verse of explanation, such as Luke 15:7, was not added by Jesus himself, but by later preachers.)

Next, Luke records the story of a woman who has lost a coin Lk 15:8-9
in her home, and who does not rest until she has found it. God is like the searching woman, says Jesus, and so am I when I spend time with outcasts.

Both parables describe the action of God. They are not intended to moralize, to tell us how we should live, but to help us realize and rejoice in the depth of God's love.

Perhaps more obvious descriptions of the action of God are
images like the mustard plant which, according to the parable, Mt 13:31-32
grows from a small seed to a large and hospitable tree. The reign of God may seem small and insignificant, but we can rely on the action of God: it cannot be stopped; it will grow.

The same point is made in the parable of the yeast. When Mt 13:34
you leave a little ball of dough in the bottom of a bowl for a while, covered by a cloth, something amazing happens. You return and whisk off the cloth and gasp, because now the little ball of dough fills the entire bowl. The reign of God is like that. It may start small, but it will surprise you by its growth, and it can't be

stopped. Even if you try to contain the dough with your fingers, it will inexorably push through them.

Surprisingly, the well-known parable of the sower is making
Mt 13:1-8// the same point. The moralizing on this parable started so long
Mk 4:1// ago, we have almost lost what many think was Jesus' original
Lk 8:4 meaning. Some scholars are convinced that the allegorical moralistic interpretation (e.g., beginning at Matthew 13:18) is not Jesus' intention (though he is presented as speaking it in all three synoptic gospels). Why do they say this? Jesus rarely used allegory (i.e., taking a story piece by piece, and giving a separate meaning to each piece). He used parables, and each parable is usually best understood as a unit: the whole story makes one point. (Only rarely is a parable double-barrelled: the parable of the prodigal son contains two stories – one about the father's kindness to the younger brother, the other about the older brother's self-righteousness – and each of them makes one point.)

The parable of the sower is not meant to teach several moral
Mt 13:18-22 lessons, such as "Don't be rootless like the seed on rocky ground; don't fall away if you face persecution; don't give in to the lure of wealth." Rather, its message is about the reign of God. Granted, there are obstacles to the growth of the reign of God, but the reign of God cannot be stopped. It will bring forth a great harvest – far greater than farmers could hope for in their wildest dreams. (A hundredfold return on a bushel of seed is unimaginable.)
Rom 8:23 Rejoice! "If God is for us, who is against us?"

Such parables about the action of God among us are intended to inspire us, to help us be happy, to give us confidence that the reign of God will bring about great results in our lives.

We Must Accept God's Invitation

Of course, many of the parables do make a moral point as well. They describe the Christian way of life and urgently demand a response from the hearer: What are you going to do, now that you are confronted with this offer from God?

The fundamental challenge is about accepting the reign of God: are you going to let God reign in your heart? If you do, your life will be transformed and you will grow towards wholeness. If you don't, you are refusing to follow the only way you can truly grow to be yourself. Jesus was not shy about the importance of the choice: if you reject me, he would say, you are choosing doom.

How good is the reign of God? It is like a treasure buried in a Mt 13:44
field. It is so great that someone who uncovers it is going to sell everything they own so they can buy the field to get the treasure. You are not supposed to worry about the ethics of deceiving the seller of the field; the parable's only point is that the reign of God is worth everything you've got – it's about the fundamental success of your life; it's about wholeness. But you must commit yourself to it. If you don't dedicate your entire life's resources to the treasure, you'll lose the opportunity. The treasure will stay buried forever.

Another parable that reminds us to make immediate decisions
is the story of the dishonest manager, a parable that has challenged Lk 16:1-8
preachers for centuries. In fact, the gospel offers at least five interpretations of Jesus' parable, likely the work of early preachers. In it, Jesus tells the story of a dishonest man who finds out that he is going to be fired. He rushes out to settle with his boss's debtors for less than they owe, so that they will owe him favours when he comes to them in future. Obviously, Jesus wasn't encouraging his followers to become embezzlers. His point is that there is one thing we should emulate in that crook's behaviour: in a crisis, he saw what he had to do, and he took immediate action. So must we, when confronted with the choice about the reign of God. We must not put off the decision. We must take action and accept the rule of God in our hearts.

The parable about the Pharisee and the tax collector empha- Lk 18:9-14a
sizes the importance of recognizing our need for God's saving power. Children, if they understand the parable at all, may be confused by it. The Pharisee is a good, devout, God-fearing, law-abiding person – and he is the villain here! Jesus disapproves of his lifestyle; he is too comfortable and self-righteous – just like so many of us who think of ourselves as respectable, church-going, God-fearing people. Jesus came to disturb the comfortable. We have to recognize our need to be saved – from our comfort and from our tendency to compare ourselves with others. If we really allow God to reign in our hearts, we will have to change. We must see ourselves in the hero of the parable: the tax collector at the back of the temple with eyes cast down, praying for mercy.

The parable of the Great Supper, as told by Luke, presents a Lk 14:16-24//
similar challenge. (Matthew's version of the parable has undergone Mt 22:1-13
significant evolution, as the tradition has turned the story into an allegory about the destruction of Jerusalem by the Romans.) In

Luke's version, which is probably closer to the original, Jesus makes one daring point: the reign of God is yours for the taking; all you have to do is accept the invitation. The story tells of a group of guests who have accepted a man's invitation for a great banquet, but who all, for whatever reason, make excuses and withdraw their acceptance on the very day of the feast. The homeowner holds the event anyway, and decides to admit anyone who will accept an invitation. One can imagine the group of derelicts and outcasts gaping as they are led into the magnificent banquet hall. The story confronts the reader with a critical choice: which group are you in – the people who refused the invitation, or the people who accepted it? The ones who accept are the people who, in some way, understand themselves to be among "the poor, the crippled, the blind and the lame." We have to recognize our need for salvation; only then will we allow God to reign in our hearts and lead us to wholeness.

One little-known parable, found in both Matthew and Luke, tells us that no excuses will be accepted: we must make up our minds and act immediately to accept God's gift of wholeness. The comment on the parable reported in both gospels gives us a remarkable glimpse into the type of accusations that Jesus had to face because his ministry upset some people:

"To what will I compare this generation?
Mt 11:15-17// *It is like children sitting in the marketplaces and calling to*
Lk 7:24 *one another,*
'We played the flute for you, and you did not dance;
we wailed, and you did not mourn.'"

In a teaching that could well be applied to many modern Christians, Jesus accuses his listeners of being like contrary children. You offer them an opportunity to do one thing, and they refuse; you offer them something totally different, and they refuse that also.

Jesus comments that John the Baptist led a demanding, ascetic life, and many people scorned him as a madman. Then Jesus came along, eating and drinking in a different house every evening as he travelled around the countryside, and many people scorned him as "a glutton and a drunkard, a friend of tax collectors and sinners." While the accusations against Jesus were undoubtedly false, it is surely true that meals were an indispensable part of this table fellowship that so frequently provided a context for his ministry.

The point of the brief parable remains: there can be no excuses, no refusals, no delaying tactics. We must decide to accept the transforming reign of God into our lives, and we must act now. If not, we are acting like the contrary children in the marketplace.

The Christian Way of Life

A classic expression of the implications of the Christian way of life is the parable of the Good Samaritan. It is told only in Luke, Lk 10:25-37
in connection with a lawyer's question about the greatest commandment in the Law of Moses. Jesus invites the lawyer to answer his own question: the man says that the two greatest commandments are to love God and to love one's neighbour. Jesus agrees with him. This man was probably a scholar of the Law of Moses, perhaps a Pharisee. The debate about the greatest commandment was a familiar one among Jewish thinkers. Jesus clearly agreed with the widely accepted point of view on this issue.

The lawyer goes on to ask Jesus, "Who is my neighbour?" This, too, was a familiar topic, for certain classes of people in society (e.g., foreigners, lepers, children) were customarily excluded.

Jesus responds not with a definition, but with a story. His parable explodes all the traditional exceptions. Samaritans were people of mixed race. The hero of the parable was someone who was scorned and rejected by his neighbours. To make the Samaritan the hero, and the priest and levite the villains of the story, was a challenging proposition.

"Who do you think deserves to be called a 'neighbour' now?" asks Jesus after the story. The lawyer chokes out a reply that does not include the hated word 'Samaritan': "The one who helped him, I suppose." "Go and do likewise," is Jesus' command to that man and to us.

Another well-known description of the Christian way of life is identified as a parable by many scholars: the 'Last Judgment' Mt 25:31-46
scene, in which "people will be separated from one another, as a shepherd separates the sheep from the goats." The basis of the separation in the parable has become a foundational expression of the type of behaviour that is expected of faithful followers of Jesus:

"I was hungry and you gave me food,
I was thirsty and you gave me something to drink,
I was a stranger and you welcomed me,
I was naked and you gave me clothing,
I was sick and you took care of me,
I was in prison and you visited me…
Truly I tell you,
just as you did it to one of the least of these
who are members of my family,
you did it to me."

One final challenging parable about the Christian way of life is that of the servant's reward. Jesus sets the scene in a wealthy landowner's dining room, and asks, "Which of you, if your slave comes in from plowing, or tending sheep in the field, would say, 'Come over here, sit down, and join me at supper?'" The expected answer in that society, of course, is "No one would." Jesus seems to accept the social structures of his time; that wasn't how you treated your slaves. Instead, the owner expects the slave, after his hard day's work, to wash up, serve dinner, and wait until the master has finished before eating anything himself. What's more, the slave wouldn't even expect a thank-you: "We have done only what we ought to have done."

Lk 17:7-10

Jesus is remarkably unsentimental about Christian life: we, his followers, are to be like the slave in the parable. There is no place for self-righteousness, no feeling that God owes us a reward. If we do all we have been ordered to do, that's fine; it's nothing special. We have only done what is expected of us.

The parables are designed to disturb the comfortable. They demand a change of heart, and they call for an immediate response.

20

THE MORAL WISDOM OF JESUS

The moral teaching of Jesus offers wisdom about a saved way of life.

The moral wisdom of the Jewish tradition is enshrined in the Law of Moses. As we saw in Chapter 8, the Law was not understood as a burden, but rather as a liberating guide for a way of life rooted in a covenant relationship with God and others.

The moral teaching of Jesus is presented not as Law, but as a goal – a call to the best possible human behaviour. Like the Jewish tradition, but in different terms, our moral tradition offers insight about a way of life that will make us truly human, civilized in the best sense, at peace, true to ourselves and faithful to God. Jesus described the way of life that is worthy of children of the kingdom of God, and demanded that his followers accept those standards of excellence and build their lives on them. Thus, the moral teaching of Jesus is both wisdom and command.

For example, when Jesus emphasizes that we must forgive one another, his teaching mustn't be seen as some kind of arbitrary, paradoxical norm or stipulation to test how obedient we are. Rather, his teaching is wisdom about what is really best for us, what will give us peace of heart, what will make us fully human. If we spend our lives taking offence at every setback, nursing grudges and making plans for revenge, we will be eaten by those inner fires. We will be angry, nasty, unhappy people. If we can bring ourselves to forgive, we will be more peaceful, more truly human, happier.

The moral teaching of Jesus does not set borders around human freedom, but rather offers a vision of the best way human beings can live with each other as faithful children of God. His teaching is always radical and visionary; he never speaks about mitigating circumstances or half measures; he sets perfection as the Christian moral standard.

In facing the uncompromising commands of Jesus, we must remember that his standards are not just ethical principles towards which we are expected to strive. Rather, Jesus promises that the only way we can grow to wholeness is by accepting the reign of God – if we will open our hearts to the saving action of God, God will lead us to wholeness. If we rely only on our own efforts, we are doomed to failure.

In dialogue with the action of God, we are creating a person by our decisions. We are shaping our *selves*, day by day. That is the moral enterprise in which every human being is engaged. As disciples of Jesus, we accept his wisdom about a way of life that is most true to ourselves, most faithful to God, most fully human. And we open our hearts to the action of God, who helps us to be wise and to make good judgments, and gives us the courage to do what we know is best and the power to love in a way that will make us truly ourselves.

Thus, Christian morality is based on responsibility: we are responsible for the person we are becoming. We try to stay rooted in the teaching of Jesus; we try to open our hearts to the saving action of God; we listen to the wisdom of our Church community; we hear viewpoints from good influences and bad in the world around us. In other words, we form our consciences, make decisions and shape our personality.

But we must remember that no one grows to wholeness in isolation. Jesus' primary moral insight was that the only way to become truly yourself is to give yourself in love to others. We rely on the community of believers for support – for challenging reminders of the demands of the gospel, for authoritative wisdom about values that must be preserved, for thoughtful discussion of the issues of the day, for community prayer, for mutual forgiveness, for the encouragement that we get from seeing other people believe as we do and try to live in love as we do.

Examples of the Moral Wisdom of Jesus

In the Sermon on the Mount, Jesus proposes six striking contrasts between his ancestral tradition and his own new and radical understanding of morality.

As the passage begins, the reader perceives that Matthew's community is struggling to express the relationship between the Law of Moses (to which many in Matthew's community remain loyal) and its fulfillment in the moral wisdom of Jesus. Jesus tells his disciples that their righteousness – their sense of what is right – must go far beyond that of the Jewish tradition. He is not accusing the scribes and Pharisees of being hypocrites; rather, he is proposing that their horizons are limited. Then Jesus takes six examples from the Law of Moses and reshapes them to express his vision of how people ought to live.

Mt 22:1-13//
Lk 14:16-24

1. *Respect*

"You have heard that it was said to those of ancient times,
'You shall not murder…'
But I say to you that if you are angry with a brother or sister,
you will be liable to judgment."

With this statement, Jesus fulfills and renews one of the Ten Commandments. The standard set by the Mosaic Law is still valid, but the Christian standard asks us to consider the root of violent behaviour. Recent tragedies in North American cities have made us realize that murderous acts are symptoms of a deep-seated anger that has seethed inside the perpetrators for years. That anger must be addressed, for it is at the root of the behaviour. Jesus knew that 2,000 years ago.

Jesus is not saying, "You shall not get angry." Jesus himself got angry. Rather, he is asking us to search our hearts to consider the sources of our anger, and to see whether our anger is justifiable or selfish. Anger, and the behaviour arising from it, can be based upon truth and upon concern for the other person, as Jesus' anger was. All our relationships need to be based on mutual respect.

Jesus' moral teaching presents the highest standards of human moral excellence, and asks us to reflect on who we are at the depths of our being.

2. *Intention*

"You have heard that it was said,
'You shall not commit adultery.'
But I say to you that everyone who looks
at a woman with lust
has already committed adultery with her in his heart."

This saying of Jesus is not only about lust; it is about all of life, and it marks a significant development beyond a morality (even later Christian morality) that focuses on borderlines. Most laws try to regulate only what people do. They do not legislate what people think or feel.

In this statement, Jesus teaches that morality is primarily interior. Action, while important, is only a symptom of intention. The moral decision happens within the person; the action expresses the decision of conscience. Jesus makes integrity the standard of Christian behaviour.

The challenge is to bring our thoughts and feelings in line with truth, and to have our deeds flow from within us, in harmony with what is truly right. We Christians are challenged to have integrity, to develop the kind of inner peace in which our thoughts and feelings and actions express the love that is at the heart of our self-understanding.

Such a standard of morality is not a different kind of law (where one can say that one has done all that is commanded), but rather a goal, a description of the best human way of life. All of us will be torn at times; all of us will experience thoughts and feelings that we know are not appropriate for followers of Jesus. The challenge is to do what is truly best, and never to stop growing towards wholeness, inner peace and integrity.

With regard to the specifically sexual content of Jesus' saying, it seems worthwhile to suggest that lust refers to sexual oppression rather than merely sexual desire. Pope John Paul II wrote that a husband could offend in such a way against his wife in this area: not that husbands shouldn't desire their wives sexually, but that even married people can be guilty of engaging in sexual oppression, sex without love, sex against the will of their spouse. Jesus is not vilifying desire or imagination. But he is challenging the believer always to seek what is right, knowing that the key to morality is what takes place within the human heart and mind.

3. *Lasting Marriage*

"It was also said, 'Whoever divorces his wife,
let him give her a certificate of divorce.'
But I say to you that anyone who divorces his wife,
except on the ground of unchastity,
Mt 5:31-32 *causes her to commit adultery."*

It is important to hear this saying of Jesus in the social context of the time. According to the Law of Moses, a man could divorce his wife simply by giving her a writ of dismissal if he found some impropriety in her; the most liberal rabbis deemed that whatever the husband considered shameful was adequate grounds for invoking the right of divorce – even if his wife's crime was only to burn his dinner! The wife could not divorce her husband under any circumstances, no matter how shameful his behaviour.

Jesus teaches that no Christian should have that kind of power over a spouse. Later in the gospel, in invoking the story of Adam and Eve, Jesus proclaims that the original or ultimate intention of God is that marriage should last for life. That is the challenge, and the demand, that Jesus places before every disciple. And who can disagree that marriage at its best should last for life?

Mt 11:18-19// Lk 7:33

The Roman Catholic tradition, in trying to remain faithful to this teaching of Jesus, has understood the teaching quite literally, as a law would be interpreted. Other Christian churches see it more as a standard of excellence, as a description of a fully saved way of life. For those churches, the demand of lifelong marriage is accepted as truly expressing God's intention. When people fall short of the standard and marriages end, those churches are able to help people to evaluate their own actions, ask God for forgiveness, and perhaps later pursue the standard of lifelong marriage in another union. Those communities may be closer to the spirit in which the teaching of Jesus was given. It is wisdom, not law, about the best way for humans to live.

4. *Honesty*

"Again, you have heard that it was said
to those of ancient times,
'You shall not swear falsely,
but carry out the vows you have made to the Lord.'
But I say to you, Do not swear at all…
Let your word be 'Yes [if you mean yes], Yes'
or 'No [if you mean no], No';
anything more than this comes from the evil one." Mt 5:33-37

According to some commentators, in the ancestral tradition, the familiar commandment "You shall not bear false witness against your neighbour" was originally a law against perjury – the crime of calling upon God to witness to the truth of a lie in court.

Jesus not only forbade perjury, he forbade oaths. Most likely, he did so out of reverence for God: a person who is profoundly aware of the greatness of God would not involve God as a witness in our petty human disputes.

Jesus' standard of excellence for Christians is simply to tell the truth because it is true: "Say 'yes' when you mean 'yes.'"

A few Christian communities (such as the Mennonites) have kept this command of Jesus literally and faithfully. They refuse to take oaths under any circumstances, because they rightly believe that Jesus taught that we should not take oaths. Most other Christian churches have compromised on this issue, and have accepted the necessity of oaths. They see Jesus' command as a goal to aim for, but find oaths to be necessary at times in a society that has not yet attained the fullness of the reign of God.

5. *Forgiveness, not Revenge*

"You have heard that it was said,
'An eye for an eye and a tooth for a tooth.'
But I say to you, Do not resist an evildoer.
Lk 10:25-37 *But if anyone strikes you on the right cheek,*
turn the other also."

The above teaching in the Law of Moses has come to be understood as a slogan advocating revenge, but in its day, the Law was a civilizing force. It was a law against vendetta. In a society where revenge had been another term for overkill, the Law of Moses limited revenge to one-for-one: "an eye for an eye...." Elsewhere in the Law, in the passage that commands "You shall love your neighbour as yourself," taking vengeance and holding a grudge are forbidden.

Jesus, in the spirit of the Leviticus passage, forbade revenge entirely. He advocated reacting to injury by being generous to the offender, and on forgiving offenders time after time – 77 times. In our world, regrettably, this is considered hopelessly idealistic and impractical. The accepted morality of our marketplace remains an eye for an eye. Everybody thinks that you have to get even, or better.

Indeed, the teaching of Jesus is idealistic; all of his insight about the way of life of the reign of God is visionary. We can never say we have done all he asked; there is always more growing to be done. But his wisdom is not impractical. It is the challenge of every Christian to apply this insight to our daily lives. The fundamental questions to ponder are these: Was Jesus right in principle? Will we have greater peace in our hearts if we can forgive, rather than nursing grudges and waiting to get even? Can we make forgiveness the foundation of our relationships?

If we do agree with Jesus in principle, we must seek to live by our principles. Our acceptance cannot be in words only. If we live in the spirit of Jesus, we will be different from many of our neighbours, and we will be perceptibly counter-cultural in our society.

This is not to suggest that Christians should surrender in the face of aggression. Jesus himself fought vigorously against his oppressors. Everyone must consider the most Christian way of acting in each situation.

At times, it feels nearly impossible to forgive or to turn the other cheek. Some offences truly seem unforgivable. Still, we must work to believe that Jesus is right. He teaches us that if we build our lives around standing up for our rights and getting even for wrongs, we will be lesser people. If we build our relationships upon a spirit of forgiveness, we will be true to ourselves, more at peace, closer to God and freer. If we forgive, especially the people we live with and work with, our lives will be more faithful to the gospel – and happier!

6. *Love Your Enemies*

"You have heard that it was said,
'You shall love your neighbour and hate your enemy.'
But I say to you, Love your enemies…
If you love those who love you, what reward do you have?
Do not even the tax collectors do the same?" Mt 5:43-46

The Law of Moses never did command people to hate their enemy. Jesus may have been repeating a popular slogan when he refers to a tradition that advocated hatred.

His remarkable statement about loving your enemies is so familiar to us, it may have lost its power to shock, but it is one of the more paradoxical and demanding of his insights about a saved way of life. Our enmities tend to be long-lasting and bitter; they can become entrenched in our psyche, occupying a significant portion of our energy and consciousness. The idea of overcoming enmity by offering love again and again is another radical command of Jesus that may seem impractical.

"Love your enemies" is a prime example of Jesus' belief that we will become most truly ourselves if we can become more self-giving. While this command is a challenge, it gives us an opportunity to rededicate ourselves to the morality of the king-dom, and to renew our openness to the transforming power of God.

The Value of Poverty, the Danger of Wealth

"If you wish to be perfect,
go, sell your possessions, and give the money to the poor...
Truly, I tell you, it will be hard for a rich person
Mt 19:21, 23 *to enter the kingdom of heaven."*

With this saying, we step outside the Sermon on the Mount to deal with another important moral issue. Jesus' attitude to money is hard to accept for many people in contemporary society. He was much more concerned about the dangers of money than he was about sexuality, though our tradition has chosen to emphasize sexuality, as if it were the more important moral issue.

Jesus knew that people tend to forget their principles in the pursuit of wealth. Though we may say that love and forgiveness are more important to us than money, we tend to compromise those values when it comes to making and spending money.

Jesus tries to make us uncomfortable about money. He points out to us the needs of people whom we would prefer not to notice. He reminds us that we can't become whole or be true to ourselves unless we are profoundly generous, unless we build our lives on giving rather than taking. He wasn't just talking about love. He was also talking about money. We see that in his conversation with the rich young man who wants to follow Jesus, but cannot leave his money.

Impossible Without God's Help

Mt 5:48 *"Be perfect, therefore, as your heavenly Father is perfect."*

The word 'perfect' is used only twice in all the gospels – in the saying reported in Matthew 19, and in this saying, which concludes the six great statements comparing Jesus' moral teaching with the Law of Moses. 'Perfect' is connected to the word 'complete'; it doesn't mean flawless, it means finished, perfected. We are invited to bring our lives as faithful people of God to successful completion – to wholeness. All of us are challenged to keep growing until we die.

With this call to fullness of life, to successful completion, Jesus summarizes the moral wisdom of the reign of God. It is a dynamic and inspiring moral teaching. We can never say that we are perfect, or that we've done all that is asked of us, or that we have loved enough. But we can continue to grow towards true wholeness; we can continue to outdo ourselves in self-giving love; we can keep growing until we die.

And because we recognize that the standard ("...as your heavenly Father is perfect") is supernatural – beyond the power of any human – we realize that the only way to keep growing is to rely on the saving, enabling power of God. Only with God's help can we become the people we are created to be. Only with God's help can we be whole. Only with God's help can we be saved.

21

THE LIFE AND LETTERS OF PAUL

The most influential member of the earliest Christian communities was a man who never met Jesus, and who did not become a follower of Jesus until at least five years after the resurrection. A brief description of his missionary activity and the genesis of his letters is found in Chapter 15.

Paul shaped the Christian proclamation, reflected on and expressed the greatness of Jesus in new ways, and brought the gospel message to the world beyond Jesus' homeland – in particular, to Europe.

He travelled and preached extensively around the Mediterranean world, eventually arriving in Rome, where a Christian community existed. During his travels, he wrote letters to several communities in which he had proclaimed the gospel. When he died in the mid-60s CE, under the persecution of Nero, none of the four gospels had yet been written.

There is debate among Scripture scholars about the authorship of some of the letters attributed to Paul. The language and concepts in Ephesians and Colossians, for example, are different from other letters that were certainly authored by Paul; the question is whether Paul's language and concepts evolved during his lifetime, or whether this and other letters were written after his death by a disciple and attributed to Paul. Ephesians and Colossians (along with Philippians and the brief note to Philemon, which were undoubtedly authored by Paul) would have to have been written while Paul was imprisoned for preaching the gospel.

A. The Conversion Experience

Paul describes himself as a devout Jew of the clan of Benjamin (the same tribe as Saul, the first of the Jewish kings, after whom he was named). He was a well-educated Pharisee, and thus a member of the academic elite in Jewish culture, which extended Phil 3:5-6 beyond the borders of Palestine into the entire Mediterranean world.

The Acts of the Apostles, the fifth book of the New Testament, is a dramatic narrative of Paul's life and missionary journeys. Acts was written by the author of the Gospel of Luke, probably sometime in the late 80s or early 90s of the first century, and therefore more than 20 years after Paul's death. The book may give us a reasonably accurate outline of the style of his ministry, but by the time Acts was written, there had been time for the story of Paul's life to evolve. This resulted in both the exaggeration of events and the expression of Paul's thought in the language of the author, rather than in Paul's own words.

This chapter will explore what we know of Paul's ministry from his own letters, rather than from a document written after his death. The Letter to the Galatians gives us the most autobiographical information about Paul.

Paul admits that, in the early years of Christianity, as a result of his dedication to the traditions of his ancestors, "I was violently Gal 1:13-14 persecuting the church of God, and was trying to destroy it." But in due time, "God was pleased to reveal his Son to me," and Paul became a Christian. Paul's only description of his conversion to Christianity is hidden in that very subdued and dignified phrase. In all his letters, there is no story of his being blinded by a flash of compare light, of being thrown from a horse, or of hearing the voice of the Acts 9:1-9 risen Lord – though in another of his letters, Paul does claim to have seen the risen Jesus "last of all," as if he were "untimely 1 Cor 15:8 born."

Thus Paul unexpectedly became a follower of Jesus some years after the resurrection. He apparently took several years to become fully familiar with Christian teaching, and to shape his personal faith and understanding. During that time, he had little contact with the original Christian community or with the friends of Jesus who were its leaders. The earliest Christians were suspicious of him; they feared that he was trying to infiltrate their communities in order to persecute them. Paul reports a time of absence from

Gal 1:17-18, 2:1 Palestine, a two-week visit to Jerusalem three years after his conversion, and a second visit after 14 years.

His missionary journeys began more than 10 years after his conversion, in the late 40s CE: first in Asia Minor and later in Macedonia and Greece. Paul's letters, the earliest written Christian documents we have, date from approximately 50 to 65 CE.

B. Some Characteristics of the Letters of Paul

Let's begin with a brief examination of the format of Paul's letters. Rather than leaving the signature until the end of the letter as we do today, letter-writers in Paul's day began with their own name.
see Rom 1:1-6 Paul's self-identification at the beginning of his letters usually isn't simply his name, but a paragraph about his credentials. At times, just as family members often do in letters and cards today, Paul identifies more than one person as the author of the letter – First Corinthians is from Paul and Sosthenes; Second Corinthians and Philemon are from Paul and Timothy; the Thessalonian letters
Gal 1:1-2 are from Paul, Silvanus and Timothy; and Galatians is from Paul and "all the members of God's family who are with me."

After the addressee is identified, a pleasant greeting follows. Almost all the letters then offer a prayer of thanks for the community's faithfulness in following the gospel since Paul left their town. The one exception to this pattern is the letter to the
Gal 1:6 Galatians: Paul was so annoyed with that community that he began his letter by expressing his dismay at their behaviour.

Paul could read and write, but like many people of his time, he probably relied on the services of professional scribes to put his thoughts into written form. Anyone who has tried to compose a lengthy document by recording it on a tape recorder will know that this is a difficult process. Speakers can sometimes stray from a strict line of thought, use language more suitable to oral expression, or make grammatical errors if they do not later reread what they have said. Such is the case in several of Paul's letters,
Rom 16:22 especially in the personal greetings that characterize the concluding paragraphs. Paul's amanuensis, Tertius, pens his own greeting as part of the lengthy farewell section in the letter to the Romans. At the end of First Corinthians and Second
1 Cor 16:21 Thessalonians, Paul takes the pen from his scribe and writes a final admonition "with my own hand." "This is the mark in every
2 Thess 3:17 letter of mine," he says; "it is the way I write." His infrequent

practice of handwriting may be inferred when he notes, "See what large letters I make when I am writing in my own hand." Gal 6:11

Notice how Paul's forceful personality comes through in his letters. He takes a stand with confidence, and expects to be obeyed. Yet his at times blustery defensiveness seems to betray personal anxiety or uncertain self-esteem.

This is my defence to those who would examine me.
Do we not have the right to our food and drink?...
Or is it only Barnabas and I who have no right to refrain from working for a living?...
Who plants a vineyard and does not eat any of its fruit?...
But I have made no use of any of these rights,
nor am I writing this so that they may be applied in my case.
Indeed, I would rather die than that – no one will deprive me of my ground for boasting! 1 Cor 9:3-15

We disciples, Paul admonishes his Corinthian community earlier in the same letter, have become a spectacle to the world:

We are fools for the sake of Christ
[he states in a sarcastic tone], *but you are wise in Christ.*
We are weak, but you are strong...
We have become like the rubbish of the world,
the dregs of all things....

1 Cor 4:10-13

I wish you would bear with me in a little foolishness...
I think that I am not in the least inferior to these super-apostles.
I may be untrained in speech, but not in knowledge...
I repeat, let no one think that I am a fool;
but if you do, then accept me as a fool,
so that I too may boast a little.
For you gladly put up with fools, being wise yourselves! 2 Cor 11:1–12:12

With that, Paul lists all the sufferings and dangers he has confronted during his ministry, and dares anybody to boast of having endured more adventures than he has. Then he emphasizes that he is boasting only about his own weakness, and that he would have accomplished nothing if not for the power of Christ at work in his life.

Here is a brief introduction to significant themes in some of Paul's letters.

C. Early Controversy: 'Kosher Christianity' and the Letter to the Galatians

One of the most significant issues of Paul's early years as a Christian was the disciples' relationship to Judaism. The Christians in Jerusalem, led by friends and relatives of Jesus, saw themselves as faithful Jews who had come to believe that Jesus was their Messiah. They continued to worship in synagogue and the Temple, and to keep the Law of Moses, including the kosher rules for dietary and ritual cleanliness. But when people joined Paul's communities, he did not require them to undergo the Jewish
Gal 2:3-10 initiation rite (circumcision, for males), nor did they have to follow the kosher rules.

Paul was concerned that Christians of Jewish heritage who adhered to the Law of Moses believed that people can earn their salvation by following that Law. Paul, on the other hand, understood salvation to be God's gift. It cannot be earned; we can never claim that God owes us a reward for the good deeds we have done. For Paul, the life, death and resurrection of Jesus – not the good deeds of believers – have accomplished the salvation of humanity.

> *If justification comes through the law*
> [meaning, the Law of Moses],
> *then Christ died for nothing.*
>
> *It is no longer I who live,*
> *but it is Christ who lives in me.*
> *And the life that I now live in the flesh*
> *I live by faith in the Son of God,*
> Gal 2:21, 20 *who loved me and gave himself for me.*

In the letter to the Galatians, Paul storms at the faction within Christianity that urges that Jewish traditions be retained. He begins
Gal 1:1 by affirming that his authority comes from God and not from any human being. He is so upset with the 'kosher faction' that he omits his customary prayer of thanks for the faithfulness of the believers to whom he is writing, and begins the body of the letter
Gal 1:6 by expressing astonishment over his readers having so quickly abandoned the gospel as he had presented it to them.

The tensions between Paul and the Jerusalem community are
Gal 2:4 visible in his references to "false believers secretly brought in" to

challenge the freedoms being allowed in Paul's communities, and
in his description of Peter, John and James the brother of the
Lord as "those who were supposed to be acknowledged leaders Gal 2:6
(what they actually were makes no difference to me)."

He reports a feisty confrontation about hypocrisy with Peter,
who accepted Paul's freedom and broke kosher rules by eating
with Gentile Christians – but only until "certain people" arrived Gal 2:11-14
from the Jerusalem community. Paul begins the third chapter by
exclaiming, "You foolish Galatians! Who has bewitched you?" Gal 3:1
And in an outburst against people who insisted on traditional
circumcision as a pre-baptism ritual, Paul expresses the devout
wish that their knife would slip and they would cut through rather Gal 5:12
than around that part of the male anatomy.

In spite of the ferocity of his scorn for the Christians who wanted to keep the Law of Moses, Paul does express some important truths in the letter to the Galatians:

> *You were called to freedom, brothers and sisters…* Gal 5:13
>
> *The whole law is summed up in a single commandment,*
> *"You shall love your neighbour as yourself."* Gal 5:14
>
> *Bear one another's burdens, and in this way you will fulfill*
> *the law of Christ.* Gal 6:2

And perhaps most memorable of his teachings in this letter,

> *If we live by the Spirit, let us also be guided by the Spirit.* Gal 5:25
>
> *The fruit of the Spirit is love, joy, peace, patience, kindness,*
> *generosity, faithfulness, gentleness, and self-control.* Gal 5:22-23

For Paul, if we see love and joy and peace in our lives we must give thanks, rather than claim credit or the right to a reward. These greatest of human characteristics should be seen as the fruit of the Holy Spirit's activity rather than as the believer's accomplishments. The recognition of the importance of God's saving action in our lives is a central insight of Paul's, and the root of his exasperated attack on 'kosher Christianity.'

D. Life Beyond Death: The First Letter to the Thessalonians

Chronologically, the first of Paul's letters are the two written to the community in Thessalonika, one of the first towns Paul entered after crossing the Hellespont from Asia into Europe.

Having preached in the synagogue and the marketplace, Paul established a community of believers with whom he stayed for a number of weeks, presumably telling them all he knew about the teaching of Jesus. Going on to other population centres, including Athens, he kept in touch with the Thessalonian community: by sending his colleague Timothy to visit them and check on their faithfulness, and writing a letter to encourage them in the ways of faith and love and to respond to questions that had arisen in the community since his departure.

1 Thess 3:1-5

One concern among members of the Thessalonian community seems to have been the fate of their loved ones who died before the expected return of the Saviour. It seems clear that the early Christians expected Jesus to return "on the clouds of heaven" soon after his resurrection, and to establish God's glorious kingdom on earth. Would their loved ones who died before Jesus returned miss out on the glorious kingdom?

Here is Paul's response, 20 years after Jesus rose from the dead, to the Thessalonians' concern:

> *We do not want you to be uninformed, brothers and sisters, about those who have died,*
> *so that you may not grieve as others do who have no hope.*
> *For since we believe that Jesus died and rose again,*
> *even so, through Jesus, God will bring with him those who have died…*
> *We who are alive* [apparently, Paul still expected to be alive at the return of the Saviour]
> *…will by no means precede those who have died.*
> *For the Lord himself…with the sound of God's trumpet, will descend from heaven,*
> *and the dead in Christ will rise first.*
> *Then we who are alive…will be caught up in the clouds…*
> *and so we will be with the Lord forever.*

1 Thess 4:13-17

When the return of the Lord might take place, Paul cannot say. He reminds his friends that "the day of the Lord will come like a thief in the night," and encourages them to have confidence, because they are all "children of light" and have nothing to fear as long as they remain faithful and ready. 1 Thess 5:2 1 Thess 5:5

In his second letter to the Thessalonians, Paul has to deal with some members who have apparently decided to rely on community charity for sustenance while they await the imminent return of the Saviour. Paul reminds them that he and his colleagues worked to support themselves while they were in Thessalonika. It was Paul who advised the early Christians to keep away from the idlers: "Anyone unwilling to work should not eat." 2 Thess 3:6-12 2 Thess 3:10

More about early Christian belief on life beyond death can be found in Chapter 26, on life everlasting.

E. The Community of Believers: The First Letter to the Corinthians

1. *The wisdom of God overcomes the wisdom of the world*

Corinth was a rough-and-tumble town on the canal that crossed the neck of land between the Greek mainland and the Peloponnesian peninsula. The backbone of the community included sailors, stevedores and the on-shore service workers who tended to their needs.

"Consider your own call," suggests Paul in beginning his letter to the group of Christians he had established in Corinth. "Not many of you were wise by human standards, not many were powerful, not many were of noble birth." But God chose people who were considered foolish and weak and low and despised, and gave them the wonderful gospel of salvation that was to transform their lives and give them meaning and purpose. 1 Cor 1:26-28

Paul marvels at the contrast between what society considers important and what God has done. Jews, with their long tradition of religious phenomena, demand signs; Greeks, with their memorable philosophical heritage, seek wisdom – and here we are, proclaiming a crucified Messiah, apparent foolishness in the eyes of both Jew and Greek; but to those who are called, the gospel truly embodies "the power of God and the wisdom of God." 1 Cor 1:22-23

2. *Marriage in the 'End-Time'*

In the absence of extensive teaching about marriage from Jesus, it could be claimed that the seventh chapter of Paul's first letter to the Corinthians has set the tone for Christian teaching on the subject for almost 2,000 years.

It is a document of mixed messages. Paul's overriding viewpoint is that

the appointed time [for the return of Jesus]
has grown short;...
the present form of this world is passing away.
I want you to be free from anxieties...
I say this for your own benefit...
1 Cor 7:29-35 *to promote unhindered devotion to the Lord.*

And heaven knows, no aspect of human life engenders more anxieties than sex.

1 Cor 7:7-8 Paul, who is unmarried, says, "I wish that all were as I myself
am." He urges people, whatever their state in life, "in view of the
impending crisis," to "remain in the condition in which you were
1 Cor 7:20, 26 called," and to dedicate their lives to pleasing God.

In this setting, Paul speaks of marriage as something to be
allowed (even though it ensures that "those who marry will
1 Cor 7:28 experience distress") if people cannot practise self-control, or if
their passions are too strong. As he puts it, "it is better to marry
1 Cor 7:9 than to be aflame with passion."

The unmarried man
is anxious about the affairs of the Lord...
but the married man is anxious about the affairs of the world,
how to please his wife.

The unmarried woman and the virgin
are anxious about the affairs of the Lord...
but the married woman is anxious about the affairs
of the world,
1 Cor 7:32-34 *how to please her husband.*

While not a ringing endorsement of married life, these words do provide a clear expression of Paul's total dedication to the gospel – a conviction that he wished everyone to share. Regrettably, it has taken almost 20 centuries for Christians to realize that Paul's sense of urgency about the impending return of the Saviour coloured his perspective about the daily lives of Christians. Only recently have we come to understand more clearly that marriage is not a distraction from total dedication to the reign of God, but is in fact the vehicle by which the majority of Christians live out their dedication to the gospel.

Other paragraphs in the same chapter offer a more positive attitude towards married life. One in particular discusses the no doubt common situation of a person who had converted to Christianity but whose spouse remained pagan or unreligious. Jewish practice would have required that the couple separate, since orthodox Jews were not permitted even to eat with Gentiles. Paul is confident that a believing partner need not fear an unbeliever who is willing to continue living in marriage:

> *For the unbelieving husband is made holy through his wife,*
> *and the unbelieving wife is made holy through her husband.*
> *Otherwise, your children would be unclean, but as it is,*
> *they are holy…*
> *Wife, for all you know, you might save your husband.* 1 Cor 7:12-16

In this very positive and encouraging approach, believers need not fear contamination from living with an 'infidel.' Instead, a grace-filled power is expected to flow from the believing spouse and transform every member of the family.

Other positive features of Pauline teaching on marriage are found in letters that may not have been written by Paul himself. "Husbands, love your wives, and never treat them harshly." (Col 3:19) "Husbands, love your wives, just as Christ loved the church and gave himself up for her." (Eph 5:25) Those wise admonitions proclaim self-giving love as the key to happy marriage, and perceive the faithful bond between married partners to be a symbol of Jesus' love for the community – a truly honourable and challenging comparison for married people.

It must be acknowledged that both of those sayings are found in a patriarchal context that is questioned by many Christians today. It is vital to keep in mind the context in which the New Testament epistles were written.

3. *Eucharist and Community Life*

On the basis of his recognition of the organic interdependence of everyone in the community, Paul offers advice about community life to the believers in Corinth and to future generations.

He has heard, for example, that when the Christians of Corinth gather in the evening to celebrate the Lord's Supper, the richer members of the group enjoy good food and plenty of wine, while poorer people drag themselves in after a day's work and are forced to watch hungrily from a corner of the room. The eucharistic rite takes place in the course of the supper, in such a context of disparity. "If this is what is going on," shouts Paul, "I don't care whether you say all the proper words of the Eucharist. It simply isn't authentic!"

When you come together, it is not really to eat the Lord's supper…
Each of you goes ahead with your own supper,
and one goes hungry and another becomes drunk.
What!… Do you show contempt for the church of God
and humiliate those who have nothing?…
[I want to remind you of the tradition] I also handed on to you,
that the Lord Jesus on the night when he was betrayed
took a loaf of bread…

Whoever eats the bread or drinks the cup of the Lord in an unworthy manner
will be answerable for the body and blood of the Lord…
For all who eat and drink without discerning the body,
1 Cor 11:20-29 *eat and drink judgment against themselves.*

The 'body' of which he speaks is not only the eucharistic presence of Jesus, but also the community of believers. According to Paul, no one can truly celebrate the Lord's Supper while ignoring the needs of other members of the body.

No doubt Paul would rage with equal force against those of us who pray in our assemblies that God will send food to the hungry while we continue to overconsume and waste food every day. For Paul, Eucharist does not simply happen in church. It is something we must live out.

4. *The community as a living organism inspired by the Spirit of love*

In this first letter to the Corinthians, Paul discusses a number of issues that have arisen in the community. In Chapter 12, he compares the church community to a living organism. A human body is amazingly complex: every part of the body has a role to

play, and must be working well. If any part of the body is in pain, 1 Cor 12:14-26
the whole person suffers.

The community of believers, says Paul, is the body of Christ. 1 Cor 12:27
The Spirit of God is like the life-principle in a human body,
activating everything that the community does. Each member 1 Cor 12:11
has a role to play, as apostle, prophet, teacher, healer or interpreter.
All may take part – Jew or Greek, slave or free person (and male 1 Cor 12:28
or female, as Paul adds in the letter to the Galatians). 1 Cor 12:13,

Then Paul focuses his teaching about community in his well- Gal 3:28
known description of love, the unifying principle of community
life:

Love is patient; love is kind;
love is not envious or boastful or arrogant or rude.
It does not insist on its own way;
it is not irritable or resentful;
it does not rejoice in wrongdoing, but rejoices in the truth.
It bears all things, believes all things, hopes all things,
endures all things.
Love never ends. 1 Cor 13:4-8

In the gospels, Jesus' sayings about love are found in the
language of commandment: "Love the Lord your God," "Love Mt 22:37-40
your neighbour as yourself," "Love your enemies," "Just as I have Mt 5:44
loved you…love one another." When Jesus talks about community Jn 13:34
(for example, in Matthew, Chapter 18), he wisely identifies forgiveness as the indispensable unifying force among the members. Mt 18:35

Paul has built upon the foundation of Jesus' teaching, giving us a beautiful descriptive reflection on the meaning of love that has inspired believers for centuries. Still today, in the age of modern social science, it stands up as a valid expression of the greatest of human values.

Later, as he is bringing this letter to a close, Paul returns to
the language of commandment in his admonition: "Let all that 1 Cor 16:14
you do be done in love."

F. Life in the Believing Community

1. *Constructive Behaviour*

Some of Paul's other letters exhort believers to live in peace with each other and to live up to the model set by Jesus.

Leaf through the letters of Paul in the Bible, reading only the opening prayers of thanks. The following passage is selected from the letter to the Philippians:

Grace to you and peace
from God our Father and the Lord Jesus Christ.
I thank my God every time I remember you...
because of your sharing in the gospel from the first day
until now...

This is my prayer,
that your love may overflow more and more
with knowledge and full insight
to help you to determine what is best,
so that in the day of Christ you may be pure and blameless,
having produced the harvest of righteousness that comes
through Jesus Christ
Phil 1:2-4, 9-11 *for the glory and praise of God.*

The letter to the Ephesians urges the community to be united in peace and love.

I pray that...[God] may grant that you may be strengthened
in your inner being
with power through his Spirit,
and that Christ may dwell in your hearts through faith,
Eph 3:16-17 *as you are being rooted and grounded in love.*

I therefore, the prisoner in the Lord,
beg you to lead a life worthy of [your] calling...
with all humility and gentleness, with patience,
bearing with one another in love,
making every effort to maintain the unity of the Spirit
Eph 4:1-3 *in the bond of peace.*

The author goes on to use an image found in First Corinthians:

Eph 4:4 *There is one body and one Spirit...*

Speaking the truth in love,
we must grow up in every way into him who is the head,
into Christ, from whom the whole body...[builds] itself up
Eph 4:15-16 *in love.*

The letter to the Colossians also offers encouragement to the community:

As God's chosen ones, holy and beloved,
clothe yourselves with compassion, kindness, humility,
meekness, and patience.
Bear with one another and, if anyone has a complaint
against another, forgive each other…
Above all, clothe yourselves with love, which binds
everything together in perfect harmony.
And let the peace of Christ rule in your hearts… Col 3:12-16

2. *Structure in the Christian Community*

Three New Testament letters (two addressed to Timothy, and one
to Titus) are known as the "pastoral epistles" since they deal with 1 Tim 1:3-6
leadership and structure in the early community. A majority of Titus 2:1-5
commentators question the authorship of these epistles. Because
they portray a community life that is more evolved than what is
depicted even in the gospels, such scholars believe that these 1 Tim 6:3-5 2 Tim 2:14
letters were written by an unknown author 40 or more years after Titus 1:10-11
Paul's death, using details about Timothy and Titus that appear
in the Acts of the Apostles.

While contemporary sensibilities find that the pastoral epistles 1 Tim 2:9-15
reveal a community life that is male-dominated, that endorses Titus 2:5
slavery and that takes racism for granted, the author does present 1 Tim 6:1-3
wise counsel about holding firm to the authentic teaching of Jesus Titus 2:9-10
and avoiding unseemly disputes.

The pastoral letters are perhaps best remembered for their depiction of developing structure in the early communities. They use specific terms for Christian leaders such as *episkopos* (literally, supervisor; now translated as 'bishop'), *presbyteros* ('elder') and *diakonos* ('deacon'). They do not use the term '*ieros* (priest) in describing early Church community structure.

The qualifications listed for bishops and deacons are both 1 Tim 3:1-13
insightful and interesting; they urge the community not to choose leaders who are violent or quarrelsome, but rather to select men who are temperate and sensible, and who have a peaceful family life. There is mention of the laying on of hands by the council of elders, which we still do when ordaining community leaders. 1 Tim 4:14

G. Who is Jesus?

Expressions of faith about the person of Jesus developed in the Christian community as a result of reflection on the resurrection. In the early years of Christianity, disciples were more concerned about the teaching that had been most important to Jesus – the reign of God and its implications for the lives of believers.

As time went on, the focus of reflection evolved towards the person of Jesus himself. Paul's letters show us some relatively early stages in the process that led to gospel affirmations like the ringing avowal in Mark of the centurion at the crucifixion ("Truly
Mk 15:39 this man was God's Son!"), the profound theological statement of John's opening chapter ("The Word became flesh and lived
Jn 1:14 among us"), and eventually to the great Nicene Creed, which declares that Jesus is "God from God, Light from Light, true God from true God, begotten not made, one in being with the Father."

One early stage in the process of reflection is found in Paul's letter to the Philippians, which was probably written in the early 60s CE. Exhorting the members of the community to be compassionate, agreeable and humble, and to think of other people before themselves, Paul urges believers to be of the same mind as Jesus, who,

> *though he was in the form of God,*
> *did not regard equality with God as something to be exploited,*
> *but emptied himself, taking the form of a slave,*
> Phil 2:6-7 *being born in human likeness.*

Paul goes on to say that Jesus "humbled himself and became obedient to the point of death," as a result of which

> *God also highly exalted him and gave him the name that is above every name:...*
> Phil 2:9, 11 *Jesus Christ is Lord, to the glory of God the Father.*

This well-known passage shows that 15 years before the first gospel was written, Christians had already come to believe that Jesus had been equal to God before he became human. They were trying to reconcile his obvious humanity with his divinity, and had developed the understanding that he had "emptied himself" to join us as a mortal human. They then understood the resurrection as a reward given by God the Father (note that Paul doesn't use the title 'Son of God' in this context), who authorizes believers to call Jesus "Lord," the title by which Jewish people addressed the God of Moses.

Another example of early Christian reflection on Jesus is found in the letter to the Colossians. This letter describes the person of Jesus using language that is not found in any other letter of Paul.

He is the image of the invisible God,
the firstborn of all creation;
for in him all things in heaven and on earth were created...
all things have been created through him and for him...
he is the beginning, the firstborn from the dead...
For in him all the fullness of God was pleased to dwell,
and through him God was pleased to reconcile to himself
all things. Col 1:15-20

Both this statement and the above quotation from Philippians can be seen as part of early Christian creeds – statements of faith about the person and mission of Jesus. The faith expressed in Colossians is based on the resurrection, but also links Jesus with the creation of the universe, as John's gospel would later do. Using vocabulary that is different from gospel language about Jesus, Colossians calls him "the image of the invisible God," in whom "the fullness of God" dwells.

In both passages, one can perceive the uncertainty and yet the profound commitment of the early disciples, who had, in the light of the resurrection, come to believe that Jesus was much more than his followers had understood before his death.

H. The Gospel According to Paul: The Glorious Freedom of the Children of God

For Paul, the good news of Jesus is that God is taking a great new initiative to set us free. Ever since the escape from Egypt in the time of Moses, the Jewish people cherished their freedom, and believed that God would continue to liberate them from oppression and enable them to set the course of their lives and to grow to wholeness as God's people. Paul was the heir of that Jewish tradition, but he believed that in the life of Jesus, God had gone beyond past blessings and was now acting in a new way, offering freedom to the whole of humanity. Rom 8:21

1. *Freedom from…*

In spite of his profound faith and loyalty to the Jewish tradition, Paul believes that this new covenant frees us from many familiar ways of thinking and living.

a) Freedom from 'salvation by striving'

As we saw earlier in this chapter, in the letter to the Galatians Paul strongly opposes the idea that we can earn our salvation by our deeds. He associates those ideas with his own heritage, according to which a person was saved by obeying the Law of Moses. Paul believes that it is the action of God that saves us, not the deeds we do.

The only thing I want to learn from you is this:
Did you receive the Spirit by doing the works of the law,
or by believing what you heard?
Are you so foolish?
Having started with God's Spirit
are you now ending with the flesh?

Gal 3:2-4

Paul does not mean that believers can do whatever they want, and then rely on God to save them. He believes we can grow towards wholeness only if we open our hearts to the action of God. If we look at our lives and see love and joy, peace and patience, we will know that God's Spirit is at work in us. We don't take credit for it; we give thanks.

If we live by the Spirit, let us also be guided by the Spirit.

Gal 5:25

As the Christian community evolved through the ages, however, it tended to ignore this important teaching and returned to the merit system, complete with self-righteous judgmental attitudes towards others.

b) Freedom from self-righteous hypocrisy

Paul hated hypocrisy. A forthright person, he would scorn the self-righteousness of some modern church-goers who claim to know the will of God but don't live the gospel.

Therefore you have no excuse, whoever you are,
when you judge others; for in passing judgment on another
you condemn yourself, because you, the judge, are doing
the very same things.

But if you call yourself a Jew [he would say the same to Christians] and boast of your relation to God and know his will and determine what is best because you are instructed in the law, and if you are sure that you are a guide to the blind, a light to those who are in darkness… you, then, that teach others, will you not teach yourself? While you preach against stealing, do you steal? You that forbid adultery, do you commit adultery? You that abhor idols, do you rob temples? You that boast in the law, do you dishonor God by breaking the law? For, as it is written, 'The name of God is blasphemed among the Gentiles because of you.' Rom 2:1, 17-24

Let us therefore no longer pass judgment on one another. Rom 14:13

Total personal integrity is a challenge to everyone who tries to be a faithful disciple of Jesus. Paul writes that people who have never heard of the law of God, if they honestly try to do what is right, are

a law unto themselves.
They show that what the law requires is written
on their hearts,
to which their own conscience also bears witness. Rom 2:14-15

Paul, in the spirit of the Old Testament prophets, believes that God will free us from empty religious observances and enable us to live lives of true integrity and love.

c) Freedom from the wisdom of the world

As noted earlier, Paul was profoundly aware of the paradoxical nature of what we believe. The wisdom of the world celebrates wealth and power, advises us to wear the finest clothes and enjoy the best foods, and always take at least an eye for an eye when somebody does us harm.

And here we are, says Paul, proclaiming a crucified Messiah. This is apparent foolishness in the eyes of both Jew and Greek, but to those who are called, the gospel truly embodies "the power of God and the wisdom of God." 1 Cor 1:22-25

We speak of these things in words not taught
by human wisdom
but taught by the Spirit,
interpreting spiritual things to those who are spiritual.

Those who are unspiritual
do not receive the gifts of God's Spirit…
for they are foolishness to them,
and they are unable to understand them.…

1 Cor 2:13-15 *Those who are spiritual discern all things…*

Paul doesn't take credit for the spiritual discernment that he treasures. He knows it is a gift of God. And he knows it is opposed to the wisdom of the world.

d) Freedom from Sin and Death (The Letter to the Romans)

To express a proper understanding of Paul's teaching, Sin and Death should both be capitalized, especially when they appear in chapters 5 and 6 of Paul's monumental letter to the people of Rome.

This greatest of his letters is a synthesis of his teaching, written before he went to Rome to assure the Christian community at the
Rom 15:22-29 heart of the Empire that he was on their side, and that the gospel he was preaching was the same as the gospel they believed. Around the Mediterranean world, Paul had a reputation for being independent, for telling it as it was. He challenged Jesus' close friends, and even Peter (the leader of the community in Rome), in the early decades after the resurrection. Now he was coming to Rome, and as a testimony of his goodwill, he summarized his teaching in a letter.

Sin, for Paul, is a powerful reality that has been unleashed on the world by human wrongdoing. In Chapter 5, Paul speaks of the primordial Sin of one man, Adam. Since Adam is symbolic of every human, Paul is describing the destructive effects of the sinful heritage of humanity:

Rom 6:23 *For the wages of Sin is Death.*

When Paul describes Death as the ultimate consequence of Sin, he means not simply physical death, but total failure, the waste of a life. Sin shatters the human quest for wholeness. It diminishes us and makes us a shell of what we might have been.

If our lives are overwhelmed by Sin, the result is Death – a wasted life.

Paul seems to see people as victims of the power of Sin, rather than perpetrators. He urges people to look at their lives; if they see the symptoms of Sin's power – "fornication, impurity, licentiousness, idolatry, enmity..." – they must change their hearts and open themselves to God's saving action. Gal 5:19-21

For the focus of Paul's words is the cosmic struggle between Sin/Death and the generous saving power of God. His great proclamation is that

The free gift of God is eternal life in Christ Jesus
our Lord. Rom 6:23

2. *Freedom by the gift of God*

In Christ God was reconciling the world to himself...
All this is from God,
who reconciled us to himself through Christ,
and has given us the ministry of reconciliation. 2 Cor 5:19, 18

God's love has been poured into our hearts through the
Holy Spirit that has been given to us. Rom 5:5

For freedom Christ has set us free. Gal 5:1

For I am not ashamed of the gospel;
it is the power of God for salvation to everyone who has
faith...
For in it the righteousness of God is revealed
through faith for faith;
as it is written, "The one who is righteous will live by faith." Rom 1:16-17

These statements, and many more, express Paul's conviction that our wholeness is God's gift to us. God took the initiative and sent Jesus to overcome our sinfulness; God poured out love into our hearts. God set us free from the power of Sin, so that we might set the course of our lives in the direction of true wholeness and be faithful followers of Jesus.

The citation above, from Romans 1, became the central slogan of the Protestant Reformation in the sixteenth century. Using Paul's ideas as a springboard, Martin Luther rebelled against the corruption of Roman Catholicism and against Christendom's return to a legalistic moral system, which more or less reduced the message of salvation to an economic system: perform certain deeds and pile up rewards; act wrongly (e.g., miss Mass on Sunday or eat meat on Friday) and you are suddenly bankrupt (all your previous good deeds are disqualified and you will be sent to hell by a vengeful God).

Luther's understanding, like Paul's, was that wholeness or salvation is God's free gift to humanity. No one can earn it; none of us can claim that God owes us a reward. What we must do is open our hearts to the power of God's love – and believe!

see Rom 3:5-8; Rom 6:1; Gal 6:7-8

There is no childish cynicism in Paul's teaching: "Believe, and it doesn't matter what you do." He often scoffs at such foolish ideas. For Paul, believing is not simply accepting a creed; it is a way of life. He constantly encourages his communities to do what is right, but reminds them that when we live in integrity, we must give thanks to God who has saved us, for it is God who has enabled us to live in a way that is true to ourselves and faithful to God.

It is no longer I who live, but it is Christ who lives in me.
And the life I now live in the flesh I live by faith in the Son of God,
who loved me and gave himself for me.

Gal 2:20

3. *Freedom for Wholeness: A Saved Way of Life*

a) Freedom to live in obedience to God

Paul offers numerous descriptions of the results of God's saving action in our lives:

If then there is any encouragement in Christ,
any consolation from love, any sharing in the Spirit,
any compassion and sympathy, make my joy complete:
be of the same mind, having the same love…
Let the same mind be in you that was in Christ Jesus,
who, though he was in the form of God…
emptied himself, taking the form of a slave,
being born in human likeness…
He humbled himself and became obedient
to the point of death – even death on a cross.
Therefore God also highly exalted him
and gave him the name that is above every name…

Phil 2:1-11

This magnificent hymn links the life of Jesus to the life of Christians: our attitude should be like Jesus'. He was obedient to truth, and lived in radical integrity and faithfulness to God.

Many believers may simply accept it as a given that Jesus should be a model for our lives. More than half of Catholic secondary school students who were asked that question in a recent survey, however, disagreed. Perhaps they felt we cannot reach Jesus' level of excellence. Yet the challenging vision of life for disciples of Jesus is that we are called to be perfect – to allow God to lead us to complete wholeness. Mt 5:48

b) Freedom to build a strong community

No one can be a faithful Christian all alone. We need each other so much that community-building is an essential Christian endeavour.

[Make] every effort to maintain the unity of the Spirit
in the bond of peace.
There is one body and one Spirit,
just as you were called to the one hope of your calling… Eph 4:3-4

But speaking the truth in love,
we must grow up in every way into him who is the head,
into Christ,
from whom the whole body, joined and knit together
by every ligament with which it is equipped,
as each part is working properly,
promotes the body's growth
in building itself up in love. Eph 4:15-16

We have already seen Paul compare the Christian community to the human body, where all the parts need to work together for the benefit of all. Paul expresses similar thoughts in Chapter 12 of his letter to the Romans: 1 Cor 12:12-26

Do not be conformed to this world,
but be transformed by the renewing of your minds,
so that you may discern what is the will of God… Rom 12:2

[S]o we, who are many,
are one body in Christ,
and individually we are members one of another. Rom 12:5

Chapters 12 to 15 of Romans describe the way of life of the Christian community, in which each member plays a constructive role. As believers, we must try to think of others first and consider especially the needs of the weakest members of the community.

c) Freedom to live in love

Love is central to Christianity. God's saving love for people is reflected in our self-giving love for each other. Jesus teaches that we can become truly ourselves only if we give ourselves generously in love for others. The Gospel of John expands on Jesus' thought in several renowned passages. Paul's hymn to love in Chapter 13 of First Corinthians beautifully explores that insight, as does his letter to the Romans:

e.g., Jn 13:34-35

Let love be genuine…
love one another with mutual affection;
outdo one another in showing honour…

Rom 12:9-10

Owe no one anything, except to love one another…
The commandments…are summed up in this word,
"Love your neighbour as yourself."
Love does no wrong to a neighbour;
therefore, love is the fulfilling of the law.

Rom 13:8-10

d) Freedom to grow in intimate communion with God

Paul's description of "the glorious freedom of the children of God" culminates in his inspiring confidence that God is entirely on our side, that God knows us better than we know ourselves, loves us as we are and leads us towards the wholeness that is our goal. Chapter 8 of the letter to the Romans is revered, particularly in the Protestant churches, as one of the most hopeful expressions of Christian faith in the New Testament.

Likewise the Spirit helps us in our weakness;
for we do not know how to pray as we ought,
but that very Spirit intercedes
with sighs too deep for words.
And God, who searches the heart,
knows what is the mind of the Spirit,
because the Spirit intercedes for the saints according to the
will of God.

Rom 8:26-27

We know that all things work together for good
for those who love God…
What then are we to say about these things?
If God is for us, who is against us? Rom 8:28, 31

For I am convinced that neither death, nor life,
nor angels, nor rulers,
nor things present, nor things to come,
nor powers, nor height, nor depth,
nor anything else in all creation,
will be able to separate us from the love of God
in Christ Jesus, our Lord. Rom 8:38-39

We close this brief exploration of Paul's letters with three examples of his prayers for the people in his communities. These prayers describe the Christian way of life, affirm God's saving intimacy with people and inspire us with confidence and hope:

I thank my God every time I remember you,
constantly praying with joy
in every one of my prayers for all of you,
because of your sharing in the gospel
from the first day until now.
I am confident of this,
that the one who began a good work among you
will bring it to completion by the day of Jesus Christ. Phil 1:3-5

And this is my prayer,
that your love may overflow more and more
with knowledge and full insight
to help you to determine what is best… Phil 1:9-11

As God's chosen ones, holy and beloved,
clothe yourselves with compassion, kindness, humility,
meekness and patience.
Bear with one another and,
if anyone has a complaint against another,
forgive each other;
just as the Lord has forgiven you, so you also must forgive.
Above all, clothe yourselves with love,
which binds everything together in perfect harmony.

And let the peace of Christ rule in your hearts,
Col 3:12-15 *to which indeed you were called in the one body.*

May the God of hope
fill you with all joy and peace in believing,
so that you may abound in hope
Rom 15:13 *by the power of the Holy Spirit.*

22

I HAVE COME THAT THEY MAY HAVE LIFE

The 'Book of Signs' in the Gospel According to John

A. The Good News According to John

The fourth gospel is so distinctive that it can best be compared to the first three gospels by listing the differences. The Gospel according to John expresses the greatness of Jesus with such a singular style and with such remarkable vocabulary that for centuries, many Christians wondered whether it should be revered as the authentic word of God.

Like every book in the Bible, the Gospel according to John is a work of faith: a complex and profound meditation on the greatness of Jesus and his importance for our lives. It is designed to convince the reader that Jesus is the living presence of God among us, and that through Jesus, God will lead us to true wholeness, happiness and peace of heart.

B. Theology Expressed in a Distinctive Style

The whole format of the fourth gospel is unique. Matthew, Mark and Luke show Jesus in action, and invite us to make up our minds about him as if we were onlookers during his ministry. John begins with a theological statement: Jesus is the Word of God who came down to live among us. John begins with the answer, and then proceeds to present Jesus: not as a small-town craftsman who did remarkable deeds, but as the living presence of God among us, revealing his glory to any who will see. Jn 1:14

The synoptic gospels begin with Jesus as an adult (in Mark),
or with the conception of Jesus in Mary's womb (in Matthew and
Luke). John has no Christmas stories at all. Instead, he begins
with the creation of the world. Read the magnificent, poetic, highly
Jn 1:1-18 theological prologue in the first 18 verses of the gospel to see
how different John is from the synoptic gospels.

In reporting the ministry of Jesus, the synoptic gospels string together many brief episodes and invite us to come to our own conclusions. They usually present the sayings of Jesus (even many of the parables) as terse, hard-hitting and memorable. A great many miracle narratives are included (about 25 in Mark, for instance); they have a beginning, middle and end, and little extra detail in between.

The pace in the Gospel of John is much more sedate. There
are only seven miracle narratives; just two of them are duplicated
in the synoptic gospels. Jesus walks on the water in John, as in
Mark and Matthew. The feeding of thousands with a few loaves
Jn 2:1-12 of bread and some fish is the one miracle reported in all four
Jn 5:1-18 gospels. Only John tells of the wedding feast at Cana, the man on
Jn 11:1-44 a stretcher who was healed at the Sheep Pool in Jerusalem, and
Jn 4:46-54 Jn 9 the raising of Lazarus from the dead. The cure of the official's son
and of the man born blind are similar to synoptic stories, but are
told differently.

Calling the miracles 'signs,' John explores their meaning through extended reflective sections. In John, Jesus offers long, flowing discourses rather than brief epigrams, and those discourses are marked by symbolic language that does not appear in the synoptic gospels.

Jn 6:1-15 As an example, in Chapter 6, John reports the feeding of the
Jn 6:16-21 5,000 and the story of Jesus walking on the water; what follows
is a long, meditative discourse on the bread of life (which he
Jn 6:35 associates with belief in Jesus), and then on the Eucharist: "Unless
you eat the flesh [note: not the 'body and blood,' but the flesh] of
Jn 6:53 the Son of Man and drink his blood, you have no life in you." In
speaking of Jesus' Last Supper, John does not even mention the
Eucharist; instead, we find a narrative about Jesus washing the
Jn 13:1-15 feet of his disciples (which does not appear in the other gospels),
and a long farewell which, for the most part, is not reported in
Jn 14–17 the other gospels. Only in John, for example, does Jesus say,

"I give you a new commandment, that you love one another.
Just as I have loved you, you also should love one another.
By this everyone will know that you are my disciples,
if you have love for one another." Jn 13:34-35

The narratives of the death and resurrection of Jesus are similar to the synoptic gospels, though John portrays Jesus' progress towards death more as a glorious revelation of his divinity than as victimization by oppressors. In particular, the last words of Jesus are not a cry of desperation, but a triumphant conclusion:

"It is finished." Jn 19:30

Overall, John is an entirely different form of gospel.

C. Theology Expressed in a Distinctive Vocabulary

The Gospel of John offers us an interpretation of the sayings of Jesus in the language of John's community. But if you believe that Jesus spoke as the synoptic gospels report, you have to conclude that Jesus did not speak in the language of John. The sayings in John give us a true sense of what Jesus meant, but in most cases, they don't give us his exact words. Gospels are not intended to be newspaper reports; they are documents of faith whose purpose is to convince the reader to share the faith expressed in them.

Examples of vocabulary that is distinctive to the Gospel of John are many; let's look at a few of them.

1. *Life*

Whereas the synoptic gospels repeatedly emphasize that Jesus came to bring the reign of God, John has Jesus saying, "I came that they may have life, and have it abundantly." Jn 10:10

'Fullness of life,' in the deepest imaginable sense, is the gift of God through Jesus, according to John. It corresponds to all the concepts surrounding the word 'salvation' as we have used it in this book. Sometimes John uses the phrase 'eternal life.' Like 'salvation,' that term does not refer only to life beyond death, but to fullness of life given by God, beginning now and continuing forever. John tells us that we have eternal life already, and we grow in life, and there will be an ultimate fullness of life.

Such profoundly symbolic language appears from beginning to end of the gospel:

What has come into being in him was life,
Jn 1:3-4 *and the life was the light of all people.*

Jn 3:36 *Whoever believes in the Son has eternal life…*

"Those who eat my flesh and drink my blood have eternal life,
Jn 6:54 *and I will raise them up on the last day."*

"I am the resurrection and the life.
Those who believe in me, even though they die, will live,
Jn 11:25-6 *and everyone who lives and believes in me will never die."*

Jn 14:6 *"I am the way, and the truth, and the life…"*

Jesus did many other signs…which are not written
in this book.
But these are written so that you may come to believe
that Jesus is the Messiah, the Son of God,
Jn 20:30-31 *and that through believing you may have life in his name.*

2. *Light*

Light has always been a symbol of divinity: it speaks of illumination, wisdom and insight as the fruit of the presence of God. Light, according to the book of Genesis, was God's first creation, bringing order into a world of chaos.

It also refers to orientation or direction in life, which is a primary aspect of faith. Think of a lighthouse; think of a light shining in a farmhouse window under a pitch-black sky; think of the crack of light around a door that gives you a sense of where you are when you wake up in the night. Light also helps us communicate. Seeing each other's facial expressions and body language deepens our conversations.

Light has been a symbol of God in many cultures for thousands of years.

The light shines in the darkness, and the darkness did not
Jn 1:5 *overcome it.*

Jn 3:21 *Those who do what is true come to the light…*

"I am the light of the world.
Whoever follows me will never walk in darkness,
but will have the light of life." Jn 8:12

"While you have the light, believe in the light,
that you may become children of light." Jn 12:36

3. *Glory*

When the Israelites escaped into the desert with Moses, they followed a pillar of cloud by day and a pillar of fire by night. They believed that they were following the visible presence of God, which they called "the glory."

For John, Jesus is the visible presence of God, obvious to any who have eyes to see, right from the beginning of his ministry.

The Word became flesh and lived among us,
and we have seen his glory,
the glory as of a father's only son,
full of grace and truth. Jn 1:14

Jesus did this, the first of his signs, in Cana of Galilee,
and he revealed his glory; and his disciples believed in him. Jn 2:11

Father, glorify me in your own presence
with the glory that I had in your presence
before the world existed. Jn 17:5

4. *I Am*

When Moses, speaking to God revealed in a burning bush, asks for the Name of God, the answer is "I am who I am.... Thus you shall say to the Israelites, 'I am' has sent me to you." The sacred Exod 3:14
Name of God is a derivative of the Hebrew verb 'to be.'

Two significant uses of this phrase referring to Jesus appear in the synoptic gospels. When Jesus walks across the water towards the terrified apostles (controlling the waters of chaos as God had done at the creation of the world), he says, "Take heart. Mk 6:50
I am. Do not be afraid." Translating the phrase simply "It is I" risks missing the writer's point. And when the priests of the Temple demand to know whether Jesus is the Messiah, the son of the living God, Jesus' remarkable answer, as reported in Mark, is "I am." With this phrase, the gospel writers are clearly stating Mk 14:62
their belief that Jesus is equal to God.

In the Gospel of John, Jesus repeatedly uses the phrase "I
am" to refer to himself. At times, no predicate is involved: "Before
Jn 8:58 Abraham was, I am." When Jesus is arrested in the garden, he
asks, "Whom are you looking for?" When the temple officials
Jn 18:4-5 respond, "Jesus of Nazareth," Jesus says, "I am he." The group
steps back and falls to the ground.

John also includes a memorable series of sayings that echo these "I am" statements:

Jn 6:35 *"I am the bread of life."*
Jn 8:12 *"I am the light of the world."*
Jn 10:11 *"I am the good shepherd."*
Jn 11:25 *"I am the resurrection and the life."*
Jn 14:6 *"I am the way, and the truth, and the life."*
Jn 15:1 *"I am the true vine."*

In no other gospel does Jesus use any of these phrases. As you read and study John's gospel, listen for its distinctive style.

D. Authorship and Process of Composition

John has always been understood to be the last of the gospels to be written. The final version found in the New Testament is usually dated within ten years before or after 100 CE.

In the past, it was believed that the author of this gospel was
John, the son of Zebedee, one of the fishermen who became a
follower and close friend of Jesus. Two problems seemed
insurmountable, however: his age at the time of composition in
an era of short average lifespans, and the idea that this profound
and elegant gospel could be written by an impetuous fisherman
whom Jesus nicknamed 'son of thunder' and who understood
Mk 3:17 Jesus' teaching so poorly that he asked for a seat of honour when
Mk 10:35-37 Jesus came into power.

Most Scripture scholars today agree that we do not know the name of the author of the fourth gospel. If there is some connection with John the fisherman, perhaps he came to preach in a certain town, and began to build a Christian community. The oral form of the Gospel according to John may have lived on and grown, until an educated member of the community decided to commit the gospel to writing, using symbolic language.

The written document also seems to have undergone revisions and additions: read what was once the ending of the document in John 20:30-31, and notice that another chapter has been added.

E. The Introductory Chapter

1. *The Prologue*

In the beginning was the Word,
and the Word was with God,
and the Word was God.
He was in the beginning with God.
All things came into being through him;
without him not one thing came into being.

What has come into being in him was life,
and the life was the light of all people.
The light shines in the darkness,
and the darkness did not overcome it. Jn 1:1-5

And the Word become flesh
and lived among us,
and we have seen his glory,
the glory as of a father's only son,
full of grace and truth. Jn 1:14

"In the beginning was the Word." The majestic introductory poem in John begins with the same phrase as the book of Genesis: "In the beginning…." Unlike any other gospel, John's reflection on the greatness of Jesus begins not with his adult life (as in Mark), or with his conception and birth (as in Matthew and Luke), but with the creation of the world.

In Genesis 1, we read that to create the world God simply spoke with power: "'Let there be light'; and there was light." The Word of God created the world. Gen 1:3

Of all the gospels, only John, in this introductory poem, calls Jesus "the Word of God." Why did he choose that term? Words have power; they can change your life. The author of John realized that the life of Jesus summarized the reality of God and powerfully expressed God's will to lead people to wholeness.

John immediately introduces two symbolic themes that will permeate the gospel: the Word brings Life to creation; and the Word enlightens.

'Fullness of life' means wholeness – the ultimate goal of every human journey. The author of John repeatedly declares that the fundamental purpose of the ministry of Jesus was to enable people to "have life in abundance."

The prologue also introduces the recurring theme of the struggle between light and darkness. Time after time in John,
Jn 3:18 when the light is revealed, some people gladly receive it, while others choose darkness.

Jn 1:14 ***"And the Word became flesh."*** This term is intended to shock the reader into a new consciousness of God's amazing initiative. 'Flesh' is almost always a negative word in the Bible. It doesn't refer only to the realm of sexuality, but to the frailty and sinfulness of humanity without God. The Word of God became flesh – he chose to share our human weakness. Later Christian scholars, thinking in Latin, called this insight of John 'incarnation' – the enfleshment of God. John also dared to use the word 'flesh' with regard to the Eucharist. In John, it is not 'the body of Christ,' but
Jn 6:53 "Unless you eat the flesh of the Son of Man…you have no life in you."

Jn 1:14 ***"And lived among us."*** The Greek word translated here means 'pitched his tent.' Readers are expected to remember that God lived in a tent among the children of Israel as they wandered in the desert after escaping from Egypt. The tent of meeting, the tabernacle, housed the ark of the covenant, the continuing sign of God's living presence among the people. In the book of Sirach, Wisdom speaks:

> *"The Creator of all things gave me a command,*
> *and my Creator chose the place for my tent.*
> Sir 24:8 *He said, 'Make your dwelling in Jacob.'"*

The Gospel of John is full of rich allusions like these: it's almost impossible to appreciate fully the depth and beauty of the gospel without some help from biblical interpreters.

Jn 1:14 ***"We have seen his glory."*** 'Glory' is another symbolic word that recurs throughout the gospel. As mentioned earlier, the Israelites called the presence of God "the glory." For John, Jesus is the visible presence of God: anyone who is willing to see it knows the truth from the beginning.

"Full of grace and truth." Hundreds of times in the Hebrew Scriptures, the words *chesed w'emeth* are used to describe God's loving-kindness and fidelity towards humanity. John brings his theological statement to a profound conclusion by declaring that Jesus, the Word of God made flesh, embodies the eternal loving-kindness and faithfulness of the God who had nurtured the Jewish people for almost 20 centuries.

2. *John the Baptist*

Every year in Advent, we are reminded about John the Baptist preparing the way for the Jesus' public ministry. Luke in particular reports that the Baptist was a blood relative of Jesus, and gives examples of John's radical and prophetic preaching style.

The Gospel according to John offers different insights on his career. The gospel insists that Jesus was far superior to John the Baptist: "There was a man sent from God, whose name was John. . .
He himself was not the light, but he came to testify to the light." Jn 1:6, 8
When priests and Levites come to the Jordan River to ask the Baptist about who he is, he replies that he is not the Messiah.

They then ask whether John is Elijah. As mentioned in Jn 1:20
Chapter 16 of this book, according to Jewish tradition, the prophet Elijah had never died, but had been taken up to God's heaven in a fiery chariot. People came to believe that Elijah would return to prepare the way before the Messiah came. In Matthew, it is reported that Jesus, in talking about the ministry of John the Baptist,
declares that "he is Elijah who is to come." But in the Gospel of Mt 11:14
John, the Baptist denies that he is the Elijah figure, and declares
that he is merely a voice crying in the wilderness. Is 40:3

The next day, Jesus enters the scene, and the Baptist identifies him with a statement of faith (reported in no other gospel) that
has found its way into Christian liturgies: "Here is the Lamb of Jn 1:29
God who takes away the sin of the world." With this image, the gospel writer wants us to recall the annual slaughter of lambs for the Passover celebration, an event that was taking place as Jesus was being crucified. The image of the lamb may also refer to
Isaiah's poem about the suffering servant of God – "He was like a Is 53:7
lamb that is led to the slaughter" – a phrase that Christians use to express the redemptive meaning of the death of Jesus.

The Gospel according to John does not report that John baptized Jesus. It is easy to theorize, since Jesus has already been presented in the gospel as the visible presence of God in the world,

that John does not understand baptism as appropriate for Jesus.
Instead, the Baptist testifies that the Holy Spirit appeared to him
Jn 1:32-34 to proclaim that Jesus is Son of God. John the Baptist is primarily
a witness to the importance and meaning of Jesus' life.

In later chapters, the gospel gives tantalizing clues about more
prosaic historical considerations. It seems possible that Jesus and
Jn 3:22-23 his friends became disciples of John the Baptist for a while, and
perhaps carried on the Baptist's ministry of preaching and
Jn 4:1-2 baptizing. Then, in the gospel, the Baptist disappears and Jesus
assumes his rightful role as Messiah and Son of God. "He must
Jn 3:30 increase, but I must decrease," says the Baptist, and he is gone.

F. The Book of Signs

Commentators divide the Gospel of John into two main sections, often called the Book of Signs and the Book of Glory.

Jn 2:1-12 Chapters 2 to 11 present the ministry of Jesus highlighted by
Jn 4:46-54 seven 'signs': the wedding in the town of Cana; the healing of a
Jn 5:1-18 royal official's son, also at Cana; the healing of a crippled man at
Jn 6:1-15 the Pool in Jerusalem; the feeding of 5,000 people on the shore of
Jn 5:16-21 the Sea of Galilee; Jesus' walking on the sea; the cure of the man
Jn 9 who had been born blind; and the raising of Lazarus.

Jn 11:1-44 Each of the signs is presented in John's distinctive style, and
is woven by the author into long dissertations presenting the
teaching of Jesus in symbolic language, with an eye to the reaction
of friend and foe to the light that has broken through the darkness.

1. The Wedding at Cana (John 2:1-12)

This episode has captured the Christian imagination for centuries.

Mary, whose name is never mentioned in John, is addressed
Jn 2:4, 12:26 here as 'Woman,' just as she is at the death of Jesus. Perhaps she
stands as the new Eve for all women, or for all humanity, or for
Judaism. She recognizes people's need at this wedding, realizes
that Jesus can abundantly fill the need, intervenes, and counsels
openness to whatever he does.

Jesus declares his independence of his roots by rebuffing her
initially; he declares that the hour (another of John's symbolic
Jn 2:4 terms referring to the climactic death and resurrection of Jesus)
has not come – and then he proceeds to do what she asks.

For the author, the transformation of water into wine symbolizes that the New Covenant has supplanted the Jewish tradition. (The gospel writer uses this event as the prelude to a long section explaining that Jesus transcends and replaces the Jewish tradition from which he came.) The abundance of wine reveals Jesus' glory (he can control nature; he is the visible presence of God) and inspires his disciples to believe.

2. *The Cleansing of the Temple (John 2:13-23)*

The author immediately goes on to describe another sign that the
Old Covenant has been replaced: Jesus marches into the Temple
at the Passover season and violently disrupts traditional Jewish
practices. When the opposition asks him for a sign, Jesus cryp-
tically says, "Destroy this temple, and in three days I will raise it Jn 2:19
up"; the author explains that Jesus is speaking about his death
and resurrection.

The other gospels report the cleansing of the Temple as having taken place in the last week of Jesus' life; they are likely more historically accurate in this regard. John has the episode at the beginning of Jesus' ministry because it strongly supports the gospel's inaugural theme of the transcending of the former covenant.

One tiny detail in the narrative provides an interesting
historical connection. Scholars agree that Herod the Great (the
Jewish king who was alive when Jesus was born) began the
renovation of the second Temple in Jerusalem around 19 BCE. If
so, the Jews' statement that "This temple has been under con- Jn 2:20
struction for 46 years" places the story in 27 CE. This helps us
determine that Jesus probably died in the late 20s CE. Since
historians agree that Herod died in 4 BCE, and since Jesus seems
to have been born before Herod died, Jesus likely died in his early
30s.

In this scene, Jesus' enemies are identified as "the Jews." Naming "the Jews" as Jesus' enemies has contributed to 20 centuries of Christian persecution of Jewish people. Why this prejudicial labelling? After all, Jesus and his friends were Jews, too. By the time the gospel was written, Christians of Jewish heritage had been "driven out of the synagogues." Since the Roman Empire permitted only Jews and those who worshipped Roman gods to practise their religion, the declaration that Christians were not Jews amounted to a death sentence for many Christians who refused to worship Roman state gods.

3. *The Conversation with Nicodemus (John 3:1-21)*

Nicodemus is presented as a good-hearted but benighted Pharisee who comes out of the darkness of night to speak with the Light of the world.

He is not the only sympathetic Pharisee in the gospels; Jesus agrees with their teachings from time to time. (See Luke 10:25-28, about the greatest commandment in the Law of Moses.) The author of John uses Nicodemus as a foil for Jesus' teaching on the importance of being born again into the life of the Spirit. John often uses the device of naive misunderstanding ("Can one enter
Jn 3:4 a second time into the mother's womb?" asks Nicodemus) to lead
Jn 7:48-52 into further teaching by the master. After a couple of such
Jn 19:39 questions, Nicodemus fades from the scene, until he reappears
Jn 7:50-52 later in the gospel in a dispute with his colleagues, and in an
Jn 19:38-42 action of support for the disciples after Jesus' death. After
Nicodemus speaks his last line in Chapter 3 ("How can this be?"), Jesus goes on to teach about the purpose of his ministry without engaging in further dialogue.

In this context, John offers a great summary of the Christian gospel:

> *God so loved the world that he gave his only Son,*
> *so that everyone who believes in him may not perish*
> Jn 3:16 *but may have eternal life.*

The saying emphasizes Christian belief that God has taken the initiative in love to lead people to wholeness or fullness of life. God's gift of eternal life is given to those who believe. Eternal life begins now and continues beyond death.

The theme of judgment also appears in this context. John always recognizes that the gift of God causes divisions among
Jn 3:19 people: some accept Jesus, and some reject him. But according to
John, the action of God is entirely positive and in no way against humanity. The Son has not come to judge, but to save. People who reject the Light condemn themselves by rejecting God's gift. Similar ideas are found in Chapter 12 of the gospel, where Jesus says,

> *I have come as light into the world,*
> *so that everyone who believes in me should not remain in the darkness...*

I came not to judge the world, but to save the world.
The one who rejects me…has a judge:
on the last day that the word I have spoken
will serve as judge… Jn 12:46-50
[God's] commandment is eternal life.

4. *The Samaritan Woman at the Well (John 4)*

In Chapter 4 of the gospel, the theme of fullness of life continues. This time, the symbol for wholeness is "living water" that will satisfy the drinker's thirst forever, and "will become in them a spring of water gushing up to eternal life." Jn 4:14

The recipient of the offer is a Samaritan woman, a person of mixed race. While most Jews despised Samaritans, Jesus was against such racial prejudice, as shown in Luke's parable of the good Samaritan. Because Samaritans and Jews engaged in continual fighting, it would take considerable courage for Jesus and his Jewish supporters to venture into Samaritan territory. John uses this incident to emphasize that Jesus exploded traditional taboos and brought fullness of life to the larger world beyond Judaism. Lk 10:30-37

That he invited a woman to be his missionary to her people is a further challenge to traditional boundaries. In Jesus' time, men did not speak to women in public unless they were relatives. This woman has been portrayed in Christian tradition as a fallen woman in whom Jesus saw potential, but it may be more accurate to see her as a victim of patriarchy. She had apparently suffered five divorces in a society where men could divorce their wives without appeal, and women could not divorce their husbands at all. Divorce was shattering for many women, especially if they had no family to return to; their only hope was to find another man to take them in. Perhaps she was repeatedly divorced because she was infertile. She still needed the protection of a man, and might have given up on marriage. This is why Jesus says, "The one you have now is not your husband." Jn 4:17-18

As he does elsewhere, Jesus reaches out to one of society's outcasts and elevates her. Responding to her expression of hope for the coming of the Messiah, he makes the first of the gospel's great "I am" declarations to this woman. Readers of John, more clearly than the woman herself, see the phrase as resonating with the story of God's self-revelation to Moses: "I am who I am." John emphasizes that Jesus is the living presence of God among us. Jn 4:25-26 Exod 3:14

The woman goes on to evangelize her townspeople, who quickly accept the gospel and eventually declare, "We have heard
Jn 4:42 for ourselves, and we know that this is truly the Saviour of the world."

The chapter concludes with the healing of a royal official's
Jn 4:53 son in Capernaum. The man accepts Jesus' word of reassurance; the son lives, and the whole household believes.

In Chapter 4, John teaches that fullness of life is offered and accepted beyond the borders of traditional Judaism.

5. *The Relationship Between the Father and the Son (John 5)*

In Chapter 5 of the gospel, Jesus returns to Jerusalem, the headquarters of the religious establishment, where he heals a man who had been ill for many years and thereby incites antagonism
Jn 5:16 among "the Jews" because the healing took place on the sabbath.

The synoptic gospels report that Jesus dissented from traditional standards of sabbath observance, advising his hearers that
Lk 13:10-11 God made the sabbath law to help people, not to tie them in
Mk 2:25, 3:5 knots, and recommending that people do good, rather than do nothing, on the sabbath.

In John, Jesus justifies his action of healing on the sabbath by
Jn 5:17 saying, "My Father is still working, and I also am working." The author reports that his opponents were enraged, because Jesus was "making himself equal to God," which is indeed what he implies. Jewish theology required all believers to do no work on the sabbath, but recognized, in spite of the famous Genesis statement that God rested on the seventh day, that God indeed had to continue to 'work' on the sabbath to keep the world in existence. When Jesus says that God works and he works, too, he is rightly understood as claiming equality to God.

The author of John offers several theological statements about the relationship between the Father and the Son, making it clear that the Son depends on the Father.

Jn 5:19-20; see also Jn 3:34, 7:28, 8:24, 8:26, 12:49

The Son can do nothing on his own,
but only what he sees the Father doing;
for whatever the Father does, the Son does likewise.
The Father loves the Son, and shows him all that he himself is doing.

Some commentators suggest that the above lines could be read without the capital letters, as a sort of parable about the relationship of any father and his apprentice son; the implication is that the normal family relationship helps us understand the relationship between God and Jesus.

In Chapter 5, the relationship extends to the two great divine roles of having/giving life and judging:

For just as the Father has life in himself, Jn 5:26-27
so he has granted the Son also to have life in himself; see also 5:21-22
and he has given him authority to execute judgment.

6. *The Bread of Life (John 6)*

Chapter 6 begins with two important signs, both of which are also reported in the synoptic gospels. Jesus feeds 5,000 people, (Jn 6:1-14) symbolically inaugurating the banquet of the Messiah by recalling the days when God fed the chosen people with manna in the wilderness. When he perceives that the crowd is planning to appoint him messiah-king to suit their political expectations, he (Jn 6:15) escapes. This time, the crowd's response to his offer of abundant life is shallow and opportunistic.

Then Jesus walks across the windswept waters of the Sea of Galilee, symbolically proclaiming his equality to the God who controlled the waters in the great creation narrative in Genesis and liberated Israel by guiding Moses and the people unharmed through the sea. "Do not be afraid: I am," he declares for a second (Jn 6:20) time.

The rest of Chapter 6 is perhaps best described as the community's reflection on the meaning of those two signs.

In verses 35-47, Jesus declares himself to be the bread of life, (Jn 6:35, 40, 45) and invites his hearers to come to him, believe in him, hear the teaching of the Father and learn from it. These verses understand the bread of life as a wise teaching that nourishes the believer's inner life. This phrase echoes the Old Testament saying that one (Deut 8:3) does not live by bread alone, but by every word that comes from (Exod 16:4) the mouth of God. Several other texts from the Hebrew Scriptures (Neh 9:15; Ps 78:24) refer to the manna that rained down from heaven to satisfy the (Ps 105:40) Israelites' hunger in the desert. John has described Jesus as the Word of God; now that Word is compared to bread that gives life to all who believe: "Whoever believes has eternal life." (Jn 6:47)

After verse 47, the metaphor evolves, as believers are repeatedly invited to eat the bread, and the bread is now understood to be the "flesh of the Son of Man." Verses 48-58 are John's statement about the Eucharist. Although John offers a lengthy report about the Last Supper, he does not even mention the Eucharist in that context. Here, using the distinctive language of 'flesh and blood,' John speaks of the spiritual nourishment that Jesus offers to the Christian community through the sacrament.

In both parts of this reflection, in which the bread of life is used to symbolize both Word (or Wisdom) and sacrament, John reports that Jesus promised to reward people who believe and who participate in the sacrament: "I will raise them up on the last
Jn 6:40 day." John's phrase has become so familiar to us, we may not
Jn 6:54 realize that Christian teaching on a final resurrection is referred
to only rarely in the synoptic gospels.

In the last few centuries before Jesus lived, some Jewish academics, such as the Pharisees, came to believe that God would raise the dead to new life at some future time. The conservative Sadducees, knowing that the hope of resurrection arose in Judaism
Mk 12:18// not from Moses but from the Persian tradition, rejected this
Mt 22:23// teaching. Jesus is reported to have agreed with the Pharisees in
Lk 20:27 the expectation of a future resurrection.

But Jesus spoke of the kingdom of God (or 'of heaven') as a reality that begins as soon as people accept the saving power of God's love. He doesn't base his moral demands primarily on a promise of future reward, but rather on the principle that we are called as children of God to do what is right. Jesus' followers
Mk 13:30// expected him to return in glory in the near future, when God's
Mt 24:34// kingdom would be established definitively on earth.

Lk 21:32 Hope in a future resurrection seems to have become more important in the early communities as the first generation of believers began to die and Jesus had not yet returned. The most explicit expression of this evolving belief is found in Paul's first letter to the people of Thessalonika. There he promises that just
1 Thess 4:14-15 as Jesus died and rose again, so will all believers who die before
he returns. The Gospel of John perpetuates that hope with its distinctive phrase about 'the last day.'

Chapter 6 concludes with John's customary presentation of the varying reactions to Jesus' words. Even his friends are divided when Jesus presents himself, Word and Sacrament, as the new bread. Peter's leadership among the Twelve is acknowledged by his beautiful statement of faith:

> *"Lord, to whom can we go?*
> *You have the words of eternal life.*
> *We have come to believe and to know*
> *that you are the Holy One of God."* Jn 6:68-69

7. *A Series of Conflicts (John 7 and 8)*

Chapters 7 and 8 of John's gospel report Jesus' ferocious conflicts with the voices of the Jerusalem religious establishment in the setting of the feast of Tabernacles (Sukkoth), an autumn harvest festival that is still celebrated today.

Memorable sayings in these chapters include the declaration
"I am the light of the world"; the promise that "if…you are truly Jn 8:12
my disciples you will know the truth, and the truth will make
you free"; and several more "I am" sayings, perhaps the most Jn 8:31-32
striking of which is "Before Abraham was, I am." Jn 8:58

At the beginning of Chapter 8, we read about Jesus' unforgettable action to save the life of a woman who was about to be Jn 8:1-11
executed for adultery. The account is consistent with Jesus' compassionate attitude towards people who suffer from discrimination at the hands of self-righteous believers. (Scholars debated for a long time whether this episode was added to the gospel later, but it is now an accepted part of the gospel, and seen as the inspired Word of God.)

8. *Seeing and Believing: The Man Born Blind (John 9)*

All four gospels report incidents of Jesus giving sight to blind people; all understand these miracles to represent not simply restoration of optical function, but more important, new vision for the human journey.

As usual, John reports the healing of a blind man in a distinctive way. Details are slightly different from any synoptic account: the man had been blind from birth; he is sent to bathe in the pool whose name means 'Sent.' But what sets John's account apart is the long, reflective narrative on the consequences and meaning of the healing.

The predominant theme in the chapter is knowledge: the Pharisees, the parents and the blind man himself all claim to know

Jn 9:17 certain things, and (sometimes defiantly) express their ignorance
of other things.

Jesus' enemies claim to know that Jesus is not from God
Jn 9:16 because he doesn't keep the sabbath, that he is a sinner, that God
Jn 9:24 spoke to Moses, and that the once-blind man was born in sin.
Jn 9:34 They express their ignorance about how the man received his
Jn 9:29 sight, and how a sinner could perform such signs. "We don't even
know where this man comes from," they say.

The Pharisees interrogate the man's parents, who declare that
they know it is their son who was healed, and that he was born
blind, but they don't know how it is that he can now see. "Ask
Jn 9:20 him yourselves," say the old couple, who are afraid of being
thrown out of the synagogue.

The man himself is portrayed as courageous and open-hearted.
Jn 9:9, 11, 15, 17, 25 He answers the interrogators honestly, stating that he believes
Jesus to be a prophet, destroying the Pharisees' arguments and
supporting Jesus. He even saucily asks the Pharisees if they're
asking so many questions because they want to become disciples
of Jesus, too.

The intricate structure of the chapter leads to the climactic
scene in which Jesus searches out the man and declares himself
to be the "Son of Man" who should be believed. The man asks for
Jn 9:35-38 a clear statement, and then declares his faith and worships Jesus.
Now he sees in a new way; now he believes.

The Pharisees, on the other hand, hear Jesus talk about
offering new vision and having it rejected by people who think
they know everything. They indict themselves by asking whether
they are the blind ones. Jesus responds that their blindness is
Jn 9:40-41 their own fault: because they claim to be able to see but accept
only their own point of view, "[their] sin remains."

Christians need to read this chapter of John in a sincere spirit of self-examination: to what extent are we wilfully blind, like the Pharisees here? (Read also John 1:38-39.) To what extent are we decent but fearful, like the man's parents? To what extent are we courageous and open to God's action, like the man born blind?

9. *The Good Shepherd (John 10)*

To express God's relationship to the people, the Bible often uses
imagery of a shepherd and his sheep. One of the more familiar
and beloved psalms begins with this image: "The LORD is my
Ps 23 shepherd." The book of Ezekiel laments the destructiveness of

leaders who have betrayed their responsibility; God rages against
the false shepherds and declares, "I myself will be the shepherd Ezek 34:15
of my sheep." God promises to send a new shepherd-prince in Ezek 34:2
the spirit of King David. Jesus tells a parable about a shepherd
who leaves 99 sheep to search for the one that is missing. In Luke, Lk 15:3-7
Jesus explains his friendships with outcasts by saying that like Mt 18:10-14
God and like the shepherd, he reaches out to those who are lost.

The tenth chapter of John offers three variations on this theme. First, verses 1-5 explore the idea of a sheepfold, which was usually an area surrounded by a stone fence where several shepherds could keep their sheep safe overnight with a minimum of labour – perhaps one guard at a time slept at the gate. When a shepherd came for his flock, the sheep followed his familiar voice. In this intriguing metaphor, the Greek term for sheepfold is the same word used for the courtyard of the Temple, where Jesus' opponents could be found. Perhaps the gatekeeper represents the Jewish religious establishment; when Jesus enters, he will call his flock out of the sheepfold of Judaism, and they will follow him wherever he takes them.

Some commentators find in this comparison a sort of self-justification by the community where the Gospel of John developed. It is different from other Christian communities; it uses different language; it thinks differently about Jesus. It believes that it is faithful to Jesus, but it is not circumscribed by stone walls and boundaries.

Later in the gospel, the role of the Holy Spirit is described in
a similar way. The Spirit not only "will remind you of all that I
have said to you," but also will "guide you into all the truth" – in Jn 14:26
some instances, a truth that no one in the community has seen Jn 16:13
before.

It is interesting that the exploratory, boundary-free spirit of John's community has become the spirit of what might be called a traditional community: the Roman Catholic Church. Catholicism strongly asserts that we must remain faithful to the past, and especially to the Scriptures, but is also open to the possibility that Jesus in the Spirit may lead the community to places it has never been. That openness is theoretical justification for the development of Catholic teachings that cannot be found in the Scriptures (e.g., the Immaculate Conception of Mary, the Assumption, papal infallibility). Of course, the same openness can be invoked by members of the community who would like to see the Church evolve in other unprecedented directions, such as the ordination of women and married men, and a more accepting attitude towards sexuality. All believers must try to be open to the leadership of the Holy Spirit, wherever this may lead us.

Jn 10:7 Second, Jesus declares himself to be "the gate for the sheep."
Jn 14:6 In the same sense that he later calls himself "the way," he now
states that all who believe will enter salvation by going through him. Here, almost exactly in the middle of the gospel, Jesus summarizes his entire mission according to John:

I came that they may have life,
Jn 10:10 *and have it abundantly.*

Finally, in verses 11-18, Jesus speaks of himself as "the good
Jn 10:14 shepherd." Continuing the theme from verse 3, he says that his
relationship with the sheep is one of personal mutual knowledge.
A new and important theme is introduced here: the good shepherd
Jn 10:15 lays down his life for his sheep. Later, John reports Jesus as saying,
Jn 15:13 "No one has greater love than this, to lay down one's life for one's
Jn 13:37 friends."

This is one of John's great expressions of the meaning of Jesus' life and death. There is no reference to the understanding that Jesus died to make up for the sin of Adam and Eve. Jesus' death and subsequent "taking up his life again" (and, indeed, his whole self-giving life before that) are seen as protecting his flock from "the wolf," and as bringing fullness of life to his people.

The gospel goes on to expand the exploration of Jesus' relationship with his Father from Chapter 5, expressing their total unity of spirit, their perfect mutual understanding.

Jn 10:18 *The Father knows me, and I know the Father.*

Jn 10:30 *The Father and I are one.*

Jn 10:18 *The Father is in me, and I am in the Father.*

In the other gospels, only one brief passage in Matthew and one in Luke use similar language to describe Jesus' relationship with God. Note that the word 'knowledge' in the Hebrew tradition is not conceptual, but experiential: only the Father can experience the unfathomable riches of the Son; only the Son can know the depths of the being of God and reveal the profound reality of God to the world.

No one knows the Son except the Father,
and no one knows the Father except the Son Mt 11:27//
and anyone to whom the Son chooses to reveal him. Lk 10:22

10. The Resurrection and the Life: The Raising of Lazarus (John 11)

The Book of Signs comes to a climactic conclusion with the raising of Lazarus, John's most dramatic presentation of Jesus as the giver of life.

Surprisingly, no other gospel reports this event. Lazarus is presented in John as the brother of Martha and Mary, two friends
of Jesus who appear in the three synoptic gospels. Matthew and Mt 21:17//
Mark both report that Jesus stayed with Martha and Mary at their Mk 11:11
home at Bethany, but Lazarus is never mentioned. They also tell of an incident in the home of Simon the leper in Bethany, where
Jesus praised an unnamed woman who poured ointment over his Mt 26:6//
head in preparation for his burial. In Chapter 12, John reports a Mk 14:3
similar incident, also at Bethany, but says it was Mary, sister of
Martha, who anointed Jesus' feet. So several historical details of Jn 12:1-8
Jesus' relationship with his friends in Bethany are at variance.

Perhaps for narrative purposes, the author presents Jesus in this chapter in a rather negative light. He delays his response to
the sisters' urgent plea in order to create a teaching opportunity, Jn 11:6
and plays with words at a distressing time ("Lazarus has fallen
asleep, but I am going there to awaken him"). On the other hand, Jn 11:11
John says that, once he was confronted with the tears of Mary and her friends, "Jesus wept. So the Jews said, 'See how he loved
him!'" Jn 11:35-36

In this chapter, as always in John, it is important to realize that the narrative is highly stylized for symbolic purposes. It is not possible to analyze Jesus' personality from this episode; the author's purpose is not historical but theological.

"I am the resurrection and the life.
Those who believe in me, even though they die, will live,
and everyone who lives and believes in me will never die." Jn 11:25-26

As he does elsewhere, John uses words with multiple levels of meaning. Here, 'live' and 'die' refer to more than physical life and death; they assure us that God will lead us to wholeness, and that God's love is stronger than death and endures beyond our death. Jesus indeed brings abundant life.

Did I not tell you that if you believed,
Jn 11:40 *you would see the glory of God?*

Jesus' gift of life arouses faith in the hearts of some, but
engenders hatred in his enemies. At Jesus' trial, the high priest
ironically declares that it is better for one man to die for the benefit
Jn 11:50 of the people, rather than having the whole nation perish. And so
Jesus' gift of life to Lazarus leads inevitably to his own death.

The stage has been set for Jesus' hour: he will be "lifted up,"
Jn 12:32 he will "draw all people to himself"; he will make it possible for
Jn 8:28 people to "know that 'I am,'" and eventually "whoever believes
Jn 3:14 will have eternal life."

11. *Summary: Who Is Jesus According to the Book of Signs?*

The first half of the Gospel of John offers an astoundingly complex portrait of Jesus. The enlightening descriptions of Jesus listed in the following paragraphs are found only in the Gospel of John.

John presents Jesus as the *Word* who powerfully expresses
Jn 1:1-2 the reality of God. The Word is the source of our being, through
whom all things were made. And the Word has become flesh,
sharing our human existence, sent by God to reveal anew God's
Jn 1:14 grace and truth.

In the course of reflection on the seven great signs in John,
Jn 1:4-5 Jesus is portrayed as the *light of the world,* overcoming the
Jn 8:12 darkness, giving meaning and direction to human lives, making
Jn 9:5 visible the guiding power of God.

Jn 4:10-14 He is the giver of *living water,* which quenches our deepest
Jn 6:35, 48 thirst and enables us to live and grow. He is the *bread of life* who
calls us to believe and nourishes our spiritual lives through both
word and sacrament.

Jn 10:11 He is the *good shepherd* who knows each of us by name, calls
us to follow him wherever he leads us, and lays down his life for
Jn 1:29 us. Conversely, he is also the *Lamb of God* who is led to the
slaughter and thereby overcomes the sinfulness of the world.

Jesus is also presented in language that is familiar to Christians
Jn 3:14 from the other three gospels: he is *Son of Man,* a human being
Jn 8:28 who shares our mortality but is expected to return in power, and
Jn 4:25-26 he is *Messiah,* fulfilling the hopes of the Jewish people in a way
that exceeds their expectation.

And Jesus is *Son of God.* In the language of John, Jesus Jn 2:11
manifests the *glory* – he is the visible, tangible presence of God Jn 1:14, 18, 34
among us. He has power equal to the Creator, changing water to Jn 2:11
wine, controlling the waters of the sea, 'working' as the Father Jn 6:20
does, even on the sabbath day. He shares God's authority to judge Jn 5:17
the world, but declares that he has come to save rather than to Jn 8:28
judge. He expresses his divinity by repeatedly invoking the name Jn 8:58
of God revealed to Moses: "I am."

Most significantly, Jesus offers *fullness of life* to all who believe. Jn 10:10
Salvation – eternal life, the wholeness that is God's gift to humanity Jn 11:25-26
– begins when people 'see' or recognize the glory that is Jesus, Jn 6:39, 54
and 'believe.' Eternal life does not end at death but conquers death and looks forward to Jesus' promise: "I will raise them up on the last day."

23

NOW THE HOUR HAS COME FOR THE SON OF MAN TO BE GLORIFIED

The 'Book of Glory' in the Gospel According to John

In the Gospel of John, the narrative leading to Jesus' death and resurrection cannot be called a 'passion,' with that word's implications of suffering and passivity.

Instead, as many commentators have noted, it is as if the already-risen Jesus purposefully takes possession of Jerusalem, inspires his followers with insight about the meaning of his mission, advances to meet his death as the consummation of his life, and returns in glory to bestow the Holy Spirit on his friends.

Jn 10:18 *No one takes my life from me, but I lay it down on my own.*
I have power to lay it down, and power to take it up again.

Thus the narrative of the last week of Jesus' life in John is often designated as The 'Book of Glory.'

Jn 12:1-50 After the anointing at Bethany, the entry into Jerusalem, and
some sayings in that context, the gospel uses the setting of the
Jn 13–17 Last Supper to offer five chapters of profound Christian reflection
that is unparalleled in the other gospels. No mention is made of
Eucharist during the Last Supper; instead, the significant gesture
Jn 13:1-15 Jesus undertakes the night before his death is washing his disciples'
feet.

In these passages, themes are introduced and explored, then disappear only to recur later. Our considerations will therefore be thematic, dealing with the meaning of death for Jesus and for Christians, the promise of the Holy Spirit, the Christian way of life, and the great farewell prayer of Jesus. We will then discuss the narratives of Jesus' death and resurrection as they are presented in John.

A. The Great Discourse at the Last Supper

1. *The Meaning of Jesus' Death: Departure and Return, Support for Believers*

Because the friends of Jesus and the earliest Christian communities felt the absence of Jesus very deeply after his death and resurrection, they needed to develop an understanding of the meaning of his untimely death. Like us, they depended on faith to reassure them that Jesus had not ultimately deserted them, and that his death was both meaningful and beneficial.

The distress of the disciples is compared to the pain of a woman in childbirth:

> *"When a woman is in labour,* Jn 16:21-22
> *she has pain because her hour has come.*
> *But when her child is born,*
> *she no longer remembers the anguish*
> *because of the joy of having brought a human being*
> *into the world.*
> *So you have pain now…"*

Jesus emphasizes that he is leaving his friends, and that they will be grief-stricken.

> *"Little children, I am with you only a little longer…*
> *'Where I am going, you cannot come.'"* Jn 13:33

> *"If you loved me,*
> *you would rejoice that I am going to the Father,*
> *because the Father is greater than I."* Jn 14:28

> *"I am leaving the world and am going to the Father."* Jn 16:28

But the most encouraging promise of Jesus is that he will return, and will inspire joy in his followers once again.

> *"But I will see you again, and your hearts will rejoice,*
> *and no one will take your joy from you."* Jn 16:22

> *"I will not leave you orphaned;*
> *I am coming to you."* Jn 14:18

"A little while, and you will no longer see me,
Jn 16:16 *and again a little while, and you will see me."*

Jn 16:20 *"Your pain will turn into joy."*

He promises that his disciples will derive benefits from his death:

"Unless a grain of wheat falls into the earth and dies,
it remains just a single grain:
Jn 12:24 *but if it dies, it bears much fruit."*

What fruit does the death of Jesus produce?

"Now is the judgment of this world;
now the ruler of this world will be driven out.
And I, when I am lifted up from the earth,
Jn 12:31-32 *will draw all people to myself."*

For John, Jesus conquers by his death the forces of evil and draws everyone to himself. John goes on to affirm that after his death, Jesus will send the Advocate to strengthen his friends. With the help of the Spirit, the disciples will lead lives based on truth and love. Jesus' death will help believers face with courage their own mortality.

2. *The Meaning of Death for Christians*

The Christian community where the Gospel of John developed had experienced decades of persecution at the hands of the Roman empire. They blamed their suffering on the Jewish religious leaders' decision to expel followers of Jesus from the synagogues. Everyone fears death; all of us struggle to believe that death is valuable and meaningful, both for ourselves and for the people we love. John's community took courage from their understanding of the value of Jesus' death, and found hope in Jesus' promise to take us to be with him:

"If the world hates you,
Jn 15:18 *be aware that it hated me before it hated you."*

"They will put you out of the synagogues.
Indeed, an hour is coming when those who kill you
Jn 16:2 *will think that by doing so they are offering worship to God."*

Jn 16:33 *"But take courage; I have conquered the world!"*

"Believe in God, believe also in me." Jn 14:1

"And if I go and prepare a place for you.
I will come again and will take you to myself,
so that where I am, you may be also." Jn 14:3

"In my Father's house there are many dwelling places." Jn 14:2

Christian believers have cherished the hope for life beyond death expressed in the Gospel of John through 20 centuries.

3. *The Coming of the Spirit of Truth*

"It is to your advantage that I go away,
for if I do not go away, the Advocate will not come to you;
but if I go, I will send him to you." Jn 16:7

The Gospel according to Luke emphasizes the role of the Holy Spirit in Jesus' life. John is more concerned about the role of the Spirit in the life of Christians, and presents distinctive ideas about the Spirit:

"When [the Advocate] comes,
he will prove the world wrong [or 'convict the world']
about sin and righteousness and judgment..." Jn 16:8-11

The verses are confusing, but the image is clearly from the legal world. The Advocate is presented as a sort of courtroom prosecutor in the conflict between Jesus and the world. Like Jesus, the Advocate will support believers as they challenge the way of the world, the morality of the marketplace. Later in the chapter, Jesus will encourage his followers, proclaiming, "I have conquered Jn 16:33
the world!" It is the risen Jesus who speaks, even though his statement is set at the Last Supper, the evening before his death.

A comparable legal image is found in Chapter 15:

"When the Advocate comes,
whom I will send to you from the Father,
the Spirit of truth who comes from the Father,
he will testify on my behalf.
You also are to testify..." Jn 15:26-27

The spectre of conflict is also present in a saying where Jesus seems to identify himself as the first Advocate or supporter for the disciples:

"I will ask the Father,
and he will give you another Advocate
to be with you forever.
This is the Spirit of truth
whom the world cannot receive,
because it neither sees him nor knows him.
You know him, because he abides with you,
Jn 14:16-17 *and he will be in you."*

The gift of the Spirit is truth. Believing is fundamentally a search for meaning in our lives, and for an understanding of the role of God in transforming our lives and helping us to be true to ourselves. Earlier in Chapter 14, Jesus declared in unforgettable words,

Jn 14:6 *"I am the way, and the truth, and the life."*

Now Jesus makes it clear that after his death and resurrection, his Spirit will live within us believers, show us the way, support our search for truth, and lead us to fullness of life.

"The Advocate, the Holy Spirit,
whom the Father will send in my name,
will teach you everything,
Jn 14:26 *and remind you of all that I have said to you."*

"I still have many things to say to you,
but you cannot bear them now.
When the Spirit of truth comes,
he will guide you into all the truth…
Jn 16:12-13 *and will declare to you the things that are to come."*

Thus, John's community believes that the Holy Spirit will not only remind believers of what Jesus taught, but also take believers where they have never been. The Christian community not only looks back with loyalty to Jesus, but also looks forward, with the Spirit's help, faithfully applying its foundational teachings to new cultures and situations through the centuries.

4. *The Christian Way of Life*

a) Shalom

"Peace I leave with you;
my peace I give to you.
Jn 14:27 *I do not give to you as the world gives."*

Shalom, the daily greeting for Jewish people, means peace of heart and more – health, wholeness, holiness, the fullness of Life. When Jesus offers *shalom*, it is no ordinary greeting. It is the foundational element and the ultimate outcome of the Christian way of life – peace of heart, fullness of life.

b) Love

Jesus is a great teacher on the value of love. His reputation derives primarily from the Gospel according to John.

The synoptic gospels report that Jesus chose two sayings from the Law of Moses ("Love the Lord your God with all your heart…" and "Love your neighbour as yourself") as the two greatest commandments in the Hebrew Scriptures. Mt 22:37-39// Lk 10:27

Jesus' words on loving our enemies (found in the synoptic gospels) are his own; this is certainly one of his more challenging and visionary teachings. In a way, his words are relevant to everyday life, since we interact with our enemies often. We are told to act lovingly towards the people who antagonize us, in the expectation that after repeated acts of love they will cease to be our enemy. It is hard to accept Jesus' teaching on love of enemies as a practical principle for daily living; we're more interested in loving our friends. Yet the Gospel of John tells us: Mt 5:43-47// Lk 6:27-36

"I give you a new commandment,
that you love one another.
Just as I have loved you, you also should love one another. Jn 13:34-35
By this everyone will know that you are my disciples,
if you have love for one another." Jn 15:12

His words are an endless challenge to the Christian community. Do people really look at us and say, "Look how they love each other!"? For Jesus, mutual love identifies his disciples. His commandment is indeed new: we are to love each other not as ourselves (according to the former tradition), but rather following the self-giving example of Jesus himself.

"No one has greater love than this,
than to lay down one's life for one's friends." Jn 15:13

This great saying, which recalls Jesus' description of himself as the good shepherd who lays down his life for his sheep, gives us another example of what it means to love "as I have loved you." In this setting, it is important to note that for Christians, laying down one's life need not involve death: married people give their whole lives to each other; priests lay down their lives for the people they serve; parents dedicate their lives to raising their children. No one has greater love than this.

c) Service

"The Son of Man came not to be served but to serve."

Mk 10:45 In Mark, Jesus defines his mission in terms of service. He linked that role in the minds of his disciples with Isaiah's poems about the Servant of God, who was gentle and dutiful, reviled and persecuted, and eventually killed. In reflecting on his sufferings, people came to realize that God was with the Servant throughout his trials, and that the people were healed by his wounds.

In the synoptic gospels, Jesus commands his followers to serve rather than dominate each other:

"Whoever wishes to become great among you
must be your servant;
and whoever wishes to be first among you must be slave of all."

Mk 10:43-44 The theme of service is renewed in the Gospel of John.

"Whoever serves me must follow me,
and where I am, there will my servant be also.
Whoever serves me, the Father will honour."

Jn 12:26 At his Last Supper, Jesus shocks his friends by taking off his robe, tying a towel around his waist, and washing and drying their feet. After he has insisted on continuing despite their objections, he teaches them:

"Do you know what I have done to you?…
If I, your Lord and Teacher, have washed your feet,
you also ought to wash one another's feet.
For I have set you an example,
that you also should do as I have done to you."

Jn 13:13-15 In John, the significant symbolic moment at the Last Supper is not the sharing and transformation of the Passover meal, but Jesus' gesture of serving his friends as a slave would. Service is an essential component of the Christian way of life.

d) Union with God

According to John, the promised result of a life of self-giving love for Christians is not simply a feeling of well-being, or even reward in life beyond death, but spiritual union with God.

The love between Jesus and the God whom he knows as Father can be shared with everyone who follows Jesus.

"As the Father has loved me, so I have loved you." Jn 15:9

"Those who keep my commandments are those who love me,
and those who love me will be loved by my Father." Jn 14:21

"Those who love me will keep my word,
and my Father will love them,
and we will come to them
and make our home with them." Jn 14:23

In his first letter to the Corinthians, Paul describes the relationship between Jesus and his community in terms of a body 1 Cor 12 with Jesus as its head, where each member has an indispensable role to play. The Gospel of John uses a similar image, describing Jesus as the life principle of a vine, and his followers as the branches, alive only as long as they stay connected to the vine.

"Just as a branch cannot bear fruit by itself
unless it abides in the vine,
neither can you unless you abide in me.
I am the vine; you are the branches.
Those who abide in me and I in them bear much fruit,
because apart from me you can do nothing.
Whoever does not abide in me
is thrown away like a branch and withers...." Jn 15:1-6

"I am in the Father and the Father is in me." Jn 14:10

"If you know me, you will know my Father also." Jn 14:7

"No one comes to the Father except through me." Jn 14:6

5. *Jesus' Great Farewell Prayer (John 17)*

John's account of the Last Supper concludes with Jesus' prayer for himself and his followers. John has no record of the Lord's Prayer, which we know from Matthew and Luke, but many of the themes of the Our Father are found in Chapter 17 of John.

'Glory' is John's language describing Jesus as the visible presence of God. Jesus' farewell begins with the prayer that in his hour of glory, he may be recognized, so that he may give eternal life to his followers.

And this is eternal life,
that they may know you, the only true God,
Jn 17:3 *and Jesus Christ whom you have sent.*

To know, in biblical language, does not mean to understand conceptually, but to experience. Union with God is the ultimate goal of the believer: "Thy kingdom come."

Jesus goes on to pray for his friends, whom he has taught and protected, and whom he is now leaving. They must remain in the world as he leaves the world; they are being sent forth to bring others to a knowledge of the truth: "Deliver them from evil."

"I am not asking you to take them out of the world,
Jn 17:15 *but I ask you to protect them from the evil one."*

Finally, Jesus prays for believers of the future, that they may live in loving unity, following the model of the mutual love of Jesus and the Father. John 3:16 states, "God so loved the world that he gave the only Son, so that everyone who believes in him...may have eternal life." Now, in his last words before he goes to meet his death, Jesus prays that his disciples will help the
Jn 17:21-23 world to believe in him. The vehicle for their successful mission will be their mutual love, based on God's love for Jesus and for each of his followers.

B. The Glorious Death of Jesus

It is in the chapters describing the last hours of Jesus' life on earth that John is most aligned with the synoptic gospels – an indication that the early Christians retold these events in great detail from a very early time, before the communities separated on their distinctive paths of reflection on the life of Jesus.

Still, John's account is consistent with his gospel's theological understanding of the greatness of Jesus, and the narrative is therefore distinctive, both in what it omits and in what it adds.

John makes no mention of Jesus' prayer of distress in the garden of Gethsemane after the Last Supper, perhaps because the feelings expressed are not consistent with John's theological presentation of Jesus as the Word of God whose divinity was visible to his followers from the beginning of his ministry. A memory of those feelings may be preserved in John, however, just after the triumphal entry into Jerusalem, when Jesus says,

"Now my soul is troubled.
And what should I say –
'Father, save me from this hour'?
No, it is for this reason that I have come to this hour.
Father, glorify your name." Jn 12:27-28

As well, a number of minor characters and incidents reported in the synoptic gospels are not mentioned in John: the healing of the servant's ear (though the amputation of it is reported in John, Jn 18:10 and only John reports the servant's name), the comments of Pilate's wife, the assistance of Simon of Cyrene, the wailing of the women on the road, the mocking of the bystanders at the cross, the dialogue with the 'good thief,' the darkening of the sun, the tearing of the temple veil, the earthquakes, and the appearances of the spirits of the dead. There is no way of knowing whether these details existed in the earlier tradition and were omitted in John, or whether they developed in the process of oral tradition in the communities where the synoptic gospels were composed.

Perhaps more significant is the omission of Jesus' cry of abandonment just before his death, which Mark and Matthew Mk 15:34 report both in Aramaic and in Greek. John's understanding of the Mt 27:46 divinity of Jesus would find the cry from the cross problematic – as do many of us.

The glorious death of Jesus is presented in John in several ways in the famous passage that has been read in Christian churches every Good Friday for centuries. It begins when Jesus is arrested.

Jesus, knowing all that was to happen to him,
came forward and asked them,
"Whom are you looking for?"
They answered, "Jesus of Nazareth."
Jesus replied, "I am he."…
When Jesus said to them, "I am he,"
they stepped back and fell to the ground. Jn 18:4-6

Thus, the story of Jesus' arrest has become for John a moment of revelation of Jesus' divinity. To translate Jesus' response simply as "I am he" underemphasizes the obvious reference to God's self-

Exod 3:14 revelation to Moses, a reference that becomes more obvious when the officers arresting him fall to the ground in awe.

Whereas the synoptic gospels report that Jesus was almost mute before his accusers ("It is you who have said it"), John shows Jesus presenting a vigorous defence, both before the council of high priests and before Pilate.

"If I have spoken wrongly, testify to the wrong.
Jn 18:23 *But if I have spoken rightly, why do you strike me?"*

"My kingdom is not from this world…
Jn 18:36-37 *For this I came into the world, to testify to the truth."*

"You would have no power over me
Jn 19:11 *unless it had been given you from above."*

The tensions between Jews and Christians that we examined in Chapter 22 of this book are particularly visible in the narrative of Jesus' last hours, as his accusers are usually referred to as "the Jews." "The one who handed me over to you is guilty of a greater
Jn 19:11 sin," says Jesus to Pilate, continuing this gospel's (and all the gospels') tendency to blame the death of Jesus on the Jewish religious leaders more than on the Romans.

John extends the theme of Jesus' kingship (and the tensions with the Jewish community) when, in response to the chief priests' objection that the charge over Jesus' head should not say that he
Jn 19:22 was "King of the Jews," Pilate says, "What I have written, I have written."

Only in the Gospel according to John is it reported that Jesus' mother was present at his death. Neither she nor "the disciple whom Jesus loved" is named, but John reports a final testament of the dying Jesus. Calling her "woman" to identify her as the new Eve, the mother of all humanity, John reports that Jesus gave Mary the role of mother of all disciples, and gave the disciple the
Jn 19:26-27 role of a faithful and protective son.

Jn 19:28 The dying Jesus cries out, "I am thirsty." The gospel writer points out that this word, like the earlier reference to casting lots for the prisoner's clothing, is a fulfillment of the Jewish Scriptures.
Ps 22:15, 18 Both references are to Psalm 22, which begins, "My God, my God, why have you forsaken me?" Two other gospels report that Jesus spoke that line while dying; John refers to the psalm, but does not quote its opening line. No doubt many of the early Christian communities reflected on the meaning of Jesus' death by using that ancient poetic prayer of a man in deep distress.

Jesus' final word according to John is the majestic "It is Jn 19:30
finished." The word used in the original Greek text is from the
same root as the word translated elsewhere as 'perfect.' John Mt 5:48
portrays Jesus as proclaiming that his work has been completed, brought to perfection, at the moment of his death.

The gospel extends its symbolic theology beyond Jesus' death
in the famous episode, reported only in John, of the piercing of Jn 19:34
Jesus' body with a Roman spear. At once blood and water pour out; the Christian reader is expected to see the symbolic reference to Eucharist and baptism, the two great rites by which the early Christian community carried forward its remembrance of Jesus and celebrated his powerful saving presence among them.

Thus is the death of Jesus presented in John as a moment of glory. In the act of dying, Jesus declares that his work has been brought to perfection, and spreads blessings to future generations of his followers.

C. The Resurrection and the Gift of the Holy Spirit

John's account of the burial of Jesus and the discovery of the empty
tomb agrees substantially with the narratives in the synoptic Jn 19:39
gospels. John reintroduces the character of Nicodemus, who
supports the friends of Jesus by contributing burial spices. Only
John reports that Jesus was buried in a garden near the place Jn 19:41
where he was crucified – a tradition preserved by the proximity of Calvary and the tomb within the Church of the Holy Sepulchre in Jerusalem.

The post-resurrection appearances of Jesus in John are unique to John. (Each gospel has different appearance stories; no single narrative is duplicated in any two gospels.) Only the fourth gospel tells of Mary Magdalene mistaking the risen Jesus for a gardener, of the gift of the Spirit for the forgiveness of sins, of doubting Thomas, of a surprising catch of fish and Jesus' cooking breakfast for his friends, and of the reconciliation scene between Jesus and Peter.

1. *Mary Magdalene*

John does not mention Mary Magdalene until she is reported to Jn 19:25
have been present at the death of Jesus. Only from Luke do we

know that Jesus had cured her of what was thought to be demonic
Lk 8:2-3 possession, and that she was among several women who were Jesus' financial supporters. Despite centuries of gossip, no gospel ever accuses her of sexual impropriety.

In John, as in Mark and Matthew, Mary of Magdala (her hometown on the shore of the Sea of Galilee) comes to the tomb at dawn on Sunday. Jesus had died late Friday afternoon; the sabbath rest began at sundown on Friday and ended at sundown on Saturday, when it would have been too dark to work inside the burial cave. On Sunday morning, the funeral process could
Jn 20:2 be completed. Mary finds the tomb empty and is dismayed and confused. Later, she meets two angels, but they offer no expla-
Jn 20:12 nation for what has happened.

When Jesus appears to the weeping Mary, she mistakes him
Jn 20:15 for a gardener. This account corresponds with narratives in the other gospels, which portray the risen Jesus as so completely transformed that his friends don't recognize him. He has not come back to life (as it was before), but has risen to new life.

But the transformed Jesus is still the same Jesus. He speaks
Jn 20:16 only Mary's name, and she recognizes him. This beautiful moment conveys the depth of their personal relationship and the sense that Jesus knows her – and each of us – by name. We, too, are invited to acknowledge the risen Jesus, who is part of our lives (though we may not recognize his presence), who knows us intimately, and who calls us by name to be true to ourselves and faithful to God.

The episode ends with Jesus commissioning Mary to bring a message to his disciples that he is ascending to the Father.

2. *The Gift of the Spirit*

Jn 16:7 Earlier, Jesus said that if he did not return to the Father, he could not send the Advocate to strengthen his followers. In Luke, Jesus progresses from resurrection to ascension and the sending of the Spirit over a period of 50 days, concluding at Pentecost.

John condenses the steps in Jesus' post-resurrection journey into the one Easter day. Jesus tells Mary that he is ascending to the Father, and "in the evening on the same day" he appears to the assembled disciples, wishes them the peace the world cannot
Jn 14:27 give, breathes on them, and says,

"Receive the Holy Spirit.
If you forgive the sins of any, they are forgiven them;
if you retain the sins of any, they are retained." Jn 20:22-23

Later Catholic tradition has understood this saying to be the institution of the sacrament of reconciliation, but the Reformed tradition and most biblical scholars agree that baptism was the only rite of forgiveness for the early Christians and for John's community. Except for the prayer for forgiveness that is still celebrated at the beginning of each Eucharist, for several centuries there was no specific Christian rite for the forgiveness of sin committed after baptism.

Most significant in this brief account is the Holy Spirit's role in forgiveness. Previously, the gospel told us that the Spirit will "convict the world of sin," lead the disciples into truth, and remind them of all Jesus taught. Now, according to John, the power of the Spirit overcomes human sinfulness, heals us, and leads us forward in life's journey towards wholeness.

3. *Doubting Thomas*

The series of appearance narratives in Chapter 20 of John
concludes with the story of Thomas, who calls for proof in the Jn 20:25
name of all who seek faith. Jesus presents evidence, but emphasizes the value of faith that does not require proof.

"Blessed are those who have not seen
and yet have come to believe." Jn 20:29

Thomas, who is mentioned in the synoptic gospels only as a
name in the lists of the Twelve, has a part to play earlier in John Jn 11:16
in the story of Lazarus, and at the Last Supper, when he says,

"Lord, we do not know where you are going.
How can we know the way?" Jn 14:5

In many ways, Thomas speaks for all of us who search for faith in a world of confusion and doubt. Jesus' answer then is still valid: "I am the way."

4. *Appendix*

It seems clear that the two closing sentences of Chapter 20 were Jn 20:30-31
at one time the end of the gospel.

Some time later, someone in John's community must have felt that the gospel was incomplete. A 21st chapter, whose language and vision (and conclusion) are different from those of the first 20 chapters, was added.

Lk 5:1-11, In an episode that has intriguing similarities to passages in
24:41-43 Luke, Jesus encourages seven followers to cast again for fish after
not catching anything all night. When they make an unexpectedly
Jn 21:1-14 large catch, Jesus cooks breakfast and shares it with his friends. This scene contains echoes of the banquet of the Messiah, the Cana miracle, the multiplication of the loaves and fish, and of course the Eucharist.

Jn 21:15-18 Next comes the story of Jesus asking Peter three times to profess his love, and commissioning Peter to "feed" both lambs and sheep in the name of the good shepherd. Since this chapter was added to the gospel at least 30 years after Peter's death, its purpose could be to support the leadership of those who have taken Peter's place in the Christian community of the late first century. The threefold profession of love is purposefully designed to counterbalance Peter's threefold denial on the evening of Jesus' arrest and trial. Jesus' forgiveness of that betrayal restores Peter's position as leader in the community, and should encourage any disciples who feel they have been unfaithful. This forgiveness overcomes our failings and restores the direction and strength of our journey towards wholeness.

5. *The Original Conclusion*

Recalling the great theme of life that streams throughout the gospel, the author ends his magnificent document of faith by restating his purpose: to enable people to believe in Jesus, and thereby to "have life in his name." John teaches that the profound gift of Jesus is fullness of life, beginning with the creation of the world and concluding with the gift of the Spirit after the resurrection.

Jn 1:4 *In him was life, and the life was the light of all people…*

"God so loved the world that [God] gave his only Son,
so that everyone who believes in him may not perish but
Jn 3:16 *may have eternal life."*

Jn 6:48 *"I am the bread of life."*

Jn 10:10 *"I came that they may have life, and have it abundantly."*

"I am the resurrection and the life." Jn 11:25

"I am the way, and the truth, and the life." Jn 14:6

And this is eternal life,
that they may know you, the only true God,
and Jesus Christ whom you have sent. Jn 17:3

And thus the gospel ends:

These are written so that you may come to believe
that Jesus is the Messiah, the Son of God,
and that through believing you may have life in his name. Jn 20:30-31

24

ODDS AND ENDS

Other New Testament Writings

The Letter to the Hebrews

A Scripture professor once said that a lector who announces at church "A reading from the Letter of Paul to the Hebrews" has already made three mistakes! It is not a letter, it was not written by Paul, and it was not written to Hebrews.

The document is not structured as a letter; it has no introduction like other New Testament letters. Near the end, the author calls it "a word of exhortation"; most commentators think of it as
Heb 13:22 a written sermon. Nowhere is the author identified in the text, and even from the early centuries of Christianity, authorities knew that Paul was not the author. The scholar Origen remarked that "only God knows" who wrote this document, and modern commentators agree. The audience may well have been of Jewish heritage, but they were surely Christian (not still adherents of the Hebrew faith tradition) by the time this exhortation was written.

The purpose of Hebrews was to support Christians of Jewish heritage in a time of persecution by the Romans for refusing to worship Roman gods. In the community to which Hebrews is addressed, a number of Christians had begun to reconsider their loyalty to Jesus, and contemplated returning to Judaism. The author builds a long and almost rabbinical argument to encourage believers to remain faithful:

Long ago God spoke to our ancestors in many and various ways by the prophets,

but in these last days [God] has
spoken to us by a Son…
through whom [God] also created the worlds. Heb 1:1

The author goes on to proclaim that because of his new covenant and sacrifice, the Son is greater than the angels, greater than Moses, and greater than the Jewish priesthood.

Since we have a great high priest,
who has passed through the heavens,
Jesus, the Son of God, let us hold fast to our confession.
For we do not have a high priest
who is unable to sympathize with our weaknesses,
but we have one who in every respect has been tested
as we are,
yet without sin. Heb 4:14-15

If that first covenant had been faultless,
there would have been no need to look for a second one.
God finds fault with [the people] when he says: Heb 8:7-8, quoting Jer 31:31
"The days are surely coming, says the Lord,
when I will establish a new covenant
with the…House of Judah."

Every [Jewish] priest stands day after day at his service,
offering again and again the same sacrifices that can never
take away sins.
But when Christ had offered for all time a single sacrifice
for sins…he has perfected for all time those who are Heb 10:11-12,
sanctified. 14

Therefore, urges the author,

Let us hold fast to the confession of our hope without
wavering,
for he who has promised is faithful.
And let us consider how to provoke one another
to love and good deeds,
not neglecting to meet together, Heb 10:23-25
as is the habit of some…

Faith is the assurance of things hoped for…. Heb 11:1

Let us look to Jesus…
[who] endured the cross…
so that you may not grow weary or lose heart. Heb 12:2-3

The relevance of Hebrews for believers today may depend on the extent to which we perceive that we, too, are living in a hostile society whose values make it very difficult for us to remain faithful to our calling as disciples of Jesus. No doubt the author would urge us also to hold on firmly to the hope we profess, to be concerned for one another, and to help one another to show love and to do good.

The Letter of James

The James who identifies himself as the author at the beginning
Mk 6:3, 3:31-34 of this document is usually thought to be the "brother of the
Gal 1:19, 2:9, 12 Lord," who was not a member of Jesus' inner group of disciples, but was a leader of the Christian community in Jerusalem after the resurrection. Not all scholars agree that James wrote this letter, but a substantial number believe that it is authentic, and therefore that it was written before the first gospel, in the early 60s CE.

At a time when apathy, disunity and materialism were afflicting Christian communities everywhere, the Letter of James reminds believers that faith means more than simply accepting a creed. Christianity is a way of life, and must be expressed in actions as well as words.

What good is it, my brothers and sisters, if you say you
have faith, but you do not have works?...
If a brother or sister is naked and lacks daily food,
and one of you says to them,
"Go in peace; keep warm and eat your fill,"
and yet you do not supply their bodily needs,
what is the good of that?
Jas 2:14-17 *So faith by itself, if it has no works, is dead.*

This passage challenges us today as we seek to be faithful to our calling as followers of Jesus. Those of us who are rich in comparison with the majority of the world's people must also respond in action to the following:

You rich people, weep and wail for the miseries
that are coming to you.
Your riches have rotted,
and your clothes are moth-eaten...
Listen! The wages of the labourers who mowed your fields,

which you have kept back by fraud,
cry out, and the cries of the harvesters have reached the
ears of the Lord of hosts. Jas 5:1-5
You have lived on the earth in luxury and in pleasure…

The rich person [should be glad] in being brought low,
because the rich will disappear like a flower in the field. Jas 1:10

Perhaps the most challenging statement of all is this:

Anyone who knows the right thing to do
and fails to do it, commits sin. Jas 4:16

The Letters of Peter

The First Letter of Peter was also written for believers living in a hostile environment. Parts of the text may be a sermon or exhortation addressed to newly baptized Christians, and to the community that is welcoming them into the Church.

You have been born anew…through the living and
enduring word of God. 1 Pet 1:23

You are a chosen race, a royal priesthood, a holy nation,
God's own people,
in order that you may proclaim the mighty acts of [God]
who has called you out of darkness into his marvellous light. 1 Pet 2:9

First Peter advocates a highly structured community based on obedience to authority: citizens are advised to accept the authority of governments; slaves, of their masters; wives, of their husbands. Husbands are to show consideration and pay honour to their wives, and all Christians are to

have unity of spirit, sympathy, love for one another,
a tender heart, and a humble mind. 1 Pet 3:8

Above all, maintain constant love for one another, for love
covers a multitude of sins. 1 Pet 4:8

In the past two centuries, the authorship of First Peter has been under debate, with some scholars accepting the traditional understanding that it was written by Peter himself before his death in the mid-60s CE, and others pointing to evidence in the text that supports a later date of composition by an author writing in the spirit of the revered friend of Jesus.

There is no such debate, however, about the Second Letter of Peter. Most scholars consider it the last New Testament document to be written, possibly as late as 100 years after the resurrection of Jesus, by an anonymous author.

Second Peter is primarily devoted to the denunciation of false teachers who were all the more dangerous because they arose from within the community. The document also deals with the community's growing realization that the hope for the second coming of Jesus is not going to be fulfilled in the short term.

Using the memorable phrase "With the Lord one day is like a
2 Pet 3:8 thousand years, and a thousand years are like one day," the author
urges believers to be steadfast in their faith in God, whose "divine
power has given us everything needed for life and godliness."
2 Pet 1:3

The Letters of John

There are three letters of John in the Bible. The second and third letters are short and add little to our understanding of early Christianity. One commentator has remarked that the only reason they have been preserved and included in the New Testament may be that they were written by the respected author of the First Letter of John.

Who that author was is a mystery. He is identified as "the elder" in the latter two letters, and is not named in any of the letters. Scholars are sure that the author is not John the son of Zebedee, who was a friend of Jesus; not the "beloved disciple" mentioned in the Gospel of John; not the author of the Gospel of John; and not the author of the Book of Revelation. The attribution of the name John to the author may indicate that he belonged to the community of believers in which the fourth gospel developed. He seems to be familiar with some themes distinctive to the fourth gospel, particularly those of eternal life, light and love.

We declare to you what was from the beginning,
what we have heard,
what we have seen with our own eyes,
what we have looked at and touched with our hands
1 Jn 1:1 *concerning the word of Life…*

This is the message we…proclaim to you,
that God is light
and in [God] there is no darkness at all. 1 Jn 1:5

These lines at the beginning of the First Letter of John introduce the theme of the opening section of the document, which tells of God's great gifts to humanity and urges believers to be faithful to the gift of God.

See what love the Father has given us,
that we should be called children of God;
and that is what we are.
…what we will be has not yet been revealed.

But the greatest legacy of First John is the famous passage about love in Chapter 4: 1 Jn 3:1-2

Beloved, let us love one another, because love is from God;
everyone who loves is born of God and knows God.
Whoever does not love does not know God, for God is love. 1 Jn 4:7-8

In this is love,
not that we loved God but that [God] loved us
and sent his Son to be the atoning sacrifice for our sins. 1 Jn 4:10

God is love, and those who abide in love abide in God,
and God abides in them. 1 Jn 4:16

There is no fear in love, but perfect love casts out fear. 1 Jn 4:18

Those who say, "I love God," and hate their brothers and
sisters, are liars…
The commandment we have…is this:
those who love God
must love their brothers and sisters also. 1 Jn 4:20-21

The Letter of Jude

The author of this brief document identifies himself as the "brother of James." The self-designation is a little curious, though: the author claims a connection with James, who was a respected figure in the early Church community, but if he was really related to James, Jude could also have identified himself as a brother of Jesus. Most scholars agree that Jude is a pseudonym. Jude 1 see Mk 6:3

The letter is a forceful attack on grumblers and malcontents
Jude 16 in the community who are indulging "their own lusts" and
rejecting authority as they justify their licentious behaviour. Jude
urges believers to support each other in faith, to have mercy on
Jude 21-22 those who are wavering (but not on these "ungodly sinners"),
and to "keep yourselves in the love of God."

The Book of Revelation

Rev 1:9 The author of the book of Revelation, also known as "The
Apocalypse," has given us his name (John) and the information that he has been exiled to the rocky Aegean island of Patmos because the Roman authorities disapproved of his proclamation of the good news of Jesus. Most scholars are convinced that this John (who claims no other credentials) is not the fisherman son of Zebedee, or the author of either the Gospel or the letters of John. Some themes (the Lamb, the Word, the water of life) that are also found in the fourth gospel may indicate that this John had contact with that community.

Apocalyptic literature expresses its ideas in dreams and symbols that are often difficult to understand – perhaps intentionally, if the ideas would be considered subversive by the ruling authorities. Sometimes such writings claim to have been composed in the past by someone who predicts what is going to happen (though the events have already happened by the time of the writing).Then the culmination of the vision – the triumphant dénouement – is set in the immediate future (as the writer sees things).

An example may be found in what is called the synoptic
Mt 24:1-44 apocalypse. Jesus seems to be predicting some kind of future
cataclysm, using imagery from the book of Daniel (Old Testament
Dan 7:13-14 apocalyptic literature). As a result of these symbolic teachings of
Dan 9:27 Jesus, the disciples expected an early return of the Son of Man on
Dan 11:31 the clouds of heaven (an image from Daniel), the end of history
Dan 12:11 as we know it, and the definitive establishment of the reign of
God on earth.

Thirty and 40 years after the resurrection, there had been no return of the Son of Man, but Jerusalem had been destroyed by the Romans. Did Jesus predict the destruction of the Temple in clear words such as "not one stone will be left upon another"? Or did he use the more ambiguous imagery from Daniel, with the disciples later applying it to the destruction of Jerusalem, and writing a prediction after the fact? Did Jesus mean to predict a literal return of the Son of Man on the clouds of heaven, or was he making use of Daniel's imagery to say that eventually the reign of God will overcome the force of evil in the world?

Mk 13:1-2
Mt 24:2

What seems certain about the book of Revelation is that we must not interpret it as predicting historical events between biblical times and the 21st century and beyond. Revelation was born of the tensions between the Empire (Babylon, the Beast) and the Christian community in the first century CE. And it is founded on the firm hope that Babylon and the Beast will be demolished, and the power of God will prevail.

Symbolism is everywhere: the Word of God is a sharp sword bringing justice; trumpets proclaim the voice of God; palms signify triumph; horns (whether on lambs or dragons) are signs of power; the sea (as in Chapter 1 of the book of Genesis) is fearsome and evil, bringing death. Numerology is filled with meaning: seven signifies perfection, while 666 signifies the Beast (the numerical values of the Hebrew letters that spell 'Caesar Nero' add up to 666).

The book of Revelation is intended to strengthen the faith of Christians in a time of persecution. It looks at believers' fear and confusion as a mystery whose meaning is known only to God, and proclaims that the power of God will overcome suffering and death. Christians can transform the world by living courageously as Jesus inspired us to do.

An inspiring promise is found in these verses:

Then I saw a new heaven and a new earth;
for the first heaven and the first earth had passed away,
and the sea was no more.
And I saw the holy city, the new Jerusalem,
coming down out of heaven from God,
prepared as a bride adorned for her husband.
And I heard a loud voice from the throne, saying,
See, the home of God is among mortals.
[God] will dwell with them as their God;
they will be his peoples,
And God himself will be with them;
[God] will wipe away every tear from their eyes.

Death will be no more;
mourning and crying and pain will be no more,
for the first things have passed away.
And the one who was seated on the throne said,
Rev 21:1-5 *"See, I am making all things new."*

Here is the positive spirit of the book of Revelation. Trying to figure out the meaning of the frightening and fabulous imagery throughout the book has become a popular pastime among some religious groups, but such speculation is doomed to be meaningless unless it finds all its answers in the first hundred years after Jesus died.

Let us close this chapter with the prayer that concludes the book of Revelation and the Holy Bible:

The one who testifies to these things says,
"Surely I am coming soon."
Amen. Come, Lord Jesus!
Rev 22:20-21 *The grace of the Lord Jesus be with all the saints. Amen.*

25

CHRISTMAS

It may seem strange to discuss the stories of Jesus' birth and childhood near the end of our treatment of the New Testament, but these stories developed later, in Christian communities that were already familiar with the adult life and teachings of Jesus. The accounts of Jesus' early years express what Christians believed about Jesus, years after his death, in the light of the resurrection.

It was on the basis of their knowledge of the reign of God and of the miracles, parables and moral wisdom of Jesus that two of the early Christian communities – Matthew and Luke – produced the Christmas stories. Mark's community may have known only of his adult ministry, and had no stories of his childhood; John was more concerned with his theology about Jesus, and began his gospel with the creation of the world rather than with the conception of Jesus.

Yet Matthew's and Luke's stories about Jesus' birth are so different from each other, they are almost incompatible. The two gospels agree on a few details, several of them theological: Jesus was believed to be a descendant of King David, born in Bethlehem. He was born during the reign of King Herod the Great, who died in 4 BCE. His parents were named Mary and Joseph (they disagree about the names of his grandparents, which are reported in different family trees in each gospel). They agree that the conception of Jesus was announced by an angel (they disagree about to whom the announcement was made: in Matthew, the angel speaks to Joseph; in Luke, to Mary). They agree that God took an active role in the conception of Jesus. And they agree that Mary was, for a time, an unmarried pregnant teenager – that Jesus was born less than nine months after Mary and Joseph were married.

No single episode is recounted in both gospels, not even the birth of the child.

Beyond the obvious conclusion that the gospel writers didn't know of each other's work, we may also infer that these narratives were developed in two different Christian communities by people who did not know Jesus as a child. There is no evidence that either of them had access to anyone who was present during Jesus' infancy. Like most stories about the childhood of heroes (compare the story of the baby Moses, who was rescued from the bulrushes and raised by an Egyptian princess), the narratives are primarily statements about the greatness of Jesus, not factual reports about what happened when he was a baby.

The stories about Jesus' childhood are among our most
treasured traditions, but they do give rise to a number of sensitive
questions. The purpose of the stories is to tell what Christians
believed about Jesus decades after the resurrection. Thus, when
the angels tell the shepherds that "to you is born this day in the
Lk 2:11 city of David a Saviour, who is the Messiah, the Lord," we are
listening to an early Christian creed: the community believed that
Jesus is Saviour, Messiah and Lord. Each title for Jesus had a
specific Christian meaning. This statement would have made very
little sense to shepherds at the time of Jesus' birth.

The Sequence of Events in Matthew

Mt 1:1 Matthew's family tree of Jesus begins with Abraham. An angel
Mt 1:20 reveals the importance of Jesus to Joseph, not to Mary. There is
Mt 1:24 no Roman census, no trip from Nazareth, and no stable in
Matthew's gospel. A literal reading of the narrative could lead to
the conclusion that the family lived in Bethlehem, and that Jesus
Mt 2:1 was born in Joseph's home there. Indeed, in contemporary
Bethlehem, Joseph's home is identified at one end of the town (to
suit Matthew's narrative), while the more famous site of Luke's
stable is commemorated elsewhere, in the Church of the Nativity.

The sages (in Greek, *magoi*) from the East are portrayed in
Mt 2:1-2 the gospel as astrologers, people who explore the skies for portents
and omens. There is no sign that they were kings, or mention of
how many of them came (though three types of gifts are listed).
There isn't even evidence that they were all men; in Greek as in
other languages, a group of one man and any number of women
would be represented by a masculine plural adjective or pronoun.

The visit of the *magoi* causes all Jerusalem to be in an uproar. Mt 2:3
The family's escape into Egypt is followed by the massacre of the Mt 2:16
infants in the region of Bethlehem; the family then returns to Mt 2:19-23
settle in Nazareth. None of these details appears in Luke in any form.

The Sequence of Events in Luke

In the Gospel of Luke, an angel announces the conception of Lk 1:5-24
John the Baptist (to Zechariah) and later of Jesus (to Mary, not to Lk 1:26-38
Joseph). Mary visits her cousin Elizabeth, the mother of John the Lk 1:39-56
Baptist. John is born and his future is proclaimed. Then Jesus is Lk 1:57-80
born, wrapped in cloths, and laid in a feeding trough for animals. Lk 2:7
(Surprisingly, the word 'stable' is not used in the gospel.) The
first visitors in Luke are the shepherds. Instead of fearing the Lk 2:8-20
authorities in Jerusalem, Jesus' parents take him to the Temple Lk 2:22-38
shortly after his birth, and again when he reaches adulthood (at Lk 2:41-52
puberty).

Luke offers a family tree of Jesus a little later in the gospel;
because of Luke's universalist interests, it takes us all the way
back to Adam, the first human. Matthew and Luke both trace Lk 3:23-38
Jesus' lineage through the kings of Judah, but their genealogies disagree on his ancestry for the period after the end of the monarchy – the 500 years before his birth.

Let's look at a few of the theological themes in the stories of Jesus' childhood.

Theological Purposes of the Christmas Stories

Who Accepts Jesus, and Who Rejects Him?

How people react to Jesus is examined throughout all the gospels. Frequently, support from the crowds is offset by conflict with opponents. Even Jesus' followers are often portrayed as responding inadequately to the reign of God: they don't understand, even though Jesus has favoured them with his friendship and extensive knowledge of his ministry.

Both Matthew and Luke begin to focus on reactions to Jesus at the beginning of their gospels. The Gospel of Luke repeatedly emphasizes Jesus' concern for the poor and the outcasts of society. This theme begins on the day of his birth, as the first people who hear and welcome the good news of the Saviour are shepherds, members of one of the lowest social classes. For Luke, the reign of God belongs to the poor, and the poor accept Jesus from the outset.

In Matthew's stories about Jesus' childhood, it is significant that the people who accept Jesus are sages from far away, presumably believers from a pagan religious tradition. Despite Matthew's preoccupation with Jesus as the fulfillment of Jewish hopes, he makes the point in the story of the magi that the good news of the reign of God is available to anyone in the world who is willing to search for God with an open mind. By contrast, Jesus is opposed by the forces in society that are devoted to preserving their own power. The fact that those forces are Jewish is intended as a reminder to Matthew's readers, many of whom were of Jewish background, that their heritage alone is no longer sufficient for salvation: the reign of God can transform anyone. All must open their hearts to God.

Miraculous Conception

Lk 1:35 Both Matthew and Luke portray the conception of Jesus as the
Mt 1:20 result of the action of the Spirit of God. Catholic tradition has
firmly maintained as historical the teaching that the life of Jesus in Mary's womb began by a miracle and not by sexual intercourse. It is unquestioned that God can do such wonders; nothing is impossible for God.

Many people are mistaken about the meaning of 'Immaculate Conception.' That term refers not to the beginning of Jesus' life without sexual intercourse, but to the conception of Mary in *her* mother's womb. At issue is not a belief in a virginal conception, but the Catholic teaching that Mary's life began free of original sin. ('Immaculate' doesn't mean non-sexual; it means 'free of sin.') The concept of Immaculate Conception is not found in the Scriptures, but is the product of theological reflection about Mary through the centuries. Other ways to express the meaning of the teaching might include the following: Mary was chosen and blessed by God from the beginning of her life; the process of salvation, by which God led Mary towards wholeness, began as soon as her life began in her mother's womb; the transforming power of God counteracted the sinful heritage of humanity in Mary's life from the beginning.

With regard to the teaching on the virginal conception of Jesus, many, particularly among Reformed Christians, wonder whether the tradition is historically factual. While respecting the legitimacy of such discussions, Catholics accept the virgin birth on faith.

At the same time, we believe that Jesus is Son of God regardless of how his life began. For example, Mark, who includes no Christmas narratives, firmly believes that Jesus is Son of God Mk 1:1
because of his teachings, his healings, his integrity, his death in Mk 15:39
self-giving love, and his resurrection. Mark displays no knowledge that Jesus was born of a virgin. For Mark, we know that Jesus is Son of God because of what he did, not because of how he was conceived. Matthew and Luke would say the same, except that they include the virginal conception to support their belief in Jesus as Son of God.

The central purpose of Matthew's and Luke's teaching about the virginal conception is that Jesus is entirely God's gift to humanity, not the product of a human family. In the life of Jesus, we believe, the saving power of God burst into the world to lead all humanity towards wholeness.

Intimations of Greatness

Luke's series of narratives about Jesus' childhood concludes with the well-known story of his family's journey to Jerusalem as he Lk 2:41-52
reached the age of maturity. The episode (not found in the other gospels) is intended to give the reader a foretaste of Jesus' greatness. The story has been romanticized in popular imagination, however, with the result that many people believe it shows that Jesus has super-human knowledge. The story in Luke says only that the teachers in the Temple were amazed at Jesus' under- Lk 2:47
standing and his answers. No doubt he was an exceptional young man, with a profound and intimate love for God and with great insight into human life, but if we think of him as knowing everything we might be left with the impression that he was only pretending to be human, rather than fully sharing our experience.

One human experience that he shared as a result of going missing for three days is tension between the generations in a family. In expressing his intuition of his future greatness, Jesus is Lk 2:49
making a personal declaration of independence from his heritage. His greatness does not come from his family, but from within him, and ultimately from God. His ministry will not be what is

expected of a dutiful family member, but will be his own doing as
God's special gift to humanity. Luke concludes the episode with
Lk 2:51-52 the moderating note that Jesus returned to family life, and
continued to grow in wisdom as an apparently obedient son. His
greatness was not to become known until almost 20 years later,
when he began to proclaim the arrival of the reign of God.

Believers often express dismay that we know so little about
the childhood and early adulthood of Jesus. All we can say is that
our ignorance about those years is a measure of his apparent
ordinariness. Jesus lived a life of more than average length as a
simple village craftsman. If there were exceptional events
surrounding his birth at Bethlehem, no one in his hometown of
Lk 3:23 Nazareth knew of them, and no one made any record of his life as
a student in the local synagogue, his skills as an artisan, his
personality, his status in the village, his attitude towards the
Romans. We know next to nothing about the first 30 years of his
life, until he burst upon the Galilean stage "in the fifteenth year
Lk 3:1 of the reign of Emperor Tiberius."

The narratives of his birth and childhood are offered in the gospels of Matthew and Luke not as factual biographical accounts, but as theological statements about his relationship with God.

26

LIFE EVERLASTING

Jewish faith was beautiful, vibrant and challenging for many centuries without any belief in life beyond death. Biblical faith taught that God loves us, sets us free, leads us to wholeness, teaches us how to live, and forgives us when we fail – but not that God promises us life after we die. There was a rather naive belief that God rewards good actions with prosperity and long life, and punishes wrongdoing, but this was always expected to happen on earth, even perhaps generations after the wrongdoing itself. The book of Job expressed serious doubt about the idea that everything bad in life is God's punishment for sin, but still did not propose life beyond death as the solution to the question of reward and punishment for our actions.

After the Babylonian exile, some 500 years before the time of Jesus, contact with Persian religion led some Jewish believers to develop hope for resurrection. The most traditional religious leaders, particularly the Sadducees, did not accept belief in life after death, because it could not be found in Torah. Other believers, particularly the Pharisees, did embrace the hope for resurrection.

Still today, many devout Jews express very little certainty about life beyond death. They believe deeply in God's loving-kindness, but they can say no more than this: "We shall know for certain only after we die."

A. What Did Jesus Say About Life Beyond Death?

Surprisingly, Jesus gave us very little teaching about life after death. Readers who remember the frequent use of 'Kingdom of heaven,' particularly in the Gospel of Matthew, may disagree, but even that phrase refers primarily to the saving action of God on earth.

In the Bible, heaven is the home of God. 'Kingdom of heaven' was used as a reverent synonym for 'kingdom of God'; its meaning might be expressed as the rule of God that comes from heaven. Thus, entering the kingdom of heaven refers not primarily to life beyond death, but to allowing the transforming power of God to influence your life and lead you towards wholeness in this life.

Lk 18:24 "How hard it is for those who have wealth to enter the kingdom
Mt 19:23 of God" is not primarily about going to heaven after death; it is about getting started on the journey towards true wholeness. The saying is a lament about the lure of wealth. According to Jesus, when people become obsessed with money, they forget that self-giving love is the key to wholeness. Wealth can prevent people from allowing God to begin to transform their lives.

The early Christians didn't have ideas about going to heaven after they died that corresponded to later ideas in European Christianity. Heaven, to them, was the realm above the sky where God lived with the angels in a heavenly court; there was no popular expectation that people would live there after death. The voice of
Mk 1:11, 7:34, 8:11, 11:30, 13:31 and parallels God was heard from heaven; people looked to heaven to give thanks or to plead; signs were sent from heaven; people tried to decide whether prophets like John the Baptist were sent from heaven or were of human origin; heaven and earth were expected to pass away at the end-time. The kingdom of heaven that Jesus proclaimed (in the language of Matthew's gospel only) was a reverent rephrasing of 'kingdom of God,' and referred to the benevolent action of God on earth, intervening in people's lives to lead them to wholeness.

When the early Christians imagined life beyond death, most of them apparently did not think of their immortal soul going to heaven to live in a spirit-world with God. (That language is based on Greek philosophy.) Rather, they seem to have imagined that Jesus would return from heaven to earth, the dead would be raised to a transformed life, and all the faithful would enjoy a glorious messianic kingdom of peace and happiness on earth.

The evidence about what Jesus said to contribute to this expectation is remarkably limited. He did speak of the return of
Mk 14:62 the Son of Man on "the clouds of heaven", but most of his teaching was directed at urging people to change their hearts, accept the rule of God in their lives, and grow towards wholeness in this life by living as he taught them.

Many contemporary Christians have grown up under the guidance of moral teaching whose primary source of motivation was to avoid punishment in hell, and to receive a heavenly reward after death. When they learn that Jesus rarely proposed reward after death as a motive for obeying his teaching, such believers often ask, "Why should I try to be good and self-giving, then?" A rabbi, after expressing both uncertainty and unconcern about his hope for life beyond death, offered this answer to the question: "Because it is God's world. We try to do what we believe God asks of us."

We do what is right because it is right, because God has imbued our nature with the desire to be a good person, to be fully human, and to be happy. Further, God offers to help us to be good, wise, courageous and loving. We do good because we are creatures of God, and it is both appropriate for us as God's children and beneficial for our own well-being to live according to the gospel. Jesus taught us how to live well. Life beyond death is part of our hope, but Jesus did not propose it as the most important reason for being a good person.

A few exceptions to the preceding paragraphs can be found in Lk 16:19-31
the Gospel of Luke, where the story of the Rich Man and Lazarus portrays the poor beggar "taken by the angels to be with Abraham," and the rich man tormented in Hades (a Greek rather than a Hebrew concept). Elsewhere in Luke, Jesus advises his hearers to invite the poor and the disabled to any banquet. "They cannot repay
you, for you will be repaid at the resurrection of the righteous." To Lk 14:14
the man dying beside him on the cross, Jesus promises, "Today
you will be with me in Paradise." Those sayings, found only in Lk 23:43
Luke, help us to understand how one first-century community understood life beyond death as motivation for good behaviour.

The Gospel of John reports one series of sayings in which Jn 6:40
Jesus promises to "raise up on the last day" people who believe in Jn 6:44
the Son, who are drawn by the Father who sent him, and who eat
his flesh and drink his blood. Later in the gospel, after raising Jn 6:54
Lazarus, Jesus proclaims that his gift of fullness of life conquers even death.

"I am the resurrection and the life.
Those who believe in me, even though they die, will live,
and everyone who lives and believes in me will never die." Jn 11:25-26

The theme of future resurrection and reward appears nowhere else in John. For example, John never connects life beyond death with Jesus' great sayings about the importance of love.

Mt 22:23-32// One episode reported by three of the gospels gives us some
Mk 12:18-27// indication of Jesus' attitude towards the Jewish hope for resurrection
Lk 20:27-38 of the dead at some future time. Jesus defended this belief against the Sadducees. In his debate with them, Jesus expressed his expectation that life after resurrection is different than life now: marriage will no longer be necessary; resurrection-life is more like the life of the angels. Other than this, we have very little knowledge of what Jesus promised about life beyond death.

B. The Earliest Christian Teaching: The First Letter to the Thessalonians

One of the questions discussed in Paul's letter to the Thessalonians is the issue of life after death. As we saw in Chapter 21, the early Christians expected Jesus to return in glory in the very near future. Apparently, in his time in Thessalonika, Paul had never dealt with the question of what would happen to believers who died before Jesus returned. He later wrote to them to address their concern, reassuring them that as Jesus died and rose again, "so, through
1 Thess 4:13-18 Jesus, God will bring with him those who have died." Paul is not imagining the resurrection of all the people who ever lived in the world, but rather of the community of believers being reunited
1 Thess 4:17 with their Lord in peace and love.

C. "With What Kind of Body Do They Come?" The First Letter to the Corinthians

In the First Letter to the Corinthians (written in the mid-50s CE), Paul proclaims his belief in the resurrection of Jesus, and declares
1 Cor 15:23 him to be the "first fruits" to be followed by "those who belong to Christ." On that basis Paul offers an extended discussion about life beyond death for Christians, saying that it is so different from
1 Cor 15:35-58 the life we know that it can't even be imagined.

He offers an analogy from nature involving both continuity and transformation – concepts we used to speak about the resurrection of Jesus. Life after death is compared to a plant growing from a seed. In a way, the plant is in the seed; they are
1 Cor 15:37 the same living thing. But the plant is so different from the seed that you could never imagine what the plant will look like from looking at the seed. Our life on earth, says Paul, is like the seed; our life after death will be like the plant – beyond imagining.

"So it is with the resurrection of the dead," he says. "What is sown is perishable, what is raised is imperishable.... It is sown a physical body, it is raised a spiritual body." (Keep in mind the Hebrew understanding of 'body' as the whole person.) 1 Cor 15:42-44

Resurrection is not a coming back to life, but a transformation.

D. Re-imagining Heaven

While Paul's analogy of the seed provides some insight, it lacks the kind of definition many contemporary searchers desire. In spite of our uncertainty about details, Christian tradition affirms that we will maintain our identity after death, that God will be fully present to us, and that we will be fully present to God and to one another.

1. *Where Is Heaven?*

As people mature, they discover that childhood images no longer satisfy them. Yet we have little imagery about life beyond death to replace our childish images. A first step is to avoid language referring to time and place.

Where is heaven? Do we have to imagine, as the scriptural writers did, that God's home is a place in the sky? We can speak instead of a new dimension of being, a spiritual way of living – living with God, living as God lives.

So where is God? We say traditionally that God is everywhere – in our hearts, in sacred places, all around the world. But 'where' is an attribute of physical things; it cannot describe spiritual reality. As a spirit-being, God lives in a different way than we body-beings do. To recall a comparison made earlier, where is love? Love is within us; love is real; love is powerful; you can't get along without love; love is everywhere in our world – and yet it can't be measured. Love is a spiritual reality, and so is God. The New Testament states that God is love. If we must try to answer the question "Where is heaven?" the response is a further question: "Where is love?" Where love is, God is. Where God is, heaven is. Heaven means living in union with God. 1 Jn 4:8

2. *Time Beyond Death*

The early Christian communities used sleep as an image for the time between death and resurrection. Especially if one thinks of dreamless sleep, it is a fascinating way to express the idea of 1 Thess 4:13

timelessness or suspension of consciousness: one goes to sleep, and the next instant of consciousness comes when one wakes up. Sleep is an interesting comparison to help adults explore the concept of timelessness beyond death. While history continues in the world of time, the dead person is beyond time.

E. The Theme of Judgment in Life Beyond Death

No discussion of life beyond death can avoid the question of reward and punishment based on judgment of our moral lives.

According to the Scriptures, the action of God is entirely to help us. God reaches into our lives to lead us to wholeness, to teach us what is required of faithful believers, to give us the wisdom and courage to make good decisions, to fill us with the power of love. With God's help, we build ourselves – the persons we are created to be – by our decisions throughout our lives. At the end of our lives, we will live forever with that identity.

Judgment at death is simply the moment of truth. At death, we realize fully who we are; God accepts that reality. If some people have been deceiving themselves about the decisions they have made, death is the moment when the deception stops. We need to avoid imagining God as a judge in court, whom we must convince of our worthiness. Our judge is reality. There will be no surprises; deep in our hearts, we know who we are and how we have lived, and God accepts our self-understanding.

It is conceivable that some people may come to the end of their lives realizing that they have been fundamentally unfaithful to themselves and to God: they have built a person who is false and evil, a travesty of who they should have been; they have wasted their lives. This is the essential meaning of mortal sin. For such people, the moment of death is the moment of final recognition of that reality, and they must live forever with that knowledge. This could be a description of hell. Images that Jesus used of being cast into the darkness, and of sadness and isolation, seem to convey well the meaning of the concept of hell.

Most people seem reassured by the realization that the idea of hell involves fundamental, deliberate, consistent unfaithfulness to oneself and God. The Roman Catholic Church has consistently taught that such total failure (popularly known as 'going to hell') must be considered a possibility, but there is no teaching that anyone has ever gone to hell – come to the end of life as a total, unforgiven failure.

Most of us will come to the moment of truth realizing that we are good people, but not as good as the we could have been. We will know that, by our own decisions, we fell short of what the gospel asks of us, but will be confident and thankful that we have tried and succeeded with God's help to be faithful disciples of Jesus.

At our moment of judgment, the light of Jesus will shine on all the corners of our lives, revealing us for who we are and calling us out of darkness. Even after death, our relationship with God will continue to grow. Hell is of our own choosing: we are free to reject God and to separate ourselves from God and our brothers and sisters.

The Gospel according to John offers its own view of judgment:

God did not send the Son into the world
to condemn the world,
but in order that the world might be saved through him…
This is the judgment,
that the light has come into the world,
and people loved darkness rather than light… Jn 3:17-19

"I do not judge anyone who hears my words
and does not keep them,
for I came not to judge the world, but to save the world.
The one who rejects me and does not receive my word
has a judge:
on the last day the word that I have spoken
will serve as judge." Jn 12:47-48

F. Reincarnation

Some of the world's great religious traditions believe in reincarnation – the teaching that human beings live a series of lives (including lives as members of other living species) as they make their way towards ultimate fulfillment in God. Variations on such beliefs are sometimes popularized by people who claim to remember previous lives. The consistent tradition of the Christian Church has been that we live only one life on earth. This teaching underlines the importance of our lives: this is the only life we have; we must make the best of it, live it fully, live it well.

27

GOD SAVES US

Jesus Lived, Died and Rose to Save Us from Our Sins

From the beginning of the biblical story, the Jewish people knew
God as Redeemer and Saviour. To redeem is to set free. From the
book of Exodus through the psalms to the prophecies of Second
Isaiah and Jeremiah, the people knew that "Our Redeemer is the
Is 41:14 Holy One of Israel." "I know that my Redeemer lives," says the
Job 19:25 book of Job, in a phrase that is sung at many Christian funerals.

"God saves us" means "God reaches into our lives to lead us to wholeness." From the time of Moses, the Jewish people knew that God acts to free us from what oppresses us, that God chooses us and we belong to God, that God loves us and invites love in return, that God teaches us how to live in a way that is worthy of God's people, and that God forgives us when we fail. After the time of Moses, the people of Israel realized that God's faithful love had begun not with Moses, not even with Abraham and Sarah, but indeed with the creation of the world.

The life of Jesus was the transcending gift of God to humanity. Everything that Jesus did brought to culmination the saving action of God that began at creation, continued through the time of the patriarchs, developed profoundly through the experience of the people with Moses, struggled through the period of political decline, and was refined through the fiery integrity of the prophets and the wisdom of the sages. Jesus' life was another monumental action of God to lead humanity towards wholeness, towards salvation.

Some 400 years after Jesus lived, an influential Christian especially
thinker interpreted certain New Testament phrases to mean that sRom 5:12
the God of the Old Testament was so outraged by the sin of the Rom 5:15
first humans that God closed the gates of heaven and demanded the death of the incarnate Son of God as recompense for that primeval offence. The theology of St. Augustine captured the mind of Christian Europe, but it did not do justice to the saving action of God, whom the Bible describes in terms of steadfast love and fidelity from the beginning of human history.

Jesus repeatedly proclaimed that he had come to bring about the reign of God. Everything he said and did was designed to show people that God was initiating a wonderful new step in the process of salvation. Through the life of Jesus, the power of God was taking over in human history and in individual human lives.

The miracles of Jesus showed that God could transform people's lives – not just by healing their physical ills, but by regenerating their hearts, giving meaning to their lives, restoring their dignity, leading them to fullness of life.

The parables of Jesus expressed the abundant generosity of Jn 10:10
God, and urgently demanded a response from his hearers.

The moral teaching of Jesus described a way of life that is fully human and truly faithful to God. Jesus urged us, his followers, to grow towards wholeness, knowing that we can meet his challenge only by opening our hearts to the Spirit of God. Everything he did was an expression of the saving power of God.

Jesus claimed to speak for God. His arguments with the voices of corrupt power in his society showed his uncompromising integrity – and cost him his life.

His death summed up his life. It was not a punishment imposed by God upon Jesus as the representative of sinful humanity. Rather, it was the ultimate expression of the self-giving love and integrity that marked Jesus' entire life. He understood
that he was giving his life – his whole life, including his death –
to set people free, to redeem them. In the Gospel of Mark, Jesus' Mk 10:45
death is the ultimate revelation that he was indeed Son of God.

The resurrection was his vindication. The resurrection shows Mk 15:39
that Jesus was right, that suffering and death are not absurd or hopeless but can be profoundly meaningful, that love and integrity are the hallmarks of human wholeness, and that the power of God's love is stronger than any evil and even overcomes death.

Believing in Jesus can lead us to wholeness. But the life, death and resurrection of Jesus are more than just assurance. We believe that through the life of Jesus, spiritual power has poured into the world. Human history has been fundamentally transformed. Each of us can open our hearts to this power of God and become whole.

Of course, complete fulfillment has not yet arrived. Sin remains a dreadful force in the world, and in each of our lives. Sin is cumulative in history. It has power over the human family; sin brings death. On an individual level, sin is every choice that diminishes us, that weakens our relationship with God, that makes us in some measure unfaithful to our true selves: less free, less loving, less human, less whole.

The saving power of God, which had been recognized from the earliest days of the Jewish tradition, exploded into the world in the life of Jesus. The power of God's love overcomes the power of sin in our lives.

Jesus is God's greatest gift to humanity. Because of the life of Jesus, no matter what happens to us, our lives have hope and meaning. Somehow, despite all the pain and despair and evil that surround us, we can grow towards wholeness with God's transforming help. Sin has already been overcome in principle by the power of God working through the life, death and resurrection of Jesus: that is how Jesus saved us from our sins.

Salvation is the fundamental gift of God, proclaimed in the Scriptures, to respond to the deepest yearning and hope of every human being. Truly, in the Bible, God's word speaks with power in a language of the heart.

GLOSSARY

Anthropomorphism: The attribution of human characteristics to God (or to anything). Borrowed from the Greek words for 'human' (*anthropos*, as in anthropology) and for 'form' (*morphos*, as in morphology). It is an anthropomorphism to say that God sits on a throne in the sky, or has a face or hands, or is angry, or disappointed – because these ideas (which may have some symbolic validity) are a projection of human qualities upon the spiritual God who is beyond our experience.

Apocalyptic writing: Literature which presents mystical, usually cataclysmic revelation; for example, descriptions of future events like the return of the Son of Man, or the end of the world. The Book of Daniel is apocalyptic literature in the Old Testament. New Testament examples include the Book of Revelation, and the statements of Jesus in the gospels about the destruction of Jerusalem and the return of the Son of Man on the clouds of heaven.

Apocrypha: Taken from the Greek word for 'hidden,' which can also mean 'not genuine.' With regard to the Bible, the word refers to certain books that are considered the authentic Word of God (i.e., *not* apocryphal) but deuterocanonical by Catholics, but are not recognized by Protestants and Jews as inspired by God (who therefore consider these books as 'apocryphal'). Such books are now included in most translations of the Bible. The deuterocanonical books include Tobit, Judith, Esther, the Wisdom of Solomon, Sirach, Baruch, Azariah, Susanna, and 1 and 2 Maccabees.

Some writings from the biblical era are considered apocryphal (i.e., not inspired by God) by both Catholics and Protestants: 1 and 2 Esdras, and the prayer of Manasseh. Even those books are studied by scholars for the information they offer about faith in the Jewish tradition at the time they were written.

BCE: See **CE**

Beelzebul: means 'Ba'al is prince,' referring to a foreign god (Ba'al). In Jesus' time, the word was used to refer to the 'chief of demons.' Religious leaders accused Jesus of casting out demons by the power of Beelzebul, meaning that his healings were done by devil power or 'black magic'.

Sometimes they changed the word slightly to add more mockery: *Beelzebub* means 'Lord of the flies.'

Canon: Refers to the list of books that are considered to be Scripture or the Word of God.

- Protestants and Catholics agree on the canon of the New Testament.
- The canon of the Hebrew Scriptures was set by Jewish scholars in the first centuries of the Common Era.
- Almost 1,500 years later, Catholics declared seven additional Jewish books to be 'canonical,' with the result that there are more Jewish books in the Catholic 'Old Testament' than there are in the Hebrew Scriptures. The additional books are known as 'deuterocanonical,' meaning 'the second canon' or 'the second list.'
- The Protestant Churches retain the Hebrew canon, but often print the additional books in Protestant Bibles and call them 'the apocrypha.'

CE: Out of respect for people of many faiths all around the world who now use the familiar year-numbering system which originated in Christian Europe, some Bible scholars prefer not to use the designations B.C. (before Christ) and A.D. (*Anno Domini*, Latin for "in the year of our Lord"). Since people who are Hindu, Sikh, Muslim, Jewish, atheist or non-religious do not think of Jesus as "Our Lord," we now use the designations CE (meaning the Common Era, the year-numbering system that is commonly accepted around the world) and BCE (Before the Common Era).

Christ: see **Messiah**

Covenant: The eternal bond initiated by God and agreed to by the people, by which God promises to be faithful to humanity, and humans agree to accept the authority of God.

Deuterocanonical: see **Canon**

Deuteronomist: A strand of Jewish tradition likely written in the northern kingdom which gave us a version of the Law of Moses (as found in the book of Deuteronomy) and of the later history of the people.

Divinity of Jesus: The belief that Jesus is divine, the Son of God, God incarnate, God made human, the presence of God on earth living a single human life.

Elohist: A strand of Jewish tradition composed in the 800s BCE in the northern kingdom. The anonymous author used the name *elohim* (the generic word 'god') for God, and the word 'Horeb' (rather than Sinai) for the mountain where Moses received the Ten Commandments. Both the strand and its author are known as the Elohist. The strand was woven into Torah after the Israelites' return from the Babylonian exile.

Etiology: Literally, the study of causes or reasons. With regard to the Bible, an etiology is a story that explains how a certain place or person got its name.

There are many familiar etiological folktales in First Nations and in every culture, such as how the Big Dipper got up in the sky or how the beaver got its flat tail.

Evangelist: The author of one of the four gospels.

Exegesis: The scholarly art and science of interpreting a text of Scripture. Pronounced 'ex-e-*gee*-sis'. Adjective: exegetical (ex-e-*jet*-ical). Exegete: a Scripture scholar.

Exodus: Generically, this word refers to any mass departure of people – as, for example, in Leon Uris' 20th-century narrative of the flight of Jewish people from Hitler's Europe.

In the Bible, it refers to the departure of the Israelites from Egypt under Moses, and the second book of the Hebrew Scriptures, which narrates the event.

More symbolically, it may refer to any exodus experience, perhaps of refugees fleeing an impoverished country, or of political sympathizers fleeing a party after a few years of unpopular governing.

Exorcism: The healing of people by casting out demons. Few people in the contemporary world would interpret disturbing phenomena as the product of demon possession, but that was a familiar diagnosis in Jesus' time. The gospel writers understood such healings as portraying the worldwide struggle of good vs. evil – and good (the power of God's love) always wins.

Galilee: The territory in northern Palestine where Jesus grew up and lived most of his life. Galilee was culturally removed from Jerusalem; it was called 'Galilee of the nations' (Isaiah 9:1), meaning that there were many non-Jewish inhabitants there. Galileans had a reputation for being uneducated and rude and unconcerned about religion.

Gentile: Anyone who is not Jewish. Sometimes translated as 'the heathens' or 'the nations' (meaning, nations other than Jewish), for example, 'The rulers of the nations lord it over their subjects....'

Gospel: The form of literary art used by the four authors who present their distinctive theologies about Jesus. Gospel (in Greek, *euangelion*) literally means 'good news.' A gospel is a document of faith, designed to persuade the reader that Jesus is "good news" for us, that he will lead his followers towards wholeness. A gospel should not be read as if it were a newspaper report or a history book or a biography. The gospels are theology books.

Heaven: In the Scriptures, the realm where God lives with the angels in a 'chamber above the waters' (which are above the dome that we call sky). See Psalm 104:2.

Later understanding saw heaven as a place of reward for human souls in life beyond death. See entries in this glossary on **Immortality** and **Resurrection**.

Immortality: Based on the Greek philosophical idea that humanity is composed of two almost opposite elements (a material body and a spiritual soul), 'immortality' refers to the concept that at death only the body dies; the soul is immortal and capable of living forever in a spiritual world which we have come to call heaven. Compare the entries in this glossary for **Heaven** and **Resurrection**.

Inspiration: The process by which God led human authors to know God and to express their insight and faith by means of various forms of literary art.

Israel: The word itself may mean 'God is strong.'

The patriarch Jacob's name was changed to Israel after he 'wrestled with God,' according to an ancient saga (Genesis 32:22-28).

Jacob/Israel was the father of 12 sons, the names of the 12 tribes of Israel.

After that, the word 'Israel' refers primarily to the Jewish people, the people of Israel, the Israelites. When the united kingdom was divided after the reign of Solomon, the secessionist territory comprising 10 of the 12 tribes, which became the northern kingdom, called itself 'Israel.' That kingdom was destroyed after less than two centuries.

When the modern Jewish state was created by the United Nations in 1948 CE, there was some debate before the nation decided to call itself Israel.

Judah: The name adopted by the smaller southern kingdom after the secession. Judah continued with the royal family of David, with its capital at Jerusalem. That kingdom was destroyed in 587 BCE by the Babylonians.

Judea: The name of the territory in southern Palestine at the time of Jesus. The Judean desert (now called the Negev, or southern desert) typifies the geography.

Jesus was born in "Bethlehem of Judea" – a desert village, fewer than 10 km south of Jerusalem.

Liturgy: Liturgy is the technical term for community worship. Literally, it means "the work of the people." Liturgical prayer is what we do when we gather to pray, as opposed to private or personal prayer.

Lord: Like the Italian word '*Signore,*' the word (*kyrios* in Greek) can mean anything from a simple 'sir' to the great God of Moses. People often address Jesus by this title in the gospels. When they did so, they probably meant no more than 'sir' or the more respectful 'rabbi' or 'master.' But the gospel writers want readers to understand the term with deeper faith than that: they want the word to imply reverence for Jesus as **Son of God** (see entry in this glossary), as when we pray "through Jesus Christ our Lord."

Messiah: From the Hebrew word for "anointed one" (in Greek, *christos*). Therefore "Christ" and "Messiah" mean the same: the great leader (king, heir of David) whom the Jews expected God to send, to set the nation free of occupying forces, to inspire the people to be faithful to God. The title had too many political overtones for Jesus to accept it wholeheartedly.

After the resurrection, **Christians** (note the term) came to believe that Jesus was indeed the Christ (**Messiah**) expected by the Jews, and that he had a very different understanding of the role of the Messiah than the people of his time. Thus "Jesus Christ" became a popular name for Jesus, even though he almost never claimed to be the Messiah, and was uncomfortable with other people using that title about him.

Messianic secret: Especially in Mark, Jesus is often quoted as urging people not to publicize what he is doing. Even when Peter professes that Jesus is the Messiah, Jesus urges him not to tell anyone. The 'secret' theme is likely built on the memory that Jesus was afraid that he would be seen as the expected political/military Messiah, and that was contrary to his self-understanding.

Myth: A traditional narrative, often including supernatural elements, dealing with profound human questions. The great myths of every culture are works of fiction or products of human imagination, but they express the culture's understanding of important human and divine realities.

The term 'myth' has evolved in popular understanding to mean something false or untrue, but that meaning is not the classical meaning, which is intended when we use the word *myth* to refer to Bible narratives.

Students will often say, "So then the story of Adam and Eve is not true?" It is difficult but necessary to convince them that, though the story is not factual or historical, it does teach important truths about the relationship of God to humanity and to the world.

Palestine: The name of Jesus' homeland in the Roman era.

Teachers in Catholic schools should be aware that many Palestinian (and other Arab) families are Christians. The parents of many children in our schools may come from Nazareth, Bethlehem, East Jerusalem, Lebanon, Egypt, Iraq, etc. They are justifiably very unhappy if teachers uncritically advocate the pro-Israel viewpoint of the U.S. media. Teachers should be educated about the Palestinian interpretation of the current situation, and should call the land 'Jesus' homeland' or 'the Holy Land.' Both 'Palestine' and 'Israel' are politically charged terms, but can be used occasionally in recognition of contemporary political reality.

Parable: A saying or story used to teach a lesson about God or about life.

The word literally means "a comparison," so even sayings that are not stories could be called 'parabolic' sayings ("I am sending you out like lambs among wolves").

Pentateuch: The Greek term for the first five books of the Bible, known in Hebrew as *Torah*.

Priestly strand: During the exile, a school of priests gathered many worship-related and legal traditions. This strand was combined into

Torah with the Yahwist, Elohist and Deuteronomist strands by editors after the exile.

Prophet: (From Greek words meaning "to speak on behalf of.") The prophets were inspired by God to interpret the events of their times according to the mind of God, and to call the people to integrity and to faithfulness to God's covenant. One minor aspect of the prophets' teaching was to promise that some day God would send a faithful leader (an anointed one, a Messiah) to unite the people and lead them to a faithful way of life.

Q: The Gospels of Matthew and Luke share verbatim many sayings of Jesus that are not reported in Mark – and yet there are enough differences between Matthew and Luke that scholars feel sure that they did not copy from each other.

That 'dilemma' led scholars to propose that both authors depended on a pre-existing written source (*Quelle* in German, hence the designation "Q") – a collection of sayings of Jesus with no narratives attached. Scholars think that Q may also have contained one miracle narrative: the story of the healing of the centurion's slave.

Resurrection: Based on the traditional Jewish idea that humans are "body-beings capable of spirituality," scriptural understanding about life beyond death speaks of God's promise to *resurrect* "on the last day" people who have died: to transform them into a spiritual way of living with God and each other. We die as physical beings; we will rise as spiritual beings. See 1 Corinthians 15:42-44 as well as entries in this glossary on **Heaven**, **Immortality**.

Samaria: The third capital city of Israel, the northern kingdom, after the division of the union.

In Jesus' time, the name of the territory of the Samaritans, a people of mixed heritage who were reviled by Jewish people and engaged in guerrilla warfare against Jews. Samaria was situated between Judea and Jerusalem in the south, and Jesus' home district of Galilee in the north.

Son of God: A very strong Christian title of honour for Jesus; a declaration of his divinity (see entry on **Divinity** in this glossary). In the Old Testament, "son of God" was used to mean "favoured one of God" about a wide variety of human beings – particularly the kings (see Psalm 2), and at times the entire nation.

If people called Jesus "Son of God" during his lifetime, the title would have had that basic meaning (favoured one). But after the resurrection, the meaning of the term evolved as the Christian communities struggled to express their belief that Jesus was more than simply a human being favoured by God, and in fact is 'divine.'

The declaration of the soldier when Jesus dies is intended to be understood in the strongest Christian sense.

Son of Man: English translation of the Hebrew *ben adam* (son of a human, or simply 'a human being'). In the NRSV Old Testament, the best English translation of the Bible often uses the word 'mortal' to translate the phrase *ben adam*.

Jesus used this phrase exclusively to refer to himself, according to Matthew-Mark-Luke. The phrase has two almost opposite meanings, and one can presume that both meanings are intended when Jesus uses the term: one refers to his mortality as a human being (*Ben adam* is going down to Jerusalem...to be crucified), the other refers to the glorious return of *ben adam* on the clouds of heaven in great power and majesty (see the book of Daniel 7:13-14 for the source of this usage).

Synoptic gospels: The Gospels of Matthew, Mark and Luke are so similar to each other that episodes can be compared side by side. [Students can purchase editions of the synoptic gospels which print every episode side by side in three columns, for the purpose of comparison.]

Scholars agree that both Matthew and Luke used Mark as a source (and also had another source in common), and made some alterations in Mark's narratives to suit the concerns of their own communities.

Syn-optic is taken from Greek: *optic* is from the Greek word for 'eye' (e.g., 'optician'); *syn* is from the Greek word for 'together, with' (e.g., 'sympathy': suffering together). The synoptic gospels can be 'seen together' 'with one eye.'

Torah: The Hebrew word for the first five books of the Hebrew Scriptures – Genesis, Exodus, Leviticus, Numbers, and Deuteronomy. [*Torah* can be translated into English as 'instruction.']

Torah took its present shape after the Babylonian exile, in the 400s BCE, when a committee of editors collected several pre-existing written strands of tradition and wove them into a single narrative. In so doing, they also created a 'priestly strand' themselves.

It was once believed that Moses himself wrote the *Torah*, including the account of his own death and its aftermath, but most Christian scholars today agree that *Torah* came into existence more than 700 years after the time of Moses.

Theology: Our understanding about God. Borrowed from Greek *theos* (God) and *logos* (literally, 'word'; extended meaning: 'understanding'). Adjective: theological.

Yahwist: The earliest written strand of traditions from the past was probably composed ca. 950 BCE by an anonymous author who freely used the sacred name of God (YHWH) in his narratives, even though it was forbidden ever to pronounce the sacred name.

In modern translations, the sacred name is usually represented as "the LORD."

Both the strand and its author are known as 'the Yahwist.'

The Yahwist strand preserved in writing (for the first time) the sagas of the earliest Jewish ancestors (Abraham and Sarah, their children, grandchildren and great-grandchildren), which had existed in oral form for as long as eight centuries.

Though the sacred name of God was apparently given to Moses around the year 1250 BCE, the Yahwist used the Name in telling the stories of the patriarchs, who had lived centuries before Moses.

The Yahwist also wrote narratives about the career of Moses, which accounts had been preserved orally for more than 300 years before they were written.

Finally under this heading, we include the story of Adam and Eve, Cain and Abel, the story of the Flood, and the Tower of Babel. All those narratives were likely composed by the Yahwist.

RECOMMENDED READING

A Selective Annotated Bibliography

Pontifical Biblical Commission. *The Interpretation of the Bible in the Church*. Boston: Pauline Books and Media, 2000. 135 pages.

This Vatican document offers principles of biblical interpretation that are accepted in mainstream Catholicism.

Brown, Raymond E., Joseph A. Fitzmyer, Roland E. Murphy, eds. *The New Jerome Biblical Commentary*. Englewood Cliffs, NJ: Prentice-Hall, 2000. 1475 pages of fine print (paperback edition).

This encyclopedic volume, edited by Roman Catholic priest-scholars, provides introductory notes and verse-by-verse commentary for every book of the Bible, as well as several articles about Old Testament and New Testament topics. A very useful reference for serious students.

Introductions to the Old Testament

Anderson, Bernhard. *Understanding the Old Testament* (fourth edition). Englewood Cliffs, NJ: Prentice-Hall, 1998.

An outstanding introduction to the Old Testament written as a university textbook with considerable academic depth. Its photographs, maps and chronological charts will help students appreciate the contributions of archaeology to biblical study; its articulate exploration of the history and meaning of the sacred texts will respond to the needs of thoughtful searchers.

Boadt, Lawrence. *Reading the Old Testament*. New York: Paulist Press, 1984. 563 pages.

This readable and complete guide to the Old Testament was written by a Roman Catholic priest-scholar. It presents background information about the world in which the Scriptures developed, a theological discussion of a number of related issues, and a thorough and specific introduction to the entire Old Testament. An excellent textbook for an introductory university course on the Old Testament.

Borg, Marcus J. *Reading the Bible Again for the First Time.* San Francisco: HarperSanFrancisco, 2001. 321 pages.

Marcus Borg is a faithful Protestant scholar who provides a generic introduction to the study of the Bible in very readable language. This book frequently discusses the difference between traditional beliefs about the Bible and contemporary understandings.

Charpentier, Etienne. *How to Read the Old Testament.* New York: Crossroad, 1981. 124 pages.

This book and its New Testament counterpart provide introductory notes that are useful for systematic reading and study of the Bible. Most sections are two to four pages long, and provide information and selected readings to help serious beginners find their way in the Scriptures.

Introductions to the New Testament

Borg, Marcus J. *Meeting Jesus Again for the First Time.* San Francisco: Harper, 1994. 150 pages.

In this book, Borg offers a readable introduction to the New Testament with many autobiographical elements, as the author describes his journey away from the beliefs of his childhood to a more adult and contemporary understanding of the Scriptures, and a deeper faith.

Brown, Raymond E. *The Virginal Conception and Bodily Resurrection of Jesus.* New York: Paulist Press, 1973. 136 pages.

The late Raymond Brown was one of the greatest Catholic Scripture scholars in North America and a member of the Pontifical Biblical Commission. His many books are outstanding for their scholarship, attention to detail and comprehensible style. This book is a fascinating discussion of two controversial New Testament issues. Readers who enjoy this book may go on to one of his two books about the Christmas stories: *The Birth of the Messiah* (for theology students) or *An Adult Christ at Christmas* (a much briefer discussion for the general reader). Brown's two-volume commentary on the *Gospel According to John* is an outstanding verse-by-verse journey through the gospel and the theology it represents. His detailed and challenging book *Jesus: God and Man* deals with two questions: Does the New Testament call Jesus God? and How much did Jesus know? For a discussion of these questions, there is not a more careful Catholic discussion available.

Johnson, Luke Timothy. *Living Jesus: Learning the Heart of the Gospel.* San Francisco: HarperSanFrancisco, 2000. 224 pages.

———. *The Real Jesus: The Misguided Quest for the Historical Jesus.* San Francisco: HarperSanFrancisco, 1997. 208 pages.

Presenting strong biblical scholarship in clear and simple language, Johnson begins with an extended reflection on the risen Jesus who lives among us today. On that basis, he offers insight about Jesus as found in the four gospels.

Meier, John P. *A Marginal Jew*. 3 volumes. New York: Doubleday/Anchor Bible Reference Library, 1991, 1994, 2001. 496, 1136, 720 pages respectively.

The first volume of this series, written by a respected Catholic priest-scholar, is a fascinating study of the contemporary background, family life and ministry of Jesus from an historical perspective. Later volumes offer a detailed study of gospel accounts of Jesus' ministry, are more challenging and require significant academic background and interest.

Senior, Donald. *Jesus: A Gospel Portrait*. New York: Paulist Press, 1992. 181 pages.

This brief, clear description of the life and work of Jesus is written for the general reader by a Roman Catholic priest-scholar-teacher.

Spoto, Donald. *The Hidden Jesus: A New Life*. New York: St. Martin's Press, 1998. 312 pages.

Donald Spoto, a former monk, is a bestselling biographer who holds a doctoral degree in theology. His 'biography' of Jesus is written with faith and makes use of strong Scripture scholarship to present a credible understanding of Jesus' ministry and teaching.

Zanzig, Thomas. *Jesus Is Lord! A Basic Christology for Adults.* Winona, MN: St Mary's Press, 1982. 207 pages.

An excellent and accessible introduction to the New Testament written in a friendly style, this book is addressed to 'ordinary' adult believers wishing to explore and reflect on the person and mission of Jesus.

ALPHABETICAL SCRIPTURE INDEX

OTHER SCRIPTURE RESOURCES FROM NOVALIS

Breaking Open the Word series

Who Knows the Reach of God? Homilies and Reflections for Year A
Who Knows the Shape of God? Homilies and Reflections for Year B
Who Knows the Colour of God? Homilies and Reflections for Year C

Corbin Eddy

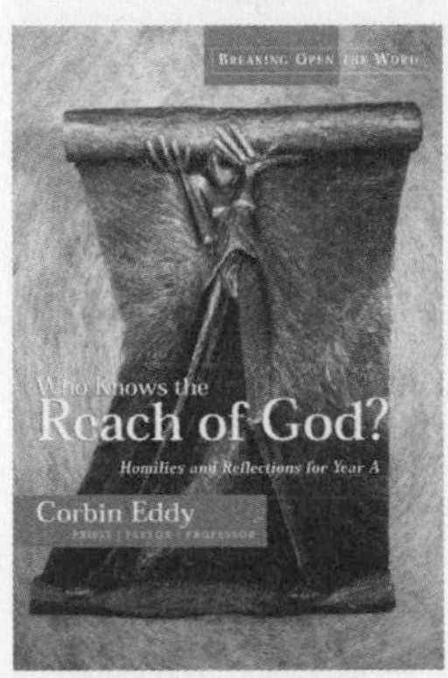

A three-volume series of homilies and reflections on the readings for each Sunday in the liturgical year, filled with deep insight, humour and faith by a popular parish priest and professor. Ideal for homilists and for all those seeking a deeper understanding of God's action in their lives.

Jesus Speaks Today series

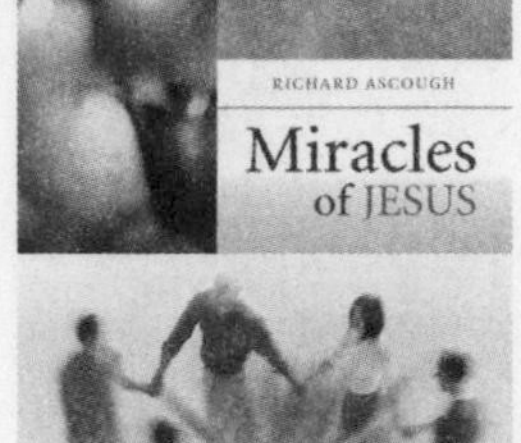

The Questions of Jesus (*John McLaughlin*)
Miracles of Jesus (*Richard Ascough*)
Parables of Jesus (available in Fall 2004)
Teachings of Jesus (available in Fall 2005)

A series of four books examining various important aspects of Jesus' ministry – questions, miracles, parables and teachings – that are just as relevant for us today as they were 2,000 years ago! An accessible approach for all readers by Canadian Scripture scholars.

Theology for Teachers

Rev. Ian Knox

A fascinating book for all Catholics, not just teachers! A highly readable, enlightening volume on Catholic theology that meets the curriculum guidelines of the Institute of Catholic Education for courses in religious education.

Singing the Lord's Song in a Foreign Land: Reclaiming Faith in a New Culture

Vivian Ligo

How can people sing the Lord's song in a new land? Theologian Vivian Ligo examines the Old Testament prophets Jeremiah, Ezekiel and Isaiah, making striking connections between these stories of exile and modern stories of immigration. Written for immigrants and those who welcome them.

Becoming Fully Human: Living the Bible with God, Each Other and the Environment

Walter Vogels

What is so special about the Bible? Becoming Fully Human guides us to the Bible, a source of wisdom and inspiration that is as relevant today as it was in ages past – and shows us how to live the Bible as we search for answers to our biggest questions.

Words of Wisdom: Proverbs for Everyday Living

Walter Vogels

Collecting and comparing proverbs from a wide array of religions and cultures, Walter Vogels skillfully demonstrates how these "spiritual nuggets" help give shape and breadth to our daily experience.

To order, contact

1-877-702-7773

or www.novalis.ca

An online course with activities to supplement *Language of the Heart* is being developed by the author and other colleagues. Using interactive strategies in ten modules which are expected to involve a total of 30 hours to complete, readers are guided through a more extended study of numerous passages and issues referred to in this book, and are given an opportunity to participate in discussion forums with other readers. At the current stage of development, we expect that the course will not be offered for credit in most cases. If you are interested in finding out more about this proposed online course, please contact the author by e-mail at nhplcoop@rogers.com.